TEN
OUT

TEN
OUT

The remarkable bowlers who have taken all
ten wickets in an innings – cricket's ultimate feat

IAN
BRAYSHAW

Hardie Grant

BOOKS

Published in 2025 by Hardie Grant Books, an imprint of Hardie Grant Publishing

Hardie Grant Books (Melbourne)
Wurundjeri Country
Level 11, 36 Wellington Street
Collingwood, Victoria 3066

Hardie Grant North America
2912 Telegraph Ave
Berkeley, California 94705

hardiegrant.com/books

Hardie Grant acknowledges the Traditional Owners of the country on which we work,
the Wurundjeri people of the Kulin nation and the Gadigal people of the Eora nation,
and recognises their continuing connection to the land, waters and culture. We pay our
respects to their Elders past and present.

 A catalogue record for this
work is available from the
National Library of Australia

Ten Out!
ISBN 978 1 76145 165 2
ISBN 978 1 76144 284 1 (ebook)

10 9 8 7 6 5 4 3 2 1

Publishing Director: Pam Brewster
Head of Editorial: Jasmin Chua

Editor: Paul Connolly
Design Manager: Kristin Thomas
Cover Design: Blue Cork, Luke Causby
Typesetter: Kirby Jones
Head of Production: Todd Rechner
Production Controller: Elly Cridland

Printed in in Australia by Griffin Press

 The paper this book is printed on is certified against the Forest
Stewardship Council® Standards. Griffin Press holds FSC® chain
of custody certification SGS-COC–001185. FSC® promotes
environmentally responsible, socially beneficial and economically
viable management of the world's forests.

To my wife, Joan,
for all the 'lost hours'.

CONTENTS

PREFACE

Since the Laws of Cricket were first recorded in 1744, more bowlers than you might expect have taken ten wickets in an innings. Some have achieved this remarkable feat in inter-school games, others in village or grade matches played from Christchurch to Manchester and all points in between. Ten-fors (to use the colloquial) have even been registered in the Test arena, though only on three occasions. As such, Jim Laker (England), Anil Kumble (India) and Ajaz Patel (New Zealand) are members of a truly exclusive club.

In researching this book I came across numerous instances of ten-fors in cricket history. They were consistently illuminating and entertaining. Consider these gems, recounted by the totemic WG Grace in his 1891 book, *Cricket*: 'Mr A Dartnell, playing for Broad Green against Thornton Heath near Croydon in 1867, captured all ten wickets and the whole side was got rid of without scoring; RC Tinley, playing for the All England Eleven against 18 of Hallam in 1860 in Sheffield, took all 17 second-innings wickets[1]; and Vyell Edgar 'VE' Walker, playing for United England XI versus 22 of Scotland in Glasgow in September, 1858, took 10-44 and James Grundy 10-31 in the same innings. They bowled unchanged for 72.1 four-ball overs!'

---

1   Tinley had a match to remember, having already taken 10-54 in Hallam's first innings. With 27 (of 36) wickets in the match, you'd have to think Tinley's single-match haul has never been bettered.

It's fun to contemplate such instances, particularly as most would be impossible in the modern, 11-a-side game. However, in these pages, we pay homage to those who have taken all ten wickets in a recognised first-class match. And this is where, historically speaking, things get tricky. What *is* a first-class game, and when did the nomenclature take its rise?

The concept was first framed in 1895, a year after a meeting of leading English clubs at Lord's. In 1947, the game's global governing body, the Imperial Cricket Conference – which later changed its name to the International Cricket Conference, and then the International Cricket Council (ICC), as it's known today – formally defined 'first-class cricket' on a global basis, and according to these set criteria, all of which must be met:

- The game has a three-day minimum planned duration
- There are 11 players on each team in the game
- There may be two innings per side
- The game is to be played on real turf, not synthetic grass
- The game is held at a location that satisfies specific standards for venues
- The game follows the Laws of Cricket, with a few minor exceptions
- The game is recognised as first-class by the applicant country's governing body for the sport; or by the ICC.

However, the ICC ruling made no attempt to decide *when* first-class cricket officially took root. Therein rested the essence of a debate that raged, until quite recently, over agreement on the start date. Historians, especially statisticians, have chewed away at the matter. Some, it has to be said, are still chewing.

One line of thinking was that the earliest first-class match was Hampshire versus England at Broadhalfpenny Down on 24–25

June 1772. At that time, cricket matches were played with a two-stump wicket and bowling was exclusively under-arm. Significantly, it's from this point that scorecards (and thus statistics) were not only routinely filled out but also kept. In 1951, however, the cricket statistician Roy Webber dipped his oar in the waters, arguing that the majority of matches prior to 1864 (the year in which over-arm bowling was legalised) 'cannot be regarded as first-class'.

Eminent statistician Bill Frindall, one of Webber's successors as the BBC's resident stats-man, challenged this opinion. He substituted his own theory, arguing that 1815 should be the start point so as to encompass the entire round-arm/over-arm phase of cricket's history (although round-arm bowling did not begin in earnest until 1827). It was Frindall's view that the inaugural first-class match should have been the opening game of the 1815 season, the match between the Marylebone Cricket Club (MCC) and Middlesex at Lord's on 31 May – 1 June.

Arguments went to and fro, like a rally in a game of tennis, until 2010 when the Association of Cricket Statisticians stepped up and endorsed the date of 1772. The fact that this date has been accepted by influential online databases CricketArchive and ESPNcricinfo, not to mention the 'bible' of cricket, *Wisden Cricketers' Almanack*, has, by and large, settled the matter.

What did this momentous decision do to the time-honoured list of cricketers with ten scalps to their name in a single innings? Well, for one, it introduced a new name at the top of the list. Previously, Edmund Hinkly had been considered the first person to snare a ten-for in a first-class match after his efforts at Lord's in 1848. John Wisden's ten-for in 1850 had him in second spot. The general acceptance of 1772 as the new starting point, however, meant that pride of place atop the adjusted list went to William Lillywhite for his feat in 1837, in a 16-a-side game. It also meant that in the 252 years since then the list expanded to 91 ten-fors achieved by 84 bowlers (with one man having claimed ten or more wickets three times, and five others twice). [2]

My worthy adviser on all matters cricket statistics, *Wisden*'s Steven Lynch, helped me break down the numbers. 'We can say it has happened 91 times in more than 62,000 first-class matches in just over 250 years,' he began. 'A rough estimate would be that those games represent 200,000 innings. That's one instance for every 690 matches. Round that up to 700, and the numbers calculate out to one ten-wicket innings haul, on average, every 2,222 innings.'

To personalise these numbers, Kent and England spinner Tich Freeman, the only man to have achieved ten-fors three times, expended a mountain of first-class overs in that pursuit; some 25,776.2 to be exact.

Central to the matter of odds are the many variables – a number of which could be filed under 'luck' – which can play an incalculable but significant role in the taking of any wickets, let alone a ten-for; variables like the weather, the condition of the pitch, the judiciousness (and eyesight) of the umpires, the fine lines between a play-and-miss and a nick behind, a held catch and a spilled one, the quality of the opposition, and the quality of one's fellow bowlers. Or indeed the kind of days they are having.

Concerning the latter, a ten-for requires an odd kind of help

---

2 I am conscious of using the word 'man' here. Accordingly, it must be pointed out that at the time of writing, no female cricketer had taken ten wickets in a first-class innings. The male game, of course, has had a profound head start on the women's game in all respects and this anomaly will surely change soon enough. That said, three Test bowlers have come mighty close. Slow left-armer Neetu David of India took 8-53 against England in Jamshedpur in 1995, Australia's Ash Gardner took 8-66 with her off-spinners against England in Nottingham in 2023, and India's Sneh Rana, also an offie, took 8-77 in Chennai against South Africa in 2024.

from the bowlers operating at the other end – bowlers who are usually doing their darnedest to take wickets of their own. For instance, in 1932, when Hedley Verity claimed a ten-for, conceding just ten runs in the process, his Yorkshire teammates, Bill Bowes and George Macaulay, both Test players, bowled 28 unrewarded overs between them at the other end. 'Thanks fellas, I couldn't have done it without you,' Verity might have said in the sheds afterwards.

All this is to say that a ten-for requires more than just the skill of an elite bowler. As I know from personal experience, a lot of puzzle pieces need to be in place.

Yes, there's no avoiding it any longer; I am one of those 84 individuals who, to date, have taken ten wickets in a first-class innings. When I consider some of the other names on this list, and the significantly longer list of bowling greats who never achieved the feat or even got close, I still cannot quite believe it myself. But look, it's recorded in *Wisden*, a tome I hold so dear, so I guess it must be true. [3]

In these pages, each member of the list, including yours truly, will be dealt with to varying degrees. Some in greater depth than others because, like Tich Freeman's, theirs is a story that cries out for deeper scrutiny (or, as in my case, because I have the memories to hand and the opportunity here to recall them). Then there are those who, incredibly, have done it more than once, and those who fit categories of my own making: the first, the most recent, the oldest, the youngest, the most unlikely, and so on.

Whenever I turned over a stone among the 84 names on the list I was constantly surprised at what turned up. As I hope you'll agree, it was a fascinating journey.

---

3   When I retired from cricket and became a broadcast journalist I obtained a leather satchel in which to carry all my cricket bits and pieces to the games. The first things I packed every time were the latest copy of *Wisden Cricketers' Almanack* and the *Wisden Book of Test Cricket*, compiled and edited by Bill Frindall. Almost anything a broadcaster would need rested within these pages. More on *Wisden* to come.

In 2025, Ian Brayshaw holds his 1967 trophy, standing before a photograph of his younger self on the day he claimed all 10 wickets in an innings.

CHAPTER 1
10 FOR 44

It's safe to say that the Western Australia squad embarked on the 1967–68 Sheffield Shield season with more hope than confidence. Our forefathers had achieved what must have seemed the near impossible by winning the Shield in 1947–48, WA's first season in the competition.[4] But in the 20 years that followed WA failed to win another title. The few highs in that time were greatly outnumbered by the lows.

As the Fifties morphed into the Sixties, however, there was a sense that we had been steadily growing into a group that had reason to believe something good might just be around the corner. Graham McKenzie's arrival in 1961 as the first WA player to be a regular in the Australian team was a positive portent.

Our 1967–68 campaign began against the reigning champion, Victoria, who had won the previous Shield with 40 points, while WA had finished fourth with 22. And there was no questioning that Victoria came to Perth with a formidable line-up, particularly in the batting department. It loomed as a real challenge for us, one articulated in an article that appeared in one of the local daily newspapers, the *Daily News*, on the eve of the game.

It was a composite story, picking up bits and pieces from various articles in the Melbourne press. It quoted some Victorian journalists

---

4   It should be noted that Western Australia played the other states only once that season, instead of twice. Their final points were calculated on a pro-rata basis.

and ex-players-turned-columnists as suggesting that the world record for a first-class innings – Victoria's 1107 against New South Wales in 1926 – was in jeopardy. According to the article, a very strong Victorian batting line-up against a modest attack on the fast WACA Ground pitch was likely to produce a huge score by the visitors.

That was more than a little bit over the top, but it is worth noting that the Victorian batting order that day included eight players who at that stage of their careers had made at least one first-class century. Leading the way was their captain, Bill Lawry, who by then had notched up 39 tons of his personal career total of 50, while Bob Cowper had 22 of his final tally of 26. At the time, the Victorian batting order boasted a tally of 92 personal centuries, out of the eventual total of 161 between them.

Whether the Vics were world-record challengers or not, we clearly had our work cut out for us.

The Shield opener started on a Saturday. I was lucky to make it. Three days out from the game I had the day off work and drove with my family to a friend's dairy farm just south of Perth for what was supposed to be a relaxed outing. And so it was until after lunch when we all went for a walk, up the road to a paddock where a horse was quietly grazing.

What did I know about horses? Nothing. Well, that's not quite true. As a boy I lived in South Perth in a house that overlooked the Swan River and the city. Looking left from our front veranda could be seen, at river level, a massive bamboo forest; to the right was what was known as the Chinese Gardens. It was there that a number of Asian-Australians lived in pretty ordinary conditions but thrived on market gardening.

One of these people was Chew. He would hook up a huge

draught horse to a cart laden with vegetables and fruit and take it plodding around the neighbourhood to sell his wares. Another horse would also come by our house on regular occasions, this one bearing goods from the local bakery. Danny Noonan's raucous cry of 'Bake!' would let us know when he had arrived. When either horse went by I was sure to stay on our side of the fence. I was always a little wary of them.

To this day I'm not sure why, but that afternoon on my friend's dairy farm I succumbed to all sorts of encouragement and agreed to climb up on that horse. No saddle, no reins, no experience. 'Just take it for a quiet walk,' they said. Absolutely crazy, when you think of it!

All was well at first as horse and rider took a slow turn around the paddock. But then we neared the open gate. At this juncture the horse decided it had had enough and it suddenly headed for home, which was some 400 metres down a bitumen road. In a few strides, the giant beast, as if trying to get home before curfew, hit what felt to me like full pace. It was all I could do but hang on for grim death while screaming 'Please stop!' I was petrified, certain that this was going to have an ugly ending.

That prospect loomed large when we neared 'home' and the horse veered sharply. Suddenly it was going in one direction while my momentum took me in another. With nothing to hang onto, a fall was inevitable. The next thing I knew I was doing a forward roll towards the bitumen and all I could see were galloping hooves which I was sure were going to land on me.

The vision of those hooves is still firmly imprinted on my mind. As is the arrival at the scene of family and friends who then saw me get to my feet in a state of shock and assess my body for damage. Not only was I uninjured, there wasn't a mark on me. It still feels like a miracle to me that a few days later I was alive enough to face the Victorians at the WACA. Where, as you'll see in due course, another miracle was about to take place.

In the moments before the match our new captain, Tony Lock, won the toss and chose to bat first. 'Bo', as he was known, was of the old school and believed in the adage, 'You win the toss ... you think about bowling ... then you bat.' So, bat we did, but in next to no time, it seemed, we were all out for 161 – a disappointing performance, to say the least. It would have been a lot worse without John Inverarity's unbeaten 76.

We went into the field in the third session of that first day. Our opening attack was left-armer Jim Hubble, into the breeze, and Test hero Graham McKenzie, downwind. 'Garth', as Graham was known universally, was WA's flag-bearer as its first regular member of the Australian team. By the time he played the last of his 60 Tests in 1971 he had 246 Test wickets to his name – just two short of Richie Benaud's then Australian record.

On his day, Hubble, a left-arm, fast-medium bowler with big swing, was also very damaging, particularly to a right-hand bat. He was good enough to have toured South Africa in 1966–67 (though he didn't play a Test) and, in 1971–72, to take 7-49 at the WACA against Queensland. On this particular afternoon, however, Jim suffered an injury early on in Victoria's innings and, sooner than expected, had to be replaced in the attack. I was chosen to take his place. This meant for me an earlier-than-usual use of the ball which, I was pleased to note when I got it in my hands, still had a good shine on it, while the seam was almost as good as new. This seriously enabled my main weapon, which was swinging the ball both ways.

Occupying both ends of the wicket at the time were the Victorian openers, Bill Lawry and Ian Redpath: one revered, the other feared; one a lefty, one a righty. Both had tremendous ability, temperament and downright doggedness, and they'd had smiles on their faces a short time earlier when they'd walked onto the WACA. They were a formidable force.

Redpath, a highly regarded top-order batsman on the international stage, was cast in the Lawry mould. A fine player, and very adaptable, he was generally very attacking, but he had the ability to accept a more defensive role when required. He could be very difficult to remove. He was a wonderful competitor, of whom Greg Chappell once said, 'While it's true most people would die for the Baggy Green, only two would kill for it: Ian Redpath and Rod Marsh.' Conversely, perhaps, Redpath was a most delightful man with a great sense of humour. A man not averse to having a friendly chat with an opponent during a game.

That was something that was definitely *not* in Bill Lawry's repertoire. No, 'Phantom' was a competitor through and through. Not only did he abstain from on-field pleasantries, he was against the delightful practice, followed by all the other states, of mingling in each other's changerooms after a day's play. Bill never came into our rooms at the close of play, and there may as well have been a sign on the Victorians' door saying 'Opposition players not welcome'. That said, one of his men, Paul Sheahan, regularly broke Bill's rule and would bring with him a couple of bottles of beer and a cheery greeting.

One-for:
Ian Redpath, bowled Brayshaw, 21
Victoria 1-22

The Victorian openers had made steady progress as the clock on the scoreboard ticked towards stumps. Then Redpath, who had scored all but one of Victoria's 22 runs, and looked as solid as the Rock of Gibraltar, was bowled. I managed to produce an inswinger that found its way through bat and pad before hitting middle and off.

Like the rest of my team I was elated at breaking the partnership, and thankful for any small mercies at that stage.

At the time I knew little about the new batsman, Ken Eastwood, other than what I saw as he took guard: that he was shortish, well-built and a left-hander. Eastwood, turns out, was a prolific run-scorer in club cricket in Melbourne and had a more than handy first-class career, making some big scores, including a double century. Had the Victorian team not been so unusually strong no doubt he would have played a lot more for them. He did play one Test, though, when he was 35, against England in 1971, having replaced Lawry who had been dropped. To me he was a quiet man who just went about his business.

When Eastwood joined his captain, not a word passed between them. I presume there was an unspoken understanding that getting to stumps without losing another wicket was their imperative.

Two-for:

Ken Eastwood, caught Vernon, bowled Brayshaw, 6
Victoria 2-28

Just six runs later Eastwood got a thick edge to one of my outswingers and was caught knee-high in the gully by Murray Vernon – a fine, up-the-order, left-hand batsman who captained WA the previous season and could easily have done well at Test-match level. The wicket of Eastwood gave me the figures of 2-2, which remained the case when stumps were called soon after.

Later, in the dressing-room, our coach, Wally Langdon, put a hand on my shoulder and said, 'Well done, two for two. If you get five for five tomorrow I'll ask Todge [the newspaper photographer] to take a picture of the board.'

And that's as good a place as any to leave my tale for the moment. It's high time we went back to the beginning.

CHAPTER 2

TRAILBLAZERS

After the hue and cry that surrounded the defining of first-class cricket, it was perhaps fitting that a man known as 'The Nonpareil' (unrivalled or matchless) was belatedly determined to have been the first player in a first-class match to take a ten-for.

A protagonist for the introduction and acceptance of round-arm bowling, **William Lillywhite (13 June 1792 – 21 August 1854)** was recognised as one of the best bowlers of his era – an era when under-arm bowling was the standard method of propelling a ball down a pitch.[5] Before we get to Lillywhite and his groundbreaking ten-for, however, it's worth exploring the evolution of bowling styles in a little more detail.

From cricket's earliest days bowlers exclusively rolled the ball down the pitch. There was no real run-up, just a half step forward and release. In the main, the ball barely, if at all, bounced. This explains the early popularity of a bat that perhaps better resembled a hockey stick. Such a bat had more wood with which to greet the ball as it rolled towards the wickets.

In time, however, new variations of bowling began to appear. One was the lob. In this case, the bowler's strategy was to under-arm

---

5 Perhaps Australian medium-pacer Trevor Chappell was merely showing he was a student of cricket history when he scandalously rolled the ball along the deck in a World Series Cup final game against New Zealand at the MCG on 1 February, 1981.

the ball into the air and challenge the batsman to either hit it on the full or after it bounced. The best lob bowlers possessed the skill to project the ball in such an arc that it would land on top of the stumps if the batsman failed to make contact.

Another variation was the under-arm skimmer. Usually, but not always, this delivery began with the bowler running up to the delivery point and releasing the ball at speed. Done right, the ball would skim along the ground like a stone on a lake.

In *Cricket*, WG Grace mentions a George Brown, born in 1783, as being the fastest 'under-hand' bowler who ever played. Said WG, 'He was so fast that two long stops were needed for him and nearly all his fieldsmen were behind the wicket.' Grace then added what could well be an apocryphal flourish: 'At Lord's a man once tried to stop [one of Brown's deliveries] with his coat, but Brown bowled through it and killed a dog on the other side.'

By the early 19th century, seismic change was in the air with bowlers like Kent cricketer John Willes sending down round-arm deliveries: deliveries where the ball was released somewhere between waist and shoulder height. Batsmen now had to deal with bounce and trajectory as well as pace. This action created considerable controversy. Round-arm bowling was not technically illegal at this time but was considered ungentlemanly (ironic when we again recall Trevor Chappell's infamous delivery, an action which saw *under*-arm bowling banned). The Laws of the Game were subsequently changed in 1816 to outlaw it.

As he demonstrated playing for Kent against the Marylebone Cricket Club (MCC) in 1822, Willes, for one, wasn't prepared to let it go. WG Grace described the moment thus: 'Mr Willes made a big bid for the introduction of round-arm bowling. He was only allowed to bowl a few balls before he was no-balled –

and he left the ground, declining to go on with the match.[6] There can be no doubt that his attempt in this match created the agitation which led to the adoption [of round-arm] a short time afterwards.'

Which brings us back to the first of our trailblazers, William Lillywhite.

Lillywhite, born in Westhampnett, a village near Chichester in West Sussex, had cricket in his veins, what with his father, FW, his brother John, and his cousin James all being accomplished players. A short, thick-set and powerful man, Lillywhite worked on improving his round-arm bowling style while playing club cricket in Brighton. In 1825, when he was in his early thirties, he made his debut for Sussex. Two years later, Lillywhite made his first appearance at Lord's – 'in the second of three matches arranged that season between Sussex and England to test the merits of underhand and round-arm bowling', as ESPNcricinfo explains.

From 1826 Lillywhite's star was on the rise, and his success as a round-armer contributed to the continuing controversy over the legality of the action. Despite its 1816 ban, the action was becoming more prevalent and as Martin Williamson writing for ESPNcricinfo noted in 2006: 'Confusion grew among players and public about what was allowed. Often it was left to individual umpires, and objections from batsmen facing round-arm bowlers was common.'

---

6   Doubt has been cast on this explanation, but the story goes that Willes had been very ill and to recover strength fell back on his beloved cricket. Not quite strong enough to bowl, however, he enlisted the aid of his sister, Christina – who had to employ a basic round-arm style due to her wide and massive skirt. Willes also noted that she gained more bounce off the pitch from turning her hand over at release. When he recovered his health he practised the technique and found he could get more work on the ball. Willes felt very strongly about the treatment of his new style at the hands of the umpires. WG Grace again: ' Unfortunately his temper was stronger than his respect for the laws – for not only did he leave the match, but he made up his mind to give up the game forever, a decision which he adhered to.'

In 1828, unable to halt evolution, the MCC tried anyway, permitting deliveries bowled as high as *elbow* height. This did little to solve the problem or the controversy. All the while Lillywhite continued to establish himself in the Sussex county side and in 1832 he took 71 wickets. From 1830 onwards, he also become a fixture in the MCC team, for whom he would take more than 400 wickets.

In 1835, the MCC, desperate to keep up with the game, modified the Laws again, finally allowing round-arm deliveries.[7]

Two years later, a year in which Lillywhite claimed 99 wickets at 8.65 apiece, his big moment arrived – though to be fair he wouldn't have known at the time just how big it was. Representing Players in a match against Gentlemen at Lord's, Lillywhite took ten wickets in helping to bowl out a 16-man team for 42 (Players, incidentally, had only 11, well, players). Despite the uneven numbers, and certain gaps in the scorecard (such as overs bowled and runs conceded by respective

---

7   The next iteration of bowling styles entered English cricket lore almost by stealth as *over*-arm bowling eased its way into being. Grumbling was pretty general at the beginning of 1862, and no-one was surprised that another explosion occurred before the end of it. The showdown that heralded further change happened at The Oval in August of that year. England was playing Surrey and the protagonist was Edgar 'Ned' Willsher – the first to be no-balled for bowling over-arm. He was called six times by umpire John Lillywhite (ironically, one of William Lillywhite's sons) for delivering the ball when his hand was above his shoulder. Like Willes before him, an outraged Willsher left the field in protest, along with the eight other professionals in his team. Lillywhite was replaced, and Willsher returned to take six wickets. Ned Willsher had had his say and won the day. Over-arm bowling was legalised in 1864.

bowlers), this game came to be recognised, much later, as a first-class fixture.

According to WG Grace, the introduction of round-arm bowling was Lillywhite's opportunity to make his mark, which he wholeheartedly embraced. 'His accuracy of pitch was something marvellous and a ball off the wicket was a rare thing,' Grace wrote. 'A wide ball from him was not expected and rarely given. He was what is called a "head" bowler, always on the lookout for a weak spot in the defence of the batsman. He knew that batsmen of that time had not been used to over after over of straight, good-length balls, and sooner or later he would tempt them to hit.'

William Lillywhite soldiered on well into his fifties, playing at one time or another for Hampshire and Middlesex, as well as Sussex. Testament to the stamina of the man (and to the paucity of games played each season), he was able to keep up with the best. For three consecutive seasons, between 1842 and 1844, when he was aged between 50 and 52, he bagged more than 100 wickets.

In a rare week in September 1847, playing for the All England Eleven, a sort of travelling professional troupe, he took ten wickets in an innings on three more occasions – in matches which were not later determined to be of the first-class variety. The first came in Newcastle against Northumberland, who had 20 players (September 20 to 22). Then, against the 22 men of Stockton and North Yorkshire at Stockton-on-Tees (September 23 to 25), he claimed ten in the first innings and 11 in the second. The following year, while again representing the All England Eleven, he also took another ten-for, against the 15 men of West Kent. His knack for spotting weaknesses in a batsman continued to pay off.

A splendid career came to an abrupt end when Lillywhite fell ill during his benefit game at Lord's on 25 July 1853. He was unable to complete the match … and did not play first-class cricket again.

At the age of 61, perhaps it *was* time for the grandfather of round-arm to draw stumps.

Lillywhite, who finished his playing days with 1576 first-class wickets at 1.54 apiece, died a year later and was buried in Highgate Cemetery. A monument, paid for by public subscription, features a shield with cross bats and stumps with a ball removing a bail. On top of the pedestal is a broken column and wreath symbolising 'a life cut short'.

Until the statisticians and record-keepers reconsidered the starting date of first-class cricket, **Edmund 'Ned' Hinkly (12 January 1817 – 8 December 1880)** was considered the first player to take a ten-for in a first-class match. The belated addition of Lillywhite pushed him down a spot to second, but he was long dead by the time that happened.

Hailing from humble beginnings in the quiet Kent countryside, Hinkly had a reputation as a fine paceman who was reputedly one of the first (if not *the* first) bowlers capable of swinging the ball away from the right-hander. And this while bowling left-arm round-arm! He was a journeyman who rose to heights that may not have been anticipated.

The son of a village postmaster, Hinkly began work as a shoemaker in his native village of Benenden, near Tunbridge Wells in Kent, before becoming a professional cricketer. From the surprisingly strong Benenden team he graduated to playing for the county. A long journey had begun.

After an uneventful three matches in 1846, he was left out of the side until 1848 when, in July, against England at Lord's, he had a match to remember. In the first innings he claimed six wickets. He followed that up with a ten-for in the second as England were dismissed for just 74 runs. One of his scalps, as it happened, was William Lillywhite, stumped for a duck.[8]

Hinkly was in and out of favour with the Kent selectors, but he enjoyed another flash of brilliance in 1849. In successive games he bagged a total of 22 wickets, six and five against Sussex at Royal Tunbridge Wells, and eight and three against England at Canterbury. Four years later in a match against Surrey at The Oval he again claimed 11 match wickets. He matched that haul once more against Sussex at Gravesend in 1856.

Relying on cricket for his income, Hinkly played as often as possible, representing Surrey (playing for whom he took 11 wickets against England at The Oval in 1849) on many occasions. He also played what might be called representative games, suiting up more than a few times for South against North. In 1857 he toured with the All England Eleven (AEE). On 31 occasions he played *against* AEE as a 'given man' (hired professional) for the 18- and 22-man squads who formed the opposition.

In 1857 he took 40 wickets against AEE in all games, notably 8-20 and 6-53 for '22 of Liverpool' at Prince's Park. Included in that haul was the wicket of George Parr, considered the greatest batsman of the day. Nine years earlier, on their first meeting, when Hinkly had taken 16 wickets for Kent against England at Lord's, he had claimed Parr's wicket twice. The records show that in all matches (not necessarily of first-class variety) they are known to have been on opposing sides he dismissed the great man 23 times.

---

8   The term 'duck' – a shortening of the term 'duck's egg' – for a score of nought (think of its shape), was probably not in use at the time. The term doesn't pop up until a reference in an 1866 English newspaper report on a cricket match in which the then Prince of Wales, the future King Edward VII, took to the crease, having earlier fielded at short leg. 'When at length expectant eyes were fixed on Britain's heir at the wicket,' *The Daily Times* correspondent reported, 'it was piteous to behold his signal failure; he was bowled out on the instant, and retired to the royal pavilion on "a duck's egg".'

Speaking as an over-arm bowler of medium pace – an action that put minimum strain on my body – I cannot imagine the stresses Hinkly placed on his frame by bowling round-arm as fast as he could. It's impressive he lasted as long as he did before, aged 57, retiring from the game in 1874. During his later years he was generally seen hobbling around in the vicinity of The Oval, a sad sight for a once vigorous man. He died in 1880 at the age of 63.

The third man in the triumvirate of trailblazers was rated the 'finest all-rounder of the day' by no less a luminary than the legendary Kent player Fuller Pilch, himself a fine hand with both bat and ball. But who knows if **John Wisden (5 September 1826 – 5 April 1884)** might have earned such lofty praise had circumstance not intervened early in his life. Wisden was only five when his father died and, as a result, was sent to live with a man named Tom Box. As it happened, Box was a fine cricketer. Indeed, he was roundly considered the greatest wicketkeeper of the 19th century. And so Wisden's schooling in cricketing life began.

Described in the chronicles of the time as a 'hungry-looking lad glad of one's sixpence for his trouble', young Wisden was a good student of the game, eager to learn and improve. Such was his success in this regard that he made his debut for Sussex at the age of 18.

Though small for a fast bowler – 'Easily the smallest fast bowler who ever made history', according to HS Altham in his 1962 book *History of Cricket* – he built up a fair head of steam and was soon considered one of the country's best. It wasn't long before he wore the nickname 'The Little Wonder' (after the winner of the Epsom Derby in 1840), and batsmen feared his fast and ripping deliveries.

Wisden stepped out for Sussex from 1846 to 1863 and posted many amazing feats. In 1848, he took 15 wickets in a match against Kent and 14 against Nottinghamshire. The following year, he nabbed 13 in a match against the MCC at Brighton. In 1850, appearing for North versus South at Lord's, his history-making moment came when claimed ten-for, all out bowled, a record that stands today. 'A very good authority who witnessed the performance told me that he kept up his break

from the off, from one to two feet, right through the innings,' WG Grace later wrote.

In the 38 matches he played that year, several against sides of more than 11 players, Wisden captured 340 wickets. In fact, he averaged 225 wickets annually for 12 years, posting a mammoth 455 in 1851, included in which was another ten-for. Playing for the All England Eleven (AEE) against Yorkshire at Sheffield, he returned figures of 10-58. Wisden had joined the AEE in 1846 and played numerous games for the outfit throughout Britain, mainly promotional affairs against teams of as many as 22 players. However, he headed a revolt against the organisation's owner, William Clarke, and formed a rival group called the United England Eleven, which began activity in 1852.

Meantime, his form with the bat showed flashes of brilliance, highlights including 100 for Sussex versus Kent in 1849 and 148 in the Sussex–Yorkshire match of 1855. As the years wore on, Wisden's pace waned. Seeing the end approaching, he began preparing for life after the game when, in 1850, he set up a cricket equipment shop in Leamington Spa. Five years later came a cricket and cigar shop in London. Managing his ageing body, Wisden slipped back to medium-pace and occasionally even reverted to under-arm. Health issues finally forced his retirement after the 1863 season, but he left some impressive figures on the ledger, having taken 1109 first-class wickets at 10.32 each.

Speaking of ledgers, of sorts, for all Wisden's achievements as a cricketer, it feels safe to say he made a more substantial contribution to the game *after* he laid down his bat and ball. A year after his retirement he launched the *Cricketer's Almanack* as a competitor to Fred Lillywhite's *The Guide to Cricketers*. [9] There has been conjecture about the authenticity of *Wisden*'s first edition (relating to doubts over whether Wisden used unattributed content from others) but a tradition had been established. *Wisden*, later given the epithet 'The Cricketer's Bible', has been a treasure of the sport ever since.

The first five editions were published as *The Cricketer's Almanack* – with the apostrophe before the 's'. In 1869 the apostrophe was shifted to after the 's'. A year later, Wisden added his name to the title, making it *John Wisden's Cricketers' Almanack*. And so it continued to be named until 1938 when it became *Wisden Cricketers' Almanack*, as it's known to this day.

After John Wisden's death in 1884 there was an occasional change of ownership, through to the current-day owners, Bloomsbury. The annual production appears each April – and invariably the reader's first port of call is *Wisden*'s anointment of its five cricketers of the year, selected for their outstanding

---

9   Fred Lillywhite was the third son of William Lillywhite, the round-armed ten-for taker discussed earlier in this chapter. Fred's brother John, a former player himself, is footnoted earlier as the umpire who no-balled Edgar Willsher for bowling over-arm in 1862. When you consider their cousin James Lillywhite became, in 1877, the first ever captain of England in a Test match, the Lillywhites were cricketing royalty.

achievements over the previous 12 months. It's an award that cannot be won more than once, and is based on performances in England.[10]

While the annual award is given to five cricketers, there have been exceptions when no awards have been given, such as during the First and Second world wars, or only a single player has been named. Three players – WG Grace (1896), Sir Pelham Warner (1921) and Sir Jack Hobbs (1926) – were the only sole recipients. And Warner and Hobbs are the only exceptions to the once-only rule, having been named twice each. At the time of writing, Australia's Neil Harvey (1954) remains the oldest surviving recipient of the very prestigious award.

In the 1913 edition there was no traditional naming of the players of the previous year. Instead, the founder was the subject of a 'special portrait' in what was the fiftieth edition of *Wisden*. What began as a figment of an inventive and determined imagination back in 1864 became, and remains, a towering influence over cricket, cricketers and followers of the great summer game. Collectors, too. A full set of originals would probably set you back over $200,000.

The aforementioned Sir Pelham Warner perhaps summed it up best, speaking after the almanack's centenary: '*Wisden* and cricket are synonymous.' And in my broadcasting days that was very true. That weighty little tome went with me everywhere and I consulted it so frequently its pages became worn and even, dare I admit to it, dog-eared. Now it sits in a prominent position on a bookshelf in my office.

---

10 For a brief period, between 2000 and 2003, the award was made based on the players' impacts on world cricket, as opposed to their performances in England. When *Wisden* reverted to its usual practice in 2004 it created a new, separate award: the *Wisden* 'Leading Cricketers in the World'.

John Wisden's ten-wicket innings haul at Lord's back in 1850 was indeed remarkable – as were those by William Lillywhite and Edmund Hinkly – but for me it plays second fiddle to his eponymous almanack which, though it's out of date by the time it is published, continues to survive in the internet age. Long may it last.

CHAPTER 3
EARLY BIRDS

Between William Lillywhite's groundbreaking ten-for in 1837 and the turn of the century, 20 other men matched his single-innings haul. Three of them achieved the feat twice.

One of these was **Vyell Edward 'VE' Walker (20 April 1837 – 3 January 1906)**, a slow, under-arm bowler once regarded as the leading amateur bowler in England. Educated at Harrow, Walker, from Southgate, was from a family with immense cricketing pedigree. His brothers John, Alfred, Frederick, Arthur, Russell and Isaac all played first-class cricket. Alfred was a deadly fast under-armer, as good as they came with that style, and on the poorly prepared wickets of the day. On three occasions all seven lined up together for the Southgate club.

The first of Walker's two official ten-fors occurred at The Oval in 1859 when, playing for Surrey, he took 10-74. The second came in 1865 at Old Trafford when Walker was playing for Middlesex versus Lancashire. Bowling a mammoth 44.2 overs – no doubt made more bearable by his modest under-arm action – he took 10-104.

Interestingly, prior to his second ten-for, Walker came close on two other occasions, the second of which was considered official – until it wasn't. The first of these came when Walker's Middlesex team played Sussex in Islington in 1864. With nine wickets already to his name Walker thought he'd had the batsman, Payne, out

stumped, and was momentarily being congratulated for his ten-for. The mode of dismissal, however, was overturned when it was determined that the batsman had, in fact, *not* been stumped but rather run out. The ball, it seemed, had rebounded off the wicketkeeper's pads and onto the stumps.

On another occasion, also in 1864, Walker took 10-37 when playing for Middlesex against Kent. For some time this ten-for *was* considered official. And when added to the other two ten-fors discussed above, it seemed Walker, with three ten-fors, was in a league of his own.

As WG Grace wrote in 1891, 'It will be thus seen that Mr VE Walker has done it thrice; no other bowler has done it more than once.'

Of course, since those words were written by WG Grace, statisticians and cricketing boffins re-drew the borders of the cricketing landscape. As such, many historical games previously considered first-class fixtures – like that 1864 fixture in which Walker took 10-37 – were stripped of that status. Walker, then, is credited with 'just' two first-class ten-fors – which has him sitting alongside WG Grace on the all-time list, as it happens – but it has hardly diminished his standing in the game's history.

Something of a prodigy, he was only 19 when selected for a Gentlemen versus Players match. This prestigious annual event pitted Gentlemen, who were amateurs (ostensibly unpaid, although WG Grace did rather well!), against Players, who were paid professionals. This match – in the early days rated as one of the highlights of the English cricket season – endured to 1962 when the distinction was abolished.

Walker was only 21 when, playing for England against Surrey, he registered his first ten-wicket haul in the first innings. He backed that up with a century in the second. It was the first time such a double had been completed in a single game. Contemporary reports also heap praise on his fielding, which, they say, superbly complemented his lob bowling: 'His sprinting powers were exceptional … and he seemed to divine where the batsman meant to place the ball.'

Walker began his bowling journey as a round-arm medium-pacer but made the switch to under-arm lob bowling and soon became renowned as its best exponent. He was inspired by the craft of William Clarke, confessing that lob bowling was 'an acquired art'. Mainly bowling round the wicket, he varied his pace and derived fair spin from the leg. Occasionally he would send one down at a considerable height – which often proved confusing for the batsman.

There was much more to Walker's contribution to the game than his prowess as an all-rounder. He was also regarded as an astute captain, and at various times he led England, Middlesex and the Gentlemen. He was captaining England in a game against Surrey in 1859 when an 18-year-old opposition player sprouting early signs of facial growth strode to the wicket. That facial growth would later sprout to become the most famous beard in the history of cricket. It was indeed a young WG Grace who made 224 not out.

When Walker retired in 1877 he then took on roles that were important in the development of the game, as treasurer and president of Middlesex, and president of the MCC in 1891 and 1892. He died at the age of 68 after an innings very well crafted.

First-class cricket in England gained momentum in the back half of the 19th century. Earlier, inter-county contests had been played, but as the game spread there was an urge to formalise and expand competition away from those chosen few teams based mainly in and around the biggest cities. The result was the official birth, in 1890, of the County Championship.

Who better, then, to turn our attention to than the man who recorded the first ten-wicket haul in the fledgling Championship, one **Henry 'Harry' Pickett (26 March 1862 – 3 October 1907)**. A powerfully built fast bowler who delivered with a high arm, he first played for Essex in 1881. In the intervening period, before the county was awarded first-class status, Pickett, who also suited up occasionally for MCC, played 127 matches for the team, taking 629 wickets at 15.08.

When, in 1895, Essex stepped up for its maiden season in county cricket, Pickett rose to the occasion. That first season, in Essex's match against Leicestershire at Leyton, Pickett returned figures of 10-32, off 27 overs no less. Despite his superb individual

performance (though, curiously, he only claimed a single second innings wicket), Essex lost the game. Pickett continued to impress that season, ending it with 51 wickets at 18.72.

Pickett's time with Essex ended after his benefit season of 1897, after which he turned to umpiring for two seasons, then coached at a private school. There is, sadly, a tragic postscript to his story. He disappeared on 27 September 1907, and some weeks later his body was washed up on a beach in Wales.

Articles found in his clothing proved his identity. His death was listed as 'suicide'.

Another ten-for player whom, very sadly, could see no other way out was **Cyril Herbert George Bland (23 May 1872 – 1 July 1950)**. In 1950, at the age of 78, Bland drowned himself in a canal at Cowbridge, near Boston, Lincolnshire.

Cyril Bland was a right-arm fast bowler who stripped for Sussex from 1897 to 1907. The pinnacle of a workmanlike career came for him in the 1899 season, when he captured ten-for (10-48) for Sussex against Kent at the Angel Ground in Tonbridge. He was the first Sussex player to achieve the feat. Contemporary reports indicated that in this game he 'bowled at a great pace and made the ball kick a good deal'.

Bland appeared in 147 first-class games for Sussex, a team-mate of such luminaries as CB Fry and KS Ranjitsinhji.[11]

---

11 Kumar Shri Ranjitsinhji, from Sadodar in Gujarat, who played for Sussex and in 15 Tests for England, has been called the 'Father of Indian Cricket' and many credit him with inventing the leg-glance. He was a *Wisden* Cricketer of the Year in 1897. After his playing days he became Maharaja of Nawanagar. All in all, an impressive CV.

One of many wonderful institutions in British sport was the annual Oxford versus Cambridge inter-varsity cricket match, which was traditionally played at Lord's. This quaint tradition took its rise from a challenge in 1827 between Oxford's captain, Christopher Wordsworth, and the Cambridge skipper, Hubert Jenner. The game was, until very recently, considered to be a first-class fixture.

Many fabled names in English cricket were printed on the scorecard at Lord's during the varsity match. One name not so well known in the years following the 1871 clash is that of **Samuel Evan Butler (15 April 1850 – 30 April 1903)**. Though his is far from a household name, in the annals of the game it still holds alone a special place today among the inter-varsity fraternity.

Butler, playing for Oxford University that year, claimed 10-38, the only time a bowler has fashioned a ten-for in the varsity match. The right-hand round-armer, who was said to produce 'great pace', also picked up five in the second innings (for match figures of 15-95), helping Oxford to win by eight wickets. Adding to the weight of the achievement is the fact that, at the time of writing, no other Oxford student has bagged a ten-for in *any* first-class fixture.

As a result of this strong performance, Butler was chosen in both Gentlemen versus Players games that year. Then, in the 1873 Varsity match, he further inflicted pain on Cambridge with a match-winning haul of 5-48.

After leaving Oxford in 1873, Butler played only two further first-class games. A career in law then took precedence over cricket but not before he'd made his mark. As his *Wisden* obituary reported, 'That one afternoon at Lord's he was unplayable'.

If you have ever been to watch a game at Lord's – or even watched via television – you would be astonished by the following description of the wicket, circa 1860: 'A rough surface, where no roller was ever used and the grass was cut by a scythe that left tufts on the surface ... with stones formed from the drying clay soil ... and balls which hit these stones could either be dead shooters or fly over the batsman's head.'

That was the sort of bowler's paradise that greeted Nottinghamshire's **George Wootton (16 October 1834 – 15 June 1924)** when he joined the Lord's ground staff team – and represented the Lord's-based MCC team in 1861. A round-arm, fast-medium left-hander of 'a good length and twist', he was almost unplayable on those surfaces ... as the return of 14-46 (bowling eight men in the first innings) in his first game for the MCC at Lord's would indicate.

While he was nowhere near as potent on grounds where the roller was employed, his best bowling figures came in 1865 at Bramall Lane in Sheffield. Representing the All England Eleven against a weak Yorkshire batting line-up, Wootton joined the ten-for club by taking 10-54 to help the MCC win by an innings and 255 runs. Two years later he enjoyed a particularly stellar season, claiming 142 wickets in only 19 games.

Although his colleagues tried in vain to convince him that he had more to offer, Wootton's playing career ended after a benefit in 1873. He then stood as a first-class umpire through to 1883, and was heard to comment, 'I liked umpiring very well, but if you made a mistake everybody is digging at you ... I couldn't stand that sort of thing.' He later watched the first Test match ever played at his home ground of Trent Bridge, an Ashes Test in 1899.

Originally a butcher by trade, Wootton on retirement took tenancy over a farm. He continued to coach youngsters in the local village club until late in life.

If a cricketer was given the chance to write his own epitaph, these words, published in *Wisden*, would perhaps do for most: 'A good batsman and a fast round-arm bowler, being altogether a cricketer above the average, and fielding generally at slip.' And if that didn't suffice, then how about, 'There were few better fast bowlers ... and he always looked a very proud man when he could get through the defence of the champion, then walk off the field in a stately fashion for a drink.'

Such were the warm, fuzzy words used to describe **William Hickton (14 December 1842 – 27 March 1900),** who played for Lancashire from 1867 to 1871 before joining Derbyshire in time to play in the newly established county's first match, ironically against his old employers. His four wickets in Lancashire's first innings might have reminded his old teammates of his talents, but they didn't need reminding. Only a year earlier Hickton had taken 10-46 in a game against Hampshire at Old Trafford, a chunk of the 144 wickets he took in his time with Lancashire.

Hickton plugged away with the ball for Derbyshire. In 1876 he snaffled 11 wickets in a match against Kent – 5-52 and 6-41. The following season he enjoyed his best form, playing all games on the fixture list and taking a total 40 wickets, with five-fors against Kent, Lancashire and Hampshire. He had one appearance for the Players at The Oval, when he claimed three wickets.

When Hickton's game faded he retired from first-class cricket in 1878, after taking only 11 wickets in as many matches. Among the tributes after his passing was that more than satisfying appraisal from *Wisden*.

In the age of under-arm bowling, there could be no conceivable way that a bowler could be no-balled for throwing. The call would be possible with round-arm bowling, where limbs could become entangled in a push for pace and movement off the wicket. But a slow left-armer?

It was a little strange, then, that the solidly successful career of **Edwin James 'Ted' Tyler (13 October 1864 – 25 January 1917)** was dogged by suspicions about the legality of his action. Was he a thrower? Was he not? These were days when there was a degree of permissiveness about such matters and, in the end, it didn't seem to matter all that much, perhaps because Tyler's bowling was so slow that there was no chance of him hurting anyone. As his *Wisden* obituary stated, 'Had he not possessed a good head and command of length he would have been cannon fodder for any quality batsman.'

Tyler was perhaps fortunate to have played most of his cricket before December 1900 when the captains of the first-class counties met to discuss what was seen as the scourge of throwing. Between

them, they compiled a list of bowlers who would be forced to step down from bowling duties for the 1901 season. 'Had he appeared after [the captains] had taken the matter of unfair bowling into their own hands,' the obituary continued, 'things might not have gone so pleasantly for him. Many offenders, much worse than Tyler, were allowed to pursue their careers quite unchecked – until the era of reform arrived.'

After playing for Worcestershire in 1885 and 1886, Tyler was a driver of Somerset's promotion to first-class ranks in 1891. With his effective bowling – plus Sammy Woods and Lionel Palairet also shining on the field – it was a fun time for Tyler, who joined the ten-for ranks in 1895 with 10-49 against Surrey at Taunton. He played for the county through until 1907, during which time he toured South Africa in 1895–1896 with England, playing one Test.

Tyler was very popular, his genial nature gaining him friends wherever he went.

There is a saying in sport that goes, 'early ripe, early rotten'. It talks both to a team and an individual, and it relates to the phenomenon of getting a flying start to a competition or a career and in the flurry of it all taking one's eye off the main game. It concerns getting ahead of oneself, losing concentration on the basics, then falling behind after everything looked so positive. A good example in Australian cricket might be Michael Clarke, who flashed on to the Test scene and then flashed off it – before coming back a much better player.

We concern ourselves here, however, with the opposite scenario, a player who had to wait so long for their opportunity they may have feared it would never come along.[12] Let's go back to 1881 and picture the situation in which **George Burton (1 May 1851 – 7 May 1930)** found himself. A slow right-handed bowler, Burton was a stalwart club cricketer around London who also had a career building coaches (as in the kind hitched to horses). There must have been many times Burton thought he'd gone as far in the

---

12 We delve elsewhere in these pages into examples of both Michael Hussey and Chris Rogers, both of whom endured an agonising wait before they finally got their chance in the Australian Test team – opportunities they grabbed with both hands.

game as he was going to – but that all changed when, aged 30, he was selected by Middlesex.

His first match was against Surrey at Lord's and he wasted no time in seizing the day, dismissing Harry Jupp with his second ball. In the second innings, in which he took 5-20, he claimed the wicket of Surrey captain John Shuter with his first delivery.

Burton went on to show a particular liking for Yorkshire. In 1888, he compiled two seven-wicket hauls against Yorkshire and, on another occasion, a 16-wicket match at Sheffield. This latter haul came the week after he claimed 10-59 against Surrey at The Oval (from a mammoth 52.3 overs), returning 13 wickets for the match.

This wasn't Burton's only ten-for (though it was the only first-class variety). He was a member of the MCC ground staff from 1883 to 1904, and in 1894, playing against Oxford City, he dismissed the entire Oxford team.

On retiring from the game, Burton spent two seasons as an umpire and was, for a number of seasons, the official scorer for the county.

Looking back on the particular – even peculiar – craft of bowling fast round-arm, you might find it difficult to conjure up a picture of what we call the 'delivery stride'. Executing such an action while standing still, I get – but taking a vigorous front-on approach, then getting into a position to project the ball in the required direction after a long, lively run-up? No way!

However, that's the formula that made **George Frederick Tarrant (7 December 1838 – 2 July 1870)** such a handful for batsmen in his heyday. And, wait for it, he specialised in bowling very fast *around* the wicket ... making the dynamics of delivery even more difficult. Remember, the round-armer must keep the bowling arm no higher than his shoulder. Yet this strong, wiry, active man was rated one of the fastest and, as WG Grace opined, one of the best. 'He was a very fast round-arm bowler and, for so little a man, astonishingly strong,' wrote Grace. 'There was no measured stately walk to the crease in his delivery. He was all over the place like a flash of lightning, never sparing himself.'

Because of his action Tarrant wasn't able to get the ball to jump sharply, but he *was* able to readily cut the ball back from the off. This resulted in more than occasional dismissals when the ball cannoned off a batsman's pads and onto the stumps. Add to all this a fiery spirit, which earned him the nickname 'Tear'em' Tarrant.

It is an odd fact that Tarrant played his first-class cricket for Cambridgeshire – a minor county team that didn't attain first-class status until 1857 – yet he was chosen to tour Australia and New Zealand with the second All England Eleven in 1863. It was that same year he bagged 10-40 playing for England against Kent at Lord's (in a match featuring more than 12 players per side).

In games for the All England Eleven against teams of 22, according to Grace, 'Tarrant terrorised timid batsmen, some of his long hops bounding over their heads, causing them to change colour and funk at the next straight one.'

Tarrant played 71 first-class games and would surely have played many more had he not died prematurely in 1870 at just 31 years of age.

CHAPTER 4
GRACE NOTES

There must be millions of words written about the 19th century cricket legend known universally as simply 'WG'. In my research to write this chapter I have read what feels like a good proportion of those words, and in them I could find no better description of Grace than that penned by the highly regarded English cricket historian HS Altham. As Altham wrote in the excellent *Barclays World of Cricket: The Game from A to Z (1980)*, 'For nearly 40 years WG Grace bestrode the world of cricket like a Colossus.'[13]

Long before exhibiting the prowess and personality that saw historian CLR James declare him 'the best known Englishman of all time', **William Gilbert 'WG' Grace (18 July 1848 – 23 October 1915)** was born into a true cricketing family. He was the fourth of five brothers (there were four older sisters), three of whom were outstanding cricketers. Indeed, they share the lovely distinction of having all played together in a Test match, the first played on English soil, against Australia at The Oval, in September, 1880.[14]

---

13 Employing a similar metaphor to describe one of Grace's distinctive physical traits, the Australian magazine *The Bulletin* said of Grace's feet that he could get two pounds a week and tucker merely to walk about in the grasshopper districts and 'kill off the pests'.

14 On two other occasions three brothers have played in the same Test match. Hanif, Mushtaq and Sadiq Mohammad all played for Pakistan against New Zealand at Karachi in October, 1969. Much earlier, in Cape Town in 1891–1892, Alec and George (GG) Hearne played for England and their brother Frank for South Africa.

The Grace brothers were also instrumental in the formation of the Gloucestershire County Cricket Club in 1871. And their combined presence projected the club to the unofficial championship title in 1876 and 1877 – 'unofficial' because the County Championship proper was established in 1890.

Their father, Henry Grace, was quite a package himself. A player, a coach, a promoter and an enthusiast of the game, he would proffer counsel to young WG along the lines of 'Have patience my boy', 'Where there's a will there's a way', and 'There is nothing you cannot attain if only you try hard enough'. That their mother, Martha, also loved cricket was of inestimable value to her cricketing sons. In fact, for years, she was the only woman to feature in the 'births and deaths' section of *Wisden*. When you consider, too, that there was a live-in uncle who taught the boys the fundamentals of technique, and the value of application through curiosity and concentration on the basics, WG was certainly raised in an environment ideal for the reaching of one's sporting potential.

As Grace himself said, the great summer game permeated his life from a very early age. 'Respect for the truth prevents me from saying that I played the first year of my existence,' he wrote. 'But I have little hesitation in declaring that I handled bat and ball before the end of my second year.'

Although WG would go on, year after year, to prove his mastery with bat in hand, he appears in these pages as a bowler. And we will come to that part of his story in due course. First, though, it's worth spending a little time looking at the coming together of the pieces that would make Grace one of the most influential cricketers in history.

The Grace family lived in Downend, a small village close to Bristol in Gloucestershire, and such was the boys' desperate enthusiasm for the game that they went as far as carving out a field among fruit trees in the backyard of their home. A special area was designated for the pitch, and it was given constant treatment to make it the best surface possible for practice. This in a day when wickets even for first-class games throughout England left a lot to be desired (and you'll recall that description of the 1880 pitch at Lord's in the previous chapter).

WG's uncle, Henry Pocock, initially instructed his young student in the basics of straight-bat play. This was an unusual technique at the time, as batsmen were slow to emerge from the cross-bat method of countering under-arm bowling. 'Keep your left shoulder well forward and get over the ball,' was the message, 'and keep your eyes fixed on the bowler and never lose sight of the ball from the time it leaves his hand.' This was rehearsed until it formed the foundation of his batting through a long and stunningly successful career.

In his book *Cricketing Reminiscences* (1899) WG answered the perennial question: Was he born a cricketer? Grace thought not, believing cricketers are made by coaching and practice, not innate ability. He did concede, however, that while he wasn't born a cricketer, he was born in the *atmosphere* of cricket, in ways we've outlined above.

There must have been more to it than that, however. There is no question that WG was a child prodigy. He emerged as a young teenager in the 1860s, when the game was in a period of evolution with the legalisation of over-arm bowling. But he thrived while others struggled to come to terms with change.

Observers say that he was equally comfortable on back or front foot – which, again, was unusual for the day. And the degree of pace didn't bother him. 'The faster the better,' he would quip. Then there was that correct style of his, a style ahead of its time. 'WG was a very correct batsman,' former teammate Colonel Frank Crozier once remarked. 'His left shoulder pointed to the bowler. He held his bat straight and brought it straight through to the ball. He was the most powerful straight driver I've ever seen. When he drove at a ball I was mighty glad I was behind the stumps.'

It all came together in a hurry for the young Grace. He was only 15 when he made 32 against an All England Eleven, and he'd just turned 18 when, playing for England against Surrey at The Oval, he scored 224 not out – after which he obtained his captain's permission to hurry off to an athletics meeting at Crystal Palace where, wouldn't you know it, he won the quarter-mile hurdles. From that day on he was the shining light in English cricket, a status he enjoyed for 44 seasons between 1865 and 1908. It's fair to say, he's a cricketing beacon that continues to cast a glow over the game.

Landmarks continued to be established as Grace, a leviathan of the game, went from strength to strength – and this in an era where, it bears repeating, Grace played on minefield pitches and for some time on grounds without boundaries, meaning every hit, including those 'into the country', as HS Altham once quipped, had to be run in full.[15] In 1868 he became only the second man to score two centuries in a match, a feat that saw one writer acclaim him as 'indisputably the cricketer of the age; the Champion'. The following year Grace was made a member of the MCC and he scored four centuries in July alone. Then came the window-dressing of a champion, the unveiling of his signature look. Turning up for the 1870 season, Grace sported an enormous black beard. His facial hair, as impressive as one of his ferocious front-foot drives, was matched by an expansion of his girth. Not especially big by today's standards, back then Grace's 15- stone (95-kilogram) frame was considered imposing. It was certainly no longer the body of a hurdler.

In 1873 he became the first to score a century before lunch, but it was three seasons later that he produced a purple patch of form that had bowlers – fast and slow – gasping for air. It started with his career-high score of 344 (the first triple-century in first-class cricket) for MCC versus Kent at Canterbury. Two days later he compiled 177 for Gloucestershire against Nottinghamshire. Two days after that he clobbered 318 not out for Gloucestershire versus Yorkshire. In all, 839 runs for two times out in three consecutive innings. Extraordinary!

---

15 Until roughly the middle of the 19th century, there was no boundary as we know it today. The only advantage to hitting the ball a long way was to create more time to run. This resulted in a first-class record that is over 180 years old. In 1842, in a game between home team Cambridge University and the MCC, Frederick Ponsonby, representing the visitors, scored nine runs from a single delivery, all without overthrows.

The general feeling as the Eighties turned into the Nineties was that WG's star must be waning; that age would have to tell. Wrong. In 1895 he enjoyed what was dubbed his 'Indian summer' and he posted his 100th first-class century shortly before turning 47.

It wasn't until April 1908 that the first-class train rolled into the terminus for the great man. Appearing for the Gentlemen of England against Surrey at The Oval, Grace, 59, opened the batting in both innings scoring 15 and 25 respectively. After that, he tucked his bat under his arm and walked off the pitch and out of the game.

It is an odd fact that for all his dominance in domestic cricket, Grace was not such a dominant figure in his 22 Test appearances, scoring his 1098 runs at an average of 32.29. He was still a man for the big occasion, though. In that first Test match on England soil – against Australia at The Oval in 1880 – he opened the batting with brother EM (with his other brother Fred coming in down the order) and scored England's first-ever century in a Test against Australia. He also made two tours to Australia, and in doing so made a significant contribution in the development of cricket Down Under.

So, what is to be said about the 'other' parts of WG's game? From all reports he was a brilliant fielder at point – and almost unpassable by straight hits off his own bowling. It's less celebrated, for obvious reasons, but he was also an excellent bowler, his round-arm action accompanied by considerable variation that proved the better of many a batsman.

The 1873 season was proof, if it was needed, of Grace's considerable ability as an all-rounder. That year he became the first to complete the double of 1000 runs and 100 wickets in a season, which he went on to achieve eight times in all:

1873 – 2139 runs and 106 wickets
1874 – 1664 runs and 140 wickets
1875 – 1498 runs and 191 wickets
1876 – 2622 runs and 129 wickets
1877 – 1474 runs and 179 wickets
1878 – 1151 runs and 152 wickets
1885 – 1688 runs and 117 wickets
1886 – 1846 runs and 122 wickets

I found WG's take on bowling, of all sorts, fascinating. The following words of wisdom, from 1891, were aimed at the young bowler. Having played as a bowler myself – and coached bowlers – I find it uncanny that these tenets are still so relevant today:

- Bowl straight
- Bowl a good length
- Vary your pace and pitch
- Try to get some break on the ball
- Learn something about the nature and condition of the wicket on which you are bowling
- Seek for the weak spots in the batsman's defence.

He adds a rider: 'Watch first-class bowlers carefully, make a note of their styles and mark their points of difference.'

Significantly, Grace played through the evolution of bowling, from the under-arm years, through the round-arm era, and on to the over-arm style that remains in place today. He only bowled round-arm himself, however, shunning the opportunity to change to the legalised over-arm style later in his career. In his early years as a round-arm bowler – which saw him develop his trademark leg-break which he called the 'leg-tweaker' – he showed lively pace before cutting back in the 1870s to something more akin to a spin-bowler's speed. In any case, the chief feature of his bowling was the excellent length that he consistently maintained.

By any manner of judgement Grace was a *proper* bowler. Indeed, twice he claimed ten-for in a first-class game. The first such occasion was in 1873 when he took 10-92 for Gentlemen of the MCC versus Kent at Canterbury. Then, in 1886 – by which time Grace began practising medicine – he returned figures of 10-49 for MCC against Oxford University at Oxford. In the latter game the indefatigable Grace had earlier made 104, then bowled out the students for 90 to seal an innings victory.

Grace, of course, wasn't as pure as the driven snow. For instance, he was said to go in for a fair bit of gamesmanship, once apparently putting the bails back on after being bowled and remarking 'Windy today, umpire?' At The Oval in 1882 he ran out Australian Sammy Jones when the batsman was out of his ground between balls patting down the pitch. The incident so riled the Aussie speedster Fred Spofforth that he took 7-44 as England – chasing 85 – were bowled out for 77. After this, the first win by Australia on English soil, British newspaper *The Sporting Times* published the infamous satirical obituary for English cricket that helped give rise to the naming of the England versus Australia contests as the Ashes.

Grace, who somewhat controversially earned huge amounts from cricket despite being a so-called 'amateur', died in 1915 after a German bombing attack on London. As you'd expect, there was no shortage of tributes, none more telling than the one offered up by KS Ranjitsinhji: 'He turned the old one-stringed instrument [that is, the cricket bat] into a multi-chorded lyre; the theory of modern batting is in all essentials the result of WG's thinking and working on the game.'

Following Grace's death, the MCC commissioned architect Sir Herbert Baker to design a pair of gates to stand as the main entrance to Lord's for MCC members. To this day, members awaiting the start of a Test match queue outside the WG Grace Memorial Gates, many of them no doubt reflecting on the lasting legacy of a true titan of the game.

It was said of **Edward Mills 'EM' Grace (28 November 1841 – 20 May 1911)** that if it hadn't been for his own brother he would have lived in cricket history as perhaps the most remarkable player the game has produced. Adding to that, barring WG, it would have been hard to name a man who was a stronger influence on a side or a more remarkable match-winner.

While EM and WG were two men from the same cricket-crazy family, they were not necessarily peas from the same pod. Seven years older than his more famous brother, something of a cavalier to his brother's more measured approach, EM was the different one. Though equally gifted, he was less inclined to take his cricket too seriously.

Playing for South Wales in 1860 and 1861, EM saw his batting blossom while he worked on his bowling, from lobs to round-arm. In one club game in 1861, for Berkeley versus Knole Park, he batted through

the innings for 100 not out, then took every wicket. That same year, for Lansdown versus Clifton, his 119 not out was followed up by another ten-for. He hit even higher spots during Canterbury Week in 1862. Playing for the MCC against Kent he scored 192 not out and then joined the first-class ten-for club with 10-69 in Kent's second innings. The critics crowned him the best cricketer in the world, lauding his talents with bat and ball and in the field, a man 'full of lusty life, cheerily gay and [with] energy inexhaustible'.

The following season EM scored 3071 runs and took 349 wickets in all matches (not just first-class) – an all-round feat that earned him a trip to Australia and New Zealand, where his form was hampered by a nasty hand injury. Plus, it was recorded, when he did bat his technique was found wanting and he reverted to reckless strokeplay. This was a problem he was unable to remedy during the tour. For all his talents, EM played just one Test match – when, as you've read, he joined his younger brothers WG and GF (Fred) in the England team for the inaugural Test on home soil at The Oval in 1880.

As a batsman, EM was unorthodox, but his wonderful eye, smart reflexes and nerve carried him to great heights. It's considered that he pioneered the pull shot – a product of his natural tendency to play across the line. As a bowler, EM first delivered by fast round-arm, then mixed that method with lobs and, finally, lobs with low flight. He kept a good length and found some spin, these balls often tempting batsmen to have a hit and offer up catches. In a game against the Players at The Oval in 1865, the Gentlemen were having a problem dismissing Harry Jupp, a noted stonewaller. EM had the solution. He sent down a very high lob that landed on the bails – while Jupp offered no stroke. Infuriated members of the crowd jumped the fence to remonstrate with the bowler, who had to fight his way to the safety of the pavilion. All in a day's play for this life and soul of the game.

The record books show that in all first-class games EM scored more than 10,000 runs and claimed in excess of 300 wickets. However, it was once assessed that his figures in *all* matches might have been as high as 76,760 runs and 12,078 wickets.

In the cricketing firmament, EM may always play second fiddle to WG, but there is no dismissing his vast talent and achievements.

CHAPTER 5

THREE TIMES

Cricket is very much a numbers game, and numbers become statistics. And statistics have fascinated those who have followed cricket since the scores were just notches on a piece of wood. For me that fascination began when my father would take me to the WACA Ground to watch a game. I suspect this was first in the summer of the 1947–48 season, when WA first entered the Sheffield Shield competition.

I took the numbers home with me – and acted out my own replay of the day's play on the pages of a birthday-present scorebook. There was a concrete staircase up to our front door, and I played cricket matches by tossing a small rubber ball against them. I would react to the bounce, left hand, right hand, then place the relevant scores down on the little scoresheet.

Keith Miller was my hero. And when it came to the 1953 Ashes tour of England I was able to follow the Australian team's fortunes – Keith Miller's in particular – via the ABC's coverage, relayed from the BBC on shortwave radio. I can still hear the distorted voices of Alan McGilvray and John Arlott, punctuated by the raucous crowd noises that tended to overwhelm their voices whenever a boundary was scored or a wicket was taken.

Commentary of that series began pretty close to my bedtime, but my parents allowed me to have our wireless tuned in so I could hear it down the passageway. I would listen, then play the appropriate shot and run up and down the passageway to score. When it was time to go to bed, I would take the wireless with me and leave it turned on. Many was the time I would wake up to the sound of white noise, signalling the fact that stumps had been drawn in England and the coverage had concluded. No such thing as 24-hour radio in those days!

Yes, numbers did tell the story for me, especially when all I could do was listen on the radio. And at that stage, for me, they were just that – numbers (not to be confused with statistics, which is the extrapolation of numbers, in cricket and elsewhere). And numbers will never go anywhere near to telling the whole story. There is the actual *doing* of it all.

When sitting down to review the career of **Alfred Percy 'Tich' Freeman (17 May 1888 – 28 January 1965),** the only player to have taken three first-class ten-fors, it was clear to me that a line must be drawn between numbers and reality. It would be too easy to allow statistics about this extraordinary career to dominate such a reverie. For this little man rose above the mere numbers game. As beguiling as the statistics are, his story is far more complex and compelling in the telling.

So, we start at the beginning. Freeman was born in Lewisham, South London. He was reared in a cricket family. His father was an assistant groundsman at the nearby Leyton ground, and his older brother John went on to have a substantial career with Essex. Freeman found his way from Essex to Kent, and in 1912 took 22 wickets at 7.7 for the county's Second XI.

Though short by any sportsman's measurement – standing 5 ft 2 in (1.57 m) – he grew to be a giant in the game, particularly in the field of wrist-spin bowling. His short stature enabled Freeman to keep a low trajectory on his deliveries, making it difficult for the batsman to get to the ball on the full.

He relied mainly on a leg-break. Pitching on a line to just miss off stump, the batsman had little choice but to play at it. Add to that a well-disguised top-spinner, now threatening the stumps. Then there was his googly, or wrong'un, which he used sparingly, especially against the better batsmen. Plus, he maintained great levels of accuracy and durability. In other words, he presented a real handful.

Freeman's shortness – hence the nickname 'Tich' – also translated to the small size of his hands. This enforced an unorthodox grip for a leggie. He gripped the ball between his thumb, middle and index fingers, rather than the more accepted method, between the palm, middle finger and index finger.

Freeman began his long and celebrated career on the professional staff at Kent in 1912, making his first-team debut in 1914 – yet another cricketer whose career was truncated by the advent of World War I. He had one return of 7-25 in that first season, but really found his feet when the County Championship resumed in 1919. His 60 wickets in that short season were followed by 102 in 1920, 166 in 1921 and 194 in 1922. The 'Tich' Freeman train was leaving the station.[16]

Freeman soon formed an almost telepathic relationship with wicketkeeper Les Ames. The first batsman in first-class cricket to be out, 'stumped Ames, bowled Freeman', was one JB Higgins

---

16 In this chapter I rely significantly on the writing of David Lemmon in his 1982 book, *Tich Freeman and the Decline of the Leg-Break Bowler* – a tome which brings to life one of cricket's immortals.

of Worcestershire, one of 261 batsmen dismissed in that manner. Ames later said that in that first game Freeman gave him a pre-arranged signal when he was about to bowl his wrong'un. But thereafter he gave no signs, and Ames had to read whatever was coming.

Ames insisted that Freeman's greatest asset lay not only in his command over length and the subtleties of flight, but in his ability to impart just the right amount of spin on the ball to beat the bat by a fraction of an inch, or to clip the edge to give the wicketkeeper or slips a chance. 'Others,' he said, 'have turned the ball more, but none has turned it to such effect, nor given the impression that they were able to control the amount of turn.'

The Freeman wrong'un was well-disguised and was instant death to the novice. Ames tells how when Freeman spotted a new and colourful cap on the head of a young man coming in he would hitch up his trousers with his forearms, in a manner characteristically his own. 'And you would know immediately that here was another victim. Two leg-breaks would be played solidly and they would not turn sufficiently to worry the young man ... then suddenly would come a vicious googly and the young man was on his way back to the pavilion.'

There's a marvellous story about Freeman's tussles with Lionel Tennyson, who captained Hampshire and England – and was the grandson of the poet Alfred, Lord Tennyson. Invariably Tennyson would leap out at Freeman, miss and be stumped – or go back, be beaten by the googly and find himself leg before wicket. Ames recalled one occasion when Tennyson won the toss on a perfect weekend at Canterbury and went back to the pavilion chuckling. 'He poked his head around the door of the Kent professionals' dressing-room and bellowed, "Where is the little bugger? It's a perfect wicket out there today ... this is the day I'm going to have you." When it was his turn to bat Tennyson came to the wicket with a gleam in his eye and shouted, "Watch out Tich, I'm going to hit you clean out of the ground."'

Tennyson's boast caused roars of laughter in the Kent side, but next over showed he was intent on following through. First he hit a magnificent shot through the covers, then he straight-drove a splendid six into the pavilion. He could not conceal his glee. Two balls later Freeman served up seemingly the same ball and Tennyson jumped out to him again, but it was tossed a little higher and it was just a little wider and with just the right amount of turn. He missed and was out, stumped Ames.

'Tennyson strode angrily from the field cursing himself,' Ames recalled. 'At the close of play he came to the Kent professionals' rooms again and said, "It's no use, Tich, you've got the better of me. If I go forward I'm stumped, if I go back it's lbw. I shall never know how to play you."'

It's a strange fact that Freeman was rarely at his best when playing for England. He toured South Africa in 1927–28, and Australia and New Zealand in 1929 – the same year he took the first of his three ten-fors, his 10-131 against Lancashire at Maidstone. Freeman also played home Tests against the West Indies and South Africa. In all, he made just 12 Test match appearances for 66 wickets – fine, by most other players, but not for somebody of Freeman's colours!

At county level, however, Freeman was almost without peer. Between 1930 and 1933 he bagged a stunning total of 951 Championship wickets – more than 55 per cent of Kent's total – averaging just 15.21 apiece. It was in this period he notched up his second and third first-class ten-fors; his 10-53 against Essex at Southend in 1930 followed, a year later, by his 10-79 against Lancashire at Old Trafford. Freeman was 43 years old by this stage.

Despite his advancing years, Freeman continued to be the leading wicket-taker in England in 1934 and 1935. In 1934, during which he turned 46, he was the only bowler to top 200 wickets. He had 205 to his name – 'Big Jim' Sims of Middlesex was next with 172. But Freeman's wickets were bought at a greater cost than they had been for many years.

The wear and tear on his tiny frame was beginning to tell. Freeman was suffering from the strain of putting his right arm through such exacting exertion. His muscles simply could not bear the workload. Wicketkeeper Howard 'Hopper' Levett well remembered Freeman's last season, 1936: 'His googly had almost disappeared. I think it hurt him, but mind you he never complained. Alf would never have said if it hurt him. We played Middlesex at Maidstone and it was the first time Tich had come up against Denis Compton, who was only a youngster at the time. He got a score in the first innings and looked to be on his way to 100 in the second. I kept saying to Alf, "Give him the googly, he's only a youngster". But he never did. That's when I realised it hurt him.'

Compton remembered that match, too. 'I had heard so much about the man that I was looking for the googly from the moment I went in. But it never came. In the end he got me caught behind off a straightforward leg-break.'

The top-spinner was Freeman's most potent weapon against the best batsmen, but the wrong'un was always effective against the left-hander, in particular, and was used with a sense of dramatic timing. Without it the end was nigh.

In 1936 Freeman played his final first-class match.[17] He left behind a legacy in inverse proportion to his tiny frame. Here are some of his most notable achievements:

---

17 He'd go on to become a professional, however, playing a number of seasons with Walsall in the Birmingham and District League. Typically, he excelled there too, establishing a club record in 1937 with 98 wickets (av. 8.27), including 10-44 versus Dudley and 9-21 versus Moseley. In 1946, aged 58, he played for Old England against Surrey at the Oval.

- 17 wickets in a match twice, in 1922 and 1932
- Ten or more wickets in a match 140 times – more than 50 per cent ahead of his nearest rival
- The most five-wicket hauls in first-class cricket – his total of 386 is 99 ahead of his nearest rival
- He is second only to Wilfred Rhodes in his aggregate of first-class wickets – accumulating his 3776 in 592 matches, while Rhodes's 4204 came in 1110 matches
- The only player to have taken three ten-fors in the history of first-class cricket.

The position of the professional cricketer has changed dramatically – and rightly so – since Freeman's day, an era of amateurs and professionals and vast class divides. Freeman saw himself as a servant in this system. And a servant knew his place and respected the master. As such, Freeman accepted his class and the position that placed him in with regard to authority. As he saw it, he was a professional cricketer, and as such was paid to do the thing that gave him the greatest pleasure in life. Those in authority had his unquestioned allegiance and they returned his loyalty with the greatest affection and admiration.

As was clear when he began playing for Kent, Freeman was neither a revolutionary, nor was he a moaner. Bryan Valentine, one of his last captains, told how the bitterest complaint that he ever heard the man make was when it was suggested that he should have a rest from bowling as there seemed little sign of a wicket falling. 'Give me a couple more, skipper,' he would plead, 'I am sure that I can get him in a minute.'

In his private life, too, Freeman was one of the ordinary folk. The pay packet was for the wife, who returned the pocket money

that she could spare. Both physically and domestically, he was dominated by his wife. Ethel ruled him, but he accepted this as the natural way of things.

He loved a drink with the lads, but not in Ethel's presence. He smoked almost endlessly, but not when Ethel was around. She did not approve. Les Ames told of slipping in to see him one evening, to find him hunched over a frugal fire. 'A voice [Ethel's] came from the hall, "Alf, I'm just going down to the shops." Immediately a packet of cigarettes was pulled from an inner pocket and Tich had a crafty drag.'

Hopper Levett always drove him to away matches when he could, because he so liked the man. On one occasion he took Tich to Lancashire and Yorkshire, where Kent were touring. On the way back they had a puncture. It took them some time to get the car moving again and they were not back in Kent till one o'clock in the morning. Tich was in a terrible state and when Ethel stormed to the door Levett knew why.

Les Ames had a similar experience some years later when, after much persuasion, he took Tich to a Test match in London. The game finished at 6.30 pm and Ames drove them back to Maidstone. When they arrived at 9 pm, Ethel was waiting on the doorstep. 'He's not going out with you again,' she cried. 'Keeping him out all night drinking.' In fact, when it was a home game, Ethel would be at the ground at the close of play in order to drive Tich home. His social life was very limited, yet in no way was he antisocial.

When on tour, off the field Freeman would look forward to his occasional surreptitious pint and his packet of cigarettes. Often in the team hotel in away matches, he would play patience for hours … waiting for the morrow when he could walk on to the field again and once more become the spider spinning the web for the destruction of the flies.

While still playing for Kent, Freeman became a partner in a coaching school in Maidstone. One of the partners was George Fenner, who had played a little for Kent and was a shrewd and efficient businessman. Freeman was neither of these things. He appeared irregularly at the coaching school, his heart always on the field rather than in the nets. Plus, he was too reticent ever to be a good coach.

So there was always a danger that, when he did appear, he would do more harm than good. Fenner was less than pleased on one occasion when a wealthy customer approached the renowned slow bowler and, pointing to a young boy he had with him, said heartily, 'This is my son, Freeman, and I'm going to give him to you because I want you to turn him into a great bowler like yourself.' Freeman was utterly unmoved. 'You can't coach bowlers,' he said and walked away.

He was also involved in a sports outfitters in Maidstone, but once more Freeman had no real interest. He concerned himself less and less with store business and both parties were happy when he relinquished his share. It was as if Freeman was entirely occupied with thoughts of cricket, and if he wasn't playing he'd be eagerly awaiting the start of the new season when, eager to get at the batsman, he could once more bustle back to the end of his five-pace run. And in he would trot, his arm coming over his head as high as he could manage, his follow through whippet-like.

What the Kent committee thought about Freeman was made apparent when they granted him a second benefit in 1934. It was a gesture not only to the man who had carried Kent bowling on his shoulders for so many years, but also to one who had raised much money for Kent charities by arranging cricket matches in which he was always a participant. Once more Kent followers had the opportunity to show their appreciation of the untiring enthusiasm of the little man who, after he retired, named his house 'Dunbowlin'.

Tich Freeman died on 28 January 1965, almost four months shy of his 77th birthday. Kent players past and present joined to honour him at his funeral. The procession was late in arriving at the chapel, however, moving an old teammate to quip, 'Ethel wouldn't let him come!' All smiled. It was neither a vindictive nor an irreligious remark, but simply an observation of affection for two people who had been part of Kent cricket, and of the lives of all those present, for so long. Later in the same year, on the Monday of Canterbury Week, a plaque was unveiled at Canterbury which honoured the man and commemorated his achievements.

From his first game at Oxford in 1914 until his last at Folkestone in 1936, Freeman gave his very best, tried his very hardest with every ball and accepted the authority of those whom, rightly or wrongly, he considered his superiors. But there was more to it than that. As a former teammate said of Tich: 'His efforts inspired love and yet he was the quietest and most undemonstrative of men. The hitch of the trousers showed determination, while the Napoleonic fold of the arms showed satisfaction.'

And well might Freeman have been satisfied.

CHAPTER 6

10 FOR 44

continued

Day two at the WACA dawned bright and clear, full spring sunshine bathing the ground and a fresh easterly breeze replacing the sou'wester of late the day before. In my experience the easterly was almost invariably a good wind for swing bowling, better even than the fabled Fremantle Doctor which came in from the Indian Ocean most summer afternoons. Recognising the changed circumstances, Tony Lock immediately changed ends for me. Now operating from the southern end, I enjoyed considerable movement through the air.

While we had made some inroads into the Victorian top order the previous evening, there was still plenty of batting to come. For a start, 'Barnacle' Bill Lawry was still at the crease. His partner, Bob Cowper, another left-hander, was no slouch with the bat either. Actually, that's underselling it. Cowper was very much in the David Gower mould. He could be a bit loose at times, but he possessed an enormous amount of talent, and if you made the mistake of bowling a little wide of off stump to him he could punish you, timing his strokes either forward or backward of point beautifully.

The son of a rugby union international (hence his nickname, 'Wallaby'), Cowper, like Lawry, was a tough competitor. He was a regular member of the Australian team, and in the 1965–66 home

Ashes series made the first triple-century in a Test in Australia. The patience he displayed in his knock – his 307 runs came from 589 deliveries in 727 minutes, and included a record 26 threes and only 20 fours – was evidence of his focus and aptitude. Cowper, who was also an effective right-arm off-break bowler who'd take 36 Test wickets at a respectable 31.63, would go on to captain Victoria to a Sheffield Shield win in 1969–70 before he surprised the cricketing world by retiring at the age of 30.

Three-for:

Bob Cowper, bowled Brayshaw, 7
Victoria 3-37

Back at the WACA, Victoria shunted along in the morning session adding just nine runs before I managed another breakthrough. Bowling to Cowper I beat him with an inswinger that found its way into the stumps. I could never reason why a player of his ability could be brought down by a slow-medium delivery – no matter how much it moved through the air. On reflection I have reached the conclusion that there has to be a certain mesmeric effect to a swinging ball. *Will that red orb ever reach me?* a batsman might think, *Oops, there it is ... too late*!

I don't recall ever being taught to swing a ball. From my earliest efforts bowling with a six-stitcher I had been blessed with the ability to make the ball deviate through the air – a skill I developed along the way by adapting the nuances of the craft. No doubt it helped me to develop a wider variety of deliveries in a bid to trick the man at the other end of the 22 yards. My mentor in the second half of my career was Ray Strauss. I had watched him make the ball go around corners bowling for WA and became a much better bowler through his guidance. In the end I worked on a repertoire of eight different deliveries. What fun!

Cowper's demise meant that was another frontline batsman ticked off, but WA's meagre total of 161 was hardly out of reach. As far as I was concerned, with a determined Lawry still going strong, the game situation was still favouring the Vics.

The unflappable Phantom welcomed his teammate Jack Potter to the crease. We knew Pottsy – and respected his ability to take an attack apart. He was a batsman who, I think it's fair to say, gave himself room. But to give him credit, he could be devastating when given anything wide of off stump. A very talented striker of the ball, Potter had made runs against us each time out the previous season. We certainly didn't want him getting up a head of steam with such a small total to defend.

Pottsy was a wonderful fielder and bowled useful wrist-spinners when occasionally called upon. He toured England in 1964, and although he never played a Test match, he was considered valuable both on and off the field. Jack referenced this himself in his 2021 autobiography *Born Lucky: The story of Jack Potter, Australia's finest 12th man.* After his playing days, he took on the role of Victoria's coach and in 1987 he had the honour of being the inaugural head coach of the Australian Cricket Academy whose ranks at the time included Shane Warne, Justin Langer and Michael Slater.

Four-for:

Jack Potter, bowled Brayshaw, 0
Victoria 4-37

For all that, this wasn't to be Jack's day – and it was increasingly becoming mine. Again, almost unaccountably, one of my big, slow inswingers did the damage as it looped in between bat and pad and hit Jack's middle stump. Now the numbers were stacking up in our favour as we were looking at the bottom of the Victorian middle order.

More from the WACA Ground soon.

CHAPTER 7

VERITY

Cricketers are not, of course, immune to the fickle hand of fate, and over the years far too many have died long before their time. Tragically, some, like Australian Phillip Hughes (aged 25), died as a result of being hit in the head by a ball on the playing field. Some, like Malcolm Marshall (41), were struck down by a deadly disease. Others, like Ben Holliake (24), have been victims of vehicular accidents.

For a number of players born at the wrong time, war not only interrupted or even curtailed their playing careers, but also brought about their untimely deaths. And so we come to the story of **Hedley Verity (18 May 1905 – 31 July 1943)**, a man who was headed towards spin-bowling immortality before he died of his wounds in a hospital in Naples in 1943, having earlier been interned in a prisoner of war

camp in Sicily. As it was, Verity only managed ten seasons of first-class cricket with Yorkshire before the breakout of World War II, but as you'll see here, he made a significant impact – not least with a stunning ten-for haul that by one measure makes it the best of the lot.

It was 15 years after Verity was born when the inaugural season of the County Championship was played in 1890. Surrey were the first winners, and they proceeded to win the title again in 1891, 1892, 1894 and 1895. Only Yorkshire (1893) prevented what almost certainly wouldn't have been called, back then, a 'five-peat'.[18] Yorkshire then set about becoming the pre-eminent team in England, winning eight of the next 19 Championship titles contested until the competition was paused for World War I. When cricket resumed in 1919, so did Yorkshire's dominance. Until World War II forced another break in proceedings in 1940, Yorkshire won another 12 Championship trophies.

Yorkshire's success in those first 50 years of the Championship was borne on the backs of three left-arm spinners. You might argue that a fourth – Ted Peate – played a big part too, putting in place the foundations of the White Rose's spin-led attack even before that first County Championship kicked off, so to speak, in 1890.

Peate played for Yorkshire in that time. Once referred to by WG Grace as 'the acknowledged best slow bowler of England', he played nine Tests for 31 wickets and took 1076 wickets at 13.49 in first-class games. He left the scene in 1886, vacating the throne for Bobby Peel, who spun away from 1884 to 1896 (20 Tests, 101 wickets at 16.98; 1775 at 16.20 in first-class cricket).

Peel's successor at Yorkshire was Wilfred Rhodes, whose reign lasted from 1899 to 1930. His 58 Tests produced 127 wickets at 26.06 apiece, while over his first-class career with Yorkshire he accumulated a whopping record 4204 victims at 16.72. Rhodes was an old man of 52 in early 1930 when he played against the West Indies. So Yorkshire went on the hunt for another who could bowl left-arm orthodox well enough to take over the reins and stretch one of modern cricket's most amazing dynasties. Rhodes

---

18 Yorkshire, aka The White Rose, proceeded to dominate the competition through to this day. At the time of writing they have a total of 32 titles, with Surrey next best on 22.

and another giant of the county, George Hirst, were charged with finding just that man.

In his youth Hedley Verity was a player of distinct promise. In 1922 Verity was 17 and playing club cricket around Leeds. He was bowling at medium-pace and could swing it both ways. He was also a more than useful batsman. In short, he was a budding all-rounder who was proving himself at club level.

Verity's first job in cricket was as the professional for Accrington in the Lancashire League. This was followed by three seasons as the pro with Middleton in the Central Lancashire League. It was during his last season with Middleton that Verity made the occasional appearance for Yorkshire.

Rhodes and Hirst, in their roles as talent scouts, had seen something in the young Verity – something more than just a handy medium-pacer who could bat a bit. Excited by his promise, they took him aside and encouraged him to concentrate on becoming a spinner, adding that if he did well in that role he would have a better chance with Yorkshire because by then Rhodes was contemplating retirement.

The metamorphosis of Hedley Verity was underway. His first-class career with Yorkshire began in 1930 when he was 25. Promise turned into performance: In 12 games he took 64 wickets at a cost of 12.42, to not only head the Yorkshire averages but the national list as well. Figures of 9-60 against Glamorgan at Swansea made a huge statement. It was his best return for that opening season. He was still a beginner at the craft of slow left-arm bowling but he was able and willing to learn from one of the very best in Rhodes.

In 1931, his first full season for Yorkshire, he struck a rich vein of form, capturing 188 wickets at a cost of 13.52 to head the county's bowling averages. He capped a great season by, on his twenty-sixth birthday no less, becoming only the second bowler in Yorkshire history to take all ten wickets in an innings, his 10-36 coming against Warwickshire at Leeds. Imagine! He was playing in only his fourteenth first-class match.

Continued good form earned Verity selection in the prestigious Gentlemen versus Players games. His season was then topped when he was rewarded by Test selection in the final two encounters with New Zealand. Four wickets in the first match was a sign of things to come. No less an authority on the game than Neville Cardus saw something special in the young Verity: 'He is gifted unmistakably.'

That stellar 1931 season earned Verity selection as one of *Wisden's* Five Cricketers of the Year – and *Wisden* had this to say of the emerging talent: 'There is no doubt that in once again carrying off the Championship, Yorkshire owed a great deal to the work accomplished by their fine left-arm bowler. It is greatly in his favour that, unspoilt by success, he realises that he still has a good deal to learn particularly in the subtle variation of his patient flight which can only come by continuous practice.'

Now to 1932 when, for the second time in consecutive seasons, Verity entered his name on the exclusive ten-for list, this time for his bowling in a match against Nottinghamshire at Headingley. In all, Verity bowled 19.4 (six-ball) overs that innings, 16 of which were maidens. He didn't concede any runs in his first nine overs, then, making full use of a drying wicket, captured seven wickets in 15 deliveries – including a hat-trick! His final figures? In what remains a first-class record, Verity claimed ten wickets for just ten runs.[19]

Here is that amazing scorecard in full:

---

19 It may be instructive to note that in Verity's two hauls of ten-for not one batsman was out bowled; 18 were caught, one stumped and one lbw.

Yorkshire v Nottinghamshire

Headingley, Leeds

9, 11, 12 July, 1932

Nottinghamshire 2nd innings

WW Keeton	c Macaulay	b Verity	21
FW Shipston	c Wood	b Verity	21
W Walker	c Macaulay	b Verity	11
AW Carr	c Barber	b Verity	0
A Staples	c Macaulay	b Verity	7
CB Harris	c Holmes	b Verity	0
GV Gunn	lbw	b Verity	0
B Lilley	not out		3
H Larwood	c Sutcliffe	b Verity	0
W Voce	c Holmes	b Verity	0
SJ Staples	st Wood	b Verity	0
Sundries			4

			67

Fall: 44 47 51 63 63 63 64 64 67 67

Bowling	O	M	R	W
WE Bowes	5	0	19	0
GG Macaulay	23	9	34	0
H Verity	19.4	16	10	10

After his stunning 10-10, Verity's star was well and truly on the rise, but the qualities that led to this achievement, not to mention his very successful early seasons with Yorkshire, were already in place.

Verity was quite tall for a slow left-armer, but he used his height and reach to wonderful advantage. His left arm creased his left ear as the bowling hand came through straight over the top. After release, he would swing forward up and over his front foot. With these factors combining he could make the ball bounce sharply. On good wickets he bowled at close to medium pace, cutting back on speed when working on a rain-affected track – at all times, though, maintaining deadly degrees of accuracy.

He worked on a line from middle-and-leg to the right-hander, spinning towards off stump. He didn't get a great amount of turn, but he got just enough. 'He is tall and much stronger than his pace needs,' wrote Scottish cricketer and cricket writer RC Robertson-Glasgow. 'His run-up, longer than most of his kind, has a measured delicacy that you would expect from this fastidious and nearly-prim craftsman. His delivery has a grace which mathematics can't explain.'

As is often the case with spin bowlers, Verity's grip was different. He placed the ball with precision and tightly gripped it across the seam by three fingers, his third finger bent almost double but under the ball. On delivery his wrist turned and the knuckles would go up and out, the ball being spun from the first finger. The ball would go up from the hand, travelling in a curve on to a good length.

Verity had three paces: slow, a normal delivery which he could bowl almost with his eyes closed; a slightly faster one; and an occasional very fast ball which tended to swing in to the right-hander – and regularly took a wicket. He worked on what he called 'the shortest length at which a batsman should play forward'. Others would say he *never* bowled a bad ball, perhaps one slightly overpitched ... but never a long hop.

What of the man? Legendary cricket writer Neville Cardus wrote that 'his art expressed the man himself, unassertive yet persuasive of speech, a student of the game, and life, with not too many words but enough seriousness of thought'. Cardus continued: 'On turf at all responsive after sun and rain, his spin had an almost abrupt angularity about it, turn and lift not surpassed by any other spinner of his day.' Another said of Verity, 'He was the ever-learning professor, justly proud yet utterly humble.' And, 'Verity had a look and carriage of a man likely to do extremely well at something that would need time and trouble. His dignity was not assumed; it was a natural reflection of mind and body harmonised and controlled. He was solid, conscientious and disciplined.'

A circumspect man, Verity made a simple plea to those who may wish to judge him: 'Do not praise me when I have taken 8-20 on a sticky wicket, but when I have got 2-100 on a perfect wicket.' In the latter conditions Verity prevented batsmen scoring runs and constantly tried new strategies in an effort to beat the conditions and take wickets.

Verity was variously described as patient, quiet (so quiet you could barely hear him appeal!), helpful, studious and reflective. He was also credited with a quiet stubbornness. This story from

Alan Hill's book *Hedley Verity – a Portrait of a Cricketer* tells of one occasion when Verity went over the top. 'The match was against Surrey at The Oval and Yorkshire, without Bowes and Macaulay, could not prevent their hosts from building a massive total. Surrey chose to bat on after lunch on the second day and Verity could not hide his disgust at the delayed declaration. To emphasise his feeling, Verity sent down two balls under-arm – each ruled a no-ball by the umpire because the bowler had not notified him of his intention to change from over-arm.'

Much has been said – and written – about the gargantuan clashes between Donald Bradman, the master batsman, and Verity, the master spin bowler of the Thirties. It is said that Verity refused to be daunted by Bradman. He dismissed the Australian champion ten times – eight times in 16 Test meetings, and twice in each innings in two of them. In fact, Bradman later paid Verity a rare compliment: 'I could never claim to have completely fathomed Hedley's strategy, for it was never static or mechanical.'

Bowling in Australian conditions on the 1932–33 Bodyline tour proved a learning curve for Verity. It was his first tour and, given England's potent pace attack, headed by Harold Larwood and Bill Voce, he found himself cast in a defensive role. In the final encounter he was freed up to be more attacking and returned a match total of eight wickets, including Bradman's.

By now well established in the England team, he charged into the 1933 County Championship with a flyer against Essex at Leyton: 17 wickets in one day, a record shared only by Colin Blythe and Tom Goddard. More was to come for the silent assassin, one performance never to be forgotten by any supporter of England teams battling for the Ashes.

This was the 1934 tour, and Australia, looking to regain the urn, won the first Test and headed to Lord's for the second, a venue at which the home team had not defeated Australia since 1896. Batting first, England may have put a loss off the menu with a total of 440. In reply the visitors were cruising at 2-192, though Verity had dismissed Bradman. It rained on the rest day (Sunday) and into Monday morning, leaving the tourists facing the prospect of batting on a 'sticky' wicket.

The conditions were tailor-made for the left-arm predator in Hedley Verity. Forced to follow on, Australia groped and threshed against one spitting delivery after another, and were finally dismissed for 118. England ended up winners by an innings and 38 runs, the Lord's bogey put to rest by Verity's spinning fingers. He added 8-43 to his first-innings return of 7-61 – remarkably having claimed 14 wickets in all in the day's play, a record that remains. Neville Cardus wrote: 'Verity settled the issue like a great bowler. His length was impeccable and he made the ball come back and lift so abruptly that most of the Australians were helpless.'

It was business as usual for Verity in 1936, with 216 wickets in County Championship games, the highest season tally of his career. But he also thrived with the bat that summer, accumulating 855 runs at 31.66, also a season high for him. Verity continued to bowl for England through to the last of his 40 Test appearances, against West Indies at Lord's in June 1939.

Included were his labours with the Gubby Allen–led tour Down Under, when England won the first two Tests, but lost the last three. Neville Cardus's coverage of the tour was carried in Australian newspapers – and he sang Verity's praises. 'He is a better bowler, I think, in this country than he is even in England. For here his flight is more ample and dangerous. In Australia the pitch is the enemy not the ally of slow left-handed bowling.'

Following the Ashes, with the dark clouds of war hanging over most of Europe, the English cricket authorities moved to clear the decks of international and internal competitions. In the last match of the season at Hove in September, Verity took 7-9 in Sussex's second innings. It would prove to be his final appearance in county cricket. And it was a fitting climax for the man himself, as Yorkshire won their seventh Championship in the decade that he had played for the club.

With World War II under way, Verity, who had enlisted in the British Army years earlier, joined up with the Green Howards infantry regiment in late 1939. He was posted to India, Persia and Egypt, on the way attaining the rank of captain. The Green Howards were involved in the Allied invasion of Sicily in July 1943. Allied forces came under heavy fire on the plains outside Catania, and Verity was hit in the chest by shrapnel.

Subsequently captured he was taken to a German field hospital where he underwent surgery. He was then transported by boat across the Strait of Messina to the Italian mainland, then by train to Naples, and finally to a military hospital in Caserta, 25 kilometres outside Naples. He had further surgery to relieve pressure from a rib on his lung, but lived only three more days and died on the afternoon of 31 July.

Verity was buried with full military honours in a cemetery outside Caserta, his coffin draped with the Union Jack and his grave marked by a stone with a white rose etched into it. His coffin was later moved to a military cemetery established by the

Commonwealth War Graves Commission. Many a diehard cricket person has made a pilgrimage to the site.

Among the many tributes to the man, there was this from Bradman, who had shared the honours in several tussles with the great left-armer: 'I cannot recall ever hearing Verity utter a word of complaint or criticism. If reports of his final sacrifice are correct, he maintained this example right through to the end.'

CHAPTER 8
LAKER'S MATCH

Until the 1961 Ashes tour, Australian teams would travel by ship to England. They'd rediscover their land legs, and touch, by playing a *lot* of cricket leading up to (and around) the regulation five Test matches. County sides lined up for the chance to play a home fixture against the tourists. So much so that the Australian team's 1956 tour included no fewer than 26 first-class games outside the Tests, plus four 'second-class' matches. That's some itinerary.

One of these tour matches was played at The Oval from May 16–18, some three weeks out from the first Test. Surrey's formidable line-up for that game included **James Charles 'Jim' Laker (9 February 1922 – 23 April 1986)** and his twin in spin, Tony Lock. Their combined performance with the ball in that game was a harbinger. Batting first, the Australians witnessed Laker at his patient best. He wheeled down 46 overs and, incredibly, took all ten wickets (10-88). Big Jim took two more in the second innings – with Lock chiming in with 7-49 – as the bemused visitors were bundled out for 107. Australia lost to the county champions by ten wickets.

By the time the first Test at Trent Bridge came around, however, Australia had recovered from the mauling, managing a draw in a rain-affected contest – though Laker *still* took six wickets in the match. In the second Test, at Lord's, the powerful Australian pace attack, led by Keith Miller (with five wickets in each innings), made

full use of a lively strip. Afterwards, England skipper Peter May said to Aussie batsman Neil Harvey, 'That's the last wicket you'll get like that.' True to that promise, the strip for the third encounter, at Leeds, strongly favoured the spin twins. Accordingly, Laker returned figures of 5-58 and 6-55, while Lock had a match total of seven wickets.

The tourists were still licking their wounds a week or so later when they prepared for what was, for them at least, something of a series decider at Old Trafford in Manchester (Australia needed to win the series outright to reclaim the Ashes). The early portents didn't look good, and May's warning rang in their ears when Ray Lindwall bowled the opening delivery. As wicketkeeper Len Maddocks recalled, 'It landed outside the off stump and came through to me accompanied by a cloud of dust. Keith Miller was at second slip, and he burst out laughing and said, "This game will be over in two days."'

England, however, made light of the conditions and amassed 459, no doubt helped by Australia's slim spin stocks which were comprised of Ian Johnson's modest offies backed up by Richie Benaud, who at that stage was still learning the craft of leg-spin.

Australia's reply did at least begin promisingly. Colin McDonald and Jim Burke weathered the new ball for an opening stand of 48 before all hell broke loose, Laker sending McDonald and Harvey (a duck in each innings) packing, before Lock claimed Burke. In retrospect it was a wicket that Lock would surely have dearly loved *not* to have had next to his name!

In later cricket parlance, the two England spin merchants were 'turning it square'; Laker from off to leg for the right-handers, left-armer Lock spinning the other way. The tourists had no answer and were all out for 84. Lock had one wicket. Laker, who was almost unplayable (Garry Sobers once remarked, 'When you batted against Jim Laker you could hear the ball fizz as he spun it'), had the other nine next to his name, his scalps including Neil Harvey, Ian Craig and Keith Miller. A ravenous ring of close-in fieldsmen seriously menaced any Australian batsman who might have thought he had half a chance of surviving, let alone scoring.

Understandably, the wicket came under scrutiny. There were cries of 'foul' from a very disgruntled Australian camp – even before the inevitable ten-wicket trouncing was completed. Late in the game Australian journalist RS Whitington got himself a good old-fashioned scoop. It was there in black and white for all to see back home. He reported in the Sydney *Sun* newspaper that Bert Flack, head groundsman at Old Trafford, had admitted to having prepared the fourth Test wicket under instruction, to help England.

Whitington wrote, 'He [Flack] confessed about half an hour before stumps yesterday, in the presence of five members of the Lancashire committee, bystanders and two cricket writers he did not recognise. Flack said, "My committee has been asking me all season to prepare wickets on which Lancashire can bat and others can't. I get one for this Test …and it causes one hell of a row and I get all the blame."'

Looking back on that infamous pitch, McDonald said, 'The Lancashire committeemen at Old Trafford said they had nothing to do with the preparation of the pitch, that it was directed from down south, from the England cricket administration. England cheated – if by cheating you include the practice of preparing wickets to suit your own purpose.' Flack, the man in the hot seat, later repeated that he had 'acted on instructions'.

Of course, the make-up of the 22 yards can be pivotal in any cricket match – but the bottom line is, whether batsman or bowler, you have to apply yourself to making the best of what is dished up. Clearly the Australian batsmen lacked the technique to handle such sharp angles off the wicket. Plus, Laker was bowling off-breaks, while Lock relied on the left-armer's natural leg-break. The Australians at that time seriously lacked experience in playing off-breaks, especially on a wicket that might have been designed for an off-spinner. Not that they were focusing on this between innings. When Flack asked the Australian captain Ian Johnson what roller he wanted ahead of Australia's second dig, Johnson is said to have replied, 'Please your effing self.'

Following on a long, long way behind, the Australians fared better – for a time, at least. Once again McDonald fought the good fight, playing what Harvey later declared to be his finest Test match innings. He reached 89, exactly the same score as he had posted during Laker's ten-for match in the county game against the tourists back in May. Harvey, however, didn't fare so well, and he became Laker's first victim, caught by Oakman for a duck. Jim Burke (33) and Ian Craig (38) also fell to Laker. McDonald and Benaud (18) aside, none of the remaining Aussie batsmen offered any resistance, and one after another they fell under the spell of the England spinner's majesty in conditions that illustrated the vagaries of Manchester weather.

When Maddocks was trapped leg before to end the innings and the match, the scorebook showed an unbelievable line: Laker – 51.2 overs, 23 maidens, 10-53. Harvey sought out his nemesis after the game. 'I shook hands with Laker and congratulated him, like everybody else did. I said, "Well done, Jimmy. You've done a great job." He said, "Well, you've got to get them when you can, don't you?" That's all he said.'

Laker, who started his career as a batsman and medium pacer,[20] had led from the front to help England to a whopping victory by an innings and 170 runs. That gave the champion match figures of 19 wickets for 90. In doing so, he had become the first to claim a ten-for in a Test match. It is no wonder that fateful Old Trafford Test has ever since been known as 'Laker's Match'. With England having already retained the urn, Laker went on to take seven wickets in the drawn fifth Test, giving him 46 wickets at 9.61 for the series. This remains an Ashes record.[21]

Laker's 19 match wickets is still unmatched in first-class cricket, let alone Tests. And the self-effacing champion of spin holds another record. Remembering he'd already taken ten-for against the Aussies when they played his Surrey team before the Test series, he's the only man to bag two ten-fors in the one season. Surely the Australians just couldn't wait to board the ship home.

Certainly Aussie opener Colin McDonald had seen enough – though he fared better than any of his teammates in both the Surrey game and Manchester Test. 'My technique was based around two things,' he explained. 'One was side-on play, and secondly, any ball that was pitched up you used your feet to get to it. Laker didn't

---

20 Before World War II, young Laker had established a reputation as a batsman, but former Yorkshire batsman and coach Benjamin Wilson saw him bowling off-breaks in the nets and suggested he take up the craft. Before returning to first-class cricket following the war, Laker, stationed in Egypt as a corporal in the British Army, worked on his bowling against Aussie servicemen in a match in Cairo. As recorded by the *Egyptian Gazette* ('Laker skittles Australians'), he returned the figures of 6-10.
21 But not a record in a Test series: SF Barnes, of England, took 49 in South Africa in 1913–14 (and he didn't even play in the fifth Test!).

throw much stuff up, so you had to largely play back against fairly prodigious off-spin.'

Another victim, Ian Craig, praised Laker's consistency: 'The great thing about Laker was that he rarely bowled a bad ball.' As for his thoughts on Laker, Craig remarked, 'He was very quiet. He wasn't an extrovert by any means. He was a nice chap. He just went about his business.'

Former Australian leg-spin wizard Arthur Mailey, however, later expressed an interesting opinion of bowlers in Laker's style. In his book *10 for 66 and All That* he wrote: 'Jim Laker was not a great bowler, but he certainly ranks with the best off-breakers of all time. A right-arm off-break bowler has limitations. He does not possess the variety or amount of spin of which the bosie leg-breakers are capable of. Consequently, he cannot reach the same heights.' As I said ... interesting.

Was the Old Trafford track manufactured to suit Laker? Perhaps it was, but there was one person who saw the lighter side. In *The Daily Express*, British cartoonist Roy Ullyett summed up the summer with an illustration of a dazed kangaroo, in Australian kit, sitting beside a headstone on which was written, 'Here lie the Aussies of '56, skittled by Laker for next to nix.' On a note (a toe-tag?) attached to the kangaroo's paw was the cheeky rejoinder: 'Never forgotten, sorry you thought our wicket rotten. Love from the ground staff.'

One fine evening many years later I drove up to a house in suburban Perth. I'd been invited to a barbecue at the home of a man called Ron Tindall, a well-credentialled soccer player with Chelsea in the top English soccer competition (he'd been brought to WA to boost the code locally in a management role) and a former quality all-rounder for regular county champions Surrey. The MCC touring party was in town so my fellow guests included Tindall's Surrey teammates Alec Bedser and Ken Barrington (both part of the MCC management, selection and coaching department) as well as Tony Lock, Peter Loader, and the one and only Jim Laker, on tour doing media work.

I can still almost feel his large mitt wrapping itself all over mine in the greeting handshake. A big man with an open face, he had an almost-reserved demeanour, a reticence I found very easy to like. In accordance with his inimitable television commentary style on English cricket's Sunday League, which I had heard and enjoyed immensely while living in England in the late Sixties, I found him that night to be a man of very few words. Any enquiries about his cricketing days were deflected like a gentle glance off leg stump.

Gentle and reticent he may have been but the man was a tiger with ball in hand. Especially in the unforgettable – for him, his teammates, his Aussie opposition, and cricket fans all over the world – summer of 1956.

FOURTH TEST

Australia v England
Old Trafford, Manchester
Second innings

CC McDonald	c Oakman	b Laker	89
JW Burke	c Lock	b Laker	33
RN Harvey	c Cowdrey	b Laker	0
ID Craig	lbw	b Laker	38
KD Mackay	c Oakman	b Laker	0
KR Miller		b Laker	0
RG Archer	c Oakman	b Laker	0
R Benaud		b Laker	18

RR Lindwall	c Lock	b Laker	8
IWG Johnson	not out		1
LV Maddocks	lbw	b Laker	2
Sundries			16

			205

Fall: 28 55 114 124 130 130 181 198 205 205

England bowling

	O	M	R	W
JB Statham	16	9	15	0
TE Bailey	20	8	31	0
JC Laker	51.2	23	53	10
GAR Lock	55	30	69	0
ASM Oakman	8	3	21	0

CHAPTER 9
BOUNCERS

In Kent County Cricket Club folklore there resides a story about the consequences of a dropped catch in a game at Northamptonshire's County Ground in 1907. Wonderful finger spinner **Colin 'Charlie' Blythe (30 May 1879 – 8 November 1917)** put down a return catch when he had thus far taken all seven wickets to fall for just one run, looking on course to set figures that would have put Hedley Verity's ten for ten in second place on the all-time list for runs conceded. Blythe did end up taking all Northants wickets in that innings, but for the comparatively expensive figures of 10-30.

There was a school of thought, among Kent ranks at least, that dropping that catch and missing a golden opportunity to skittle the opposition for a record-low score was something Blythe wore for some time. But then one shouldn't feel too sorry for him. He *did* also take seven second-innings wickets in the same day's play, giving him a match aggregate of 17-48 (and good judges later said that Blythe could easily have taken all 20 that day).

If Blythe's dropped catch was, for him, a so-called sliding doors moment, so too was the choice the then 18-year-old made on the morning of 17 July 1897. Finding himself with nothing to do, Blythe decided to go to the Rectory Field at Blackheath, not far from his home, to watch the last day of a match between Kent and Somerset. Asked to send a few down in the nets before play,

he made such an impression on the team coach that he was asked to come to the nets another day.

And so it was that Charlie Blythe became immersed in what would no doubt today be called the Kent development program. The club kept notes on triallists, and these words summed up the promising youngster: 'Bowls slow left. Very useful bowler.' In 1897 he joined the county staff and on his first-class debut, on 21 August of that year, at the Angel Ground in Tonbridge, took a wicket with his first delivery. A superb career had been launched and it continued to gain altitude through to his famous 1907 ten-for and then on to 1914 when World War I intervened – in circumstances we'll come to shortly.

Blythe's secret of success in the craft of left-arm orthodox bowling was built on a gentle run-up, an easy turn of the arm and devastating spin – said to have been helped by his highly proficient violin playing, which strengthened his fingers, thus helping him impart sharp spin on the ball. Add to those virtues his variable flight and unerring accuracy and he proved himself a handful on even the most docile playing surfaces.

These nailed-down skills took him to lofty heights. In 1900 he pocketed 114 wickets, helping Kent to third in the Championship, their best placing in ten years. Continued good form won him selection for the 1901–02 Ashes tour. He took 7-56 runs in the first Test at the SCG, and when England won he was presented with a gold pocket watch, engraved with his bowling figures. In all, he played 19 Tests. Though he presented well in each campaign, some believed his 'artistic temperament' and epilepsy were not necessarily a good match for Test cricket.

Blythe's outstanding first-class career, which saw him claim 2503 wickets at 16.81, was not without some controversy. Blythe had the occasional practice of sending down a high full toss, aimed at the off bail, a ploy apparently used in an attempt to break a batsman's concentration. Opposing players suggested that on one occasion, late in a day's play at Canterbury, it was used to lose the ball's flight against the setting sun.

Prominent England personality CB Fry actually appealed about the practice to the umpire and to Kent's captain, but nothing came of it.

Blythe remained the spearhead of Kent's attack right through to the onset of World War I – which was to bring down the curtain on many sporting careers. Before the season was ended a month ahead of schedule, Blythe collected a haul of 9-97 as Surrey defeated Kent at Lord's in August 1914. Ladder positions (determined in part by win percentages) at the time of the season cancellation were used to declare that year's champions: Surrey. And the season's top wicket-taker with 159 scalps? Colin Blythe.

Though fighting a constant battle with his own health, Blythe promptly volunteered for service in the army and was used as a publicity figure when conscription came into being. He embarked for France and his battalion was involved in the Second Battle of Passchendaele, in the Ypres Salient sector of the front. He was mainly involved in laying and maintaining railway lines. But on 8

November 1917, Blythe was one of a working party under enemy fire when shrapnel from a shell-burst pierced his chest and killed him instantly.

Blythe took 100 or more wickets in 14 of his 16 seasons, including 215 in 1909. On top of his ten-for haul, five times he captured nine wickets in an innings and twice took a hat-trick, both within the same fortnight. His total of 2503 wickets in first-class games places him in stellar company. There can be no greater compliment than to say he was regarded as 'simple and unassuming, loath to speak of himself and rather deprecating of his own talents'.

It is a fact that through the devastating events that were the two world wars of the 20th century, England cricket paid a high price with the loss of two wonderful left-arm orthodox bowlers. RIP Colin Blythe and Hedley Verity.

Should a captain be granted a 'wish list' of all the qualities they'd like their leading pace bowler to have, all of the following would surely feature: a short run and a beautifully easy action; a stock ball that moves naturally from the off; a variety ball that comes straight through; a leg-cutter that pitches middle and leg and leaves the bat sharply; and the ability to swing the new ball.

Does that sound too good to be true? Not if it is said of **George Geary (9 July 1893 – 6 March 1981)**. This tall and solidly built medium-paced right-armer had all the qualities a captain could wish for – and you can add dogged persistence to the list. For example, in the last Test of the 1928–29 Ashes tour, on a flat track at the MCG, Geary bowled 81 overs and took five wickets (including Don Bradman – for 123) in one innings. He was sometimes unfairly sold short as a stock bowler because he was such a workhorse – but on his day Geary was one of the best bowlers in the world.

CHURCHMAN'S CIGARETTES

G. GEARY

Geary's first-class career began with Leicestershire in 1912, and in 1914 he made a statement with 114 wickets at just over 20. War, of course, then intervened, and Geary was not spared. While serving in the Air Force he suffered a freak injury when his leg was seriously cut by an aeroplane propeller. When cricket resumed in 1919 Geary was still not recovered enough and he drifted off to play as a professional in the Lancashire League.

In 1923, a year after he resumed playing in Leicestershire's county side, he regained his best form, claiming 115 wickets. The following season he made his Test debut in a dead-rubber game against South Africa at Old Trafford. In 1925 things looked even brighter – a maiden century, and 14-wicket hauls against both Hampshire and Lancashire.

On the matting wickets in South Africa in 1927–28 Geary's work with the ball in the first Test at Johannesburg evoked memories of the great SF Barnes. His match haul of 12 for 130 set up victory for England. Sadly he suffered a severe arm injury and missed the last three Tests, but, following surgery on his arm, better was to come Down Under in 1928–29. In the second Test at Sydney he claimed seven wickets.

Geary was in and out of fitness and form, but rode high in 1929, his best season, at the age of 36. He exceeded 150 wickets – and, in Leicestershire's match against Glamorgan at Pontypridd, he racked up what was then the cheapest ten-for of all time. Better yet, Glamorgan, batting last, needed only 84 runs to win the game. Geary, however, got the ball rolling by trapping opener AH Dyson in front for a duck with the score on eight. With his seamers proving too tricky he made regular breakthroughs and skittled the home side for just 68. His figures of 10-18 (which gave him 16-96 for the match) sit only behind Verity's 10-10 in the all-time list.

After Geary's death in 1981 (at 87), *Wisden's* obituary noted he was as popular and respected as any professional: 'No-one ever saw him out of temper, he was always cheerful and smiling and had a wonderful sense of humour which made him a splendid raconteur.' Future England captain Peter May, who was coached by Geary at Charterhouse, said, 'George really fired me with the enthusiasm and ambition to play first-class cricket and get to the top. He told me, "You will be judged by your scores ... never give your wicket away." I shall always have the happiest memories of this great man.'

Leg-spin maestro Arthur Mailey openly opined that medium-pace bowling was a blight on the game. Mailey believed you bowled either all-out pace or spin – nothing in between. But surely medium-pace bowling can't be *that* bad, right? You've just read the story of George Geary, a medium-pacer, finding a way right through a batting line-up while conceding just 18 runs. An exception to Mailey's rule? Perhaps, but what sort of bowler comes in right after

Geary on the all-time ten-for list (ranked by economy)? Why it's **Premangsu Mohan Chatterjee (10 August 1927 – 12 July 2011),** another medium-pacer with a bag of tricks!

Chatterjee – of whom it was said he could 'swing the ball all day' – played for Bengal in India's Ranji Trophy between 1946–47 and 1959–60. He made a statement in the 1955–56 campaign with a return of 15-109 (7-50 and 8-59) against Madhya Pradesh in a semifinal of the Ranji. He also took 7-101 in the first innings of the final against Bombay, who went on to win. For his efforts over the season Chatterjee was named a cricketer of the year by the *Indian Cricket Annual.*

However, it was in January 1957, playing his first game since the Ranji final, against Assam at Jorhat, that he cleaned up the whole of the opposition's first innings for just 20 runs. This remains the best innings return outside the United Kingdom and the third-best ten-for of all time.

Those who played against Chatterjee, a left-armer who often operated around the wicket, talk of the ball 'curving and dipping, almost with a life of its own'. Another suggested that 'he was a medium-pacer, but even that was an exaggeration …and the fact that he bowled in glasses probably made him look innocuous'. His control, however, 'was impeccable – and he could make use of even the slightest gust of wind, even with the old ball'.

Testament to Chatterjee's control of line and length lies in the breakdown of his effort in taking ten-for. First, his bowling analysis: 19 overs, 11 maidens, 10-20. Second, only one of his victims was caught while six were bowled, with three trapped leg-before.

For his type of bowler, often operating on surfaces not known for being friendly to medium-pacers, Chatterjee performed grandly. A question often asked was, why was he constantly overlooked by the Indian selectors? Maybe because, as we have seen, he just did not look very threatening.

It is a fact that while England has over the years produced a raft of quality finger-spinners – Rhodes, Verity, Blythe et al – there haven't been as many who have delivered the ball over the wrist. Strangely, it has been something of the opposite from an Australian experience (offie Nathan Lyon being the standout exception), with Clarrie Grimmett, Bill O'Reilly, Arthur Mailey, Stuart MacGill and Shane Warne leading the way as leggies.

One who confounded this theory in English cricket was **James Morton 'Jim' Sims (13 May 1903 – 27 April 1973)**, who found a way into the England team as a leg-spinner in the mid-Thirties – before World War II curtailed his activities. He made four Test appearances without setting the world on fire, but carved out a reputation during 381 first-class games for Middlesex.

Originally regarded as a batsman who could bowl, he often opened the innings. But particularly after the war, bowling was his strong suit. Eight times he claimed more than 100 wickets in a season, and in 1949 he collected 159 at 20.30. In 1948 he joined

the ten-for list playing in an end-of-season festival game for East versus West at Kingston-upon-Thames. West were chasing an unlikely 403 for the win but managed just 179 due to Sims's perfect ten – 10-90 to be exact. It was a feat he had gone close to performing 15 years earlier at Old Trafford, when disposing of nine Lancashire batsmen for 92 runs. He also took a hat-trick for Middlesex against the South Africans at Lord's in 1947.

Sims was noted for his ability to unleash a biting, curling wrong'un. However, his efforts with the bat over the journey with Middlesex made him an even more important contributor. His career produced a grand total of 8983 runs at 17.30 with four centuries. Not too bad!

Above all, Jim Sims was one of cricket's true personalities – tall, lean and humorous, never tiring of telling a story delivered from the side of his mouth. Typical of this, after dismissing a good batsman with a wrong'un, he remarked quietly to the nearest fieldsman, 'I'd been keeping that one warm all through winter!' Another time, padded up to face Harold Larwood, he was asked if he was nervous. 'Not exactly nervous,' came the answer, 'just a trifle apprehensive.'

He retired in 1952, taking up a coaching role with Middlesex's second eleven, before assuming the role of scorer for the first team.

The history books tell us that – Jim Laker's extraordinary 19-wicket haul at Old Trafford in 1956 aside – few members of the ten-for club have fared prominently in the *other* innings of their game. In fact, in some cases, mine included, trying to back up has resulted in a real let-down. Not so for **Pradeep Sunderam (21 March 1960 –)**, a right-arm medium-pacer for Rajasthan in India.

Playing in a Ranji Trophy match against Vidarbha at Jodhpur in 1985–86, he claimed 10-78 in the first innings (just the second in the competition after Chatterjee in 1957) – and buttered up with six wickets in the second innings. His match figures of 16-154 were then the best for the competition. This mark was subsequently surpassed by Anil Kumble, with figures of 16-99 (eight in each innings) for Karnataka versus Kerala in 1994–95.

Pradeep was one of four children of Gundibail, a former fast bowler for Rajasthan who played two Tests for India. Sadly, for both father and son, you'd expect, Pradeep was unable to win a place in the Indian Test team.

Since retiring, he has held a variety of coaching positions, including head coach of the Mumbai Cricket Association Academy, and coach of Mumbai's under-23 team. Later the Rajasthan Cricket Association appointed him head coach of their Ranji Trophy team. He remains a talent scout for the Mumbai Cricket Association.

Another who made the most of a purple patch of form was Kent fast bowler **George Christopher Collins (21 September 1889 – 23 January 1949)**. He claimed six wickets in the *first* innings and 10-65 in the second.

The game was against Nottinghamshire at Dover in 1922 and his match return of 16-83 was second-best for Kent at the time. Described as 'a splendid right-arm fast bowler who kept a good

length and came quickly off the ground, also a useful left-hand batsman', Collins added to a more than useful result with the ball over his career to score 6280 runs at 22.11. He was also a handy wicketkeeper, having once made a stumping off the bowling of Tich Freeman.

Collins's father, Christopher, and uncle George both turned out for Kent, Christopher having played at Cobham under the captaincy of Ivo Bligh, who led England's team to Australia in 1882 on a successful bid to regain the new-found Ashes.

Collins himself was a member of the MCC team that visited West Indies in 1925–26. However, he did not figure in a Test match.

Further to his all-round skills at cricket, George Collins was also a bell-ringer at Milton-next-Gravesend – an article in *The Ringing World* in 1913 suggesting he may be 'the only first-class cricketer who is a bell-ringer in this country'.[22] The magazine added that former Australian captain (and dentist) Monty Noble was also a bell-ringer.

Not all cricketers – whether batters, bowlers or wicketkeepers – who take the leap into the big sea that is first-class cricket are there to make it their mission in life. While for some it is a long journey that ends up in middle life, for others playing cricket is a passing phase. For **Anthony John Grayhurst 'Tony' Pearson (30 December 1941 –)** it was very much the latter – though that didn't stop him getting on the ten-for list, much to the chagrin of some others who didn't or haven't, you might suppose.

A tall medium-pace opening bowler with plenty of natural ability, Tony Pearson was above all a student who played cricket to pass the time on his way to a professional life away from the game. However,

---

22 According to its own website, *The Ringing World* – a magazine for bell-ringers and, one assumes, bell-ringing enthusiasts – was not only first published in 1911 but has been printed *every week* since that time.

while playing for Cambridge University against Leicestershire at Loughborough in July 1961, he claimed 10-78. Did I mention he was only 19, at the time the youngest player in the club's history?

The last nine wickets fell for 39 runs, with Pearson receiving excellent support from Mike Brearley, the man who would later captain England with distinction, taking three catches. Pearson joined Sammy Woods (who bagged them all in 1890) as the only two to have achieved the feat while playing for the university.

The self-effacing Pearson downplayed his achievement, saying, 'It was pure luck. On what was basically a spinner's wicket, everything went my way ... even down to the last wicket, where a batsman was dropped in the previous over.'

That summer of 1961 Pearson gathered 62 wickets at 26.16; the following season 50 at 31.74. His brief career with Cambridge, and six games for Somerset (for 26 wickets at 19.50), spanned 1961–63. Then it was time for him to put the six-stitcher to one side and reach for the stethoscope, having qualified as a doctor.

Did he ever have regrets at not going on with his cricket career? 'None,' he said. 'I just wasn't good enough.'

They say 'good things come to those who are prepared to wait' – and, of course, are still fit and strong and playing well while they wait. One such story with a happy ending is that of **Norman Ian Thomson (23 January 1929 – 1 August 2021)**. Thomson, who played for Sussex and the MCC, was just weeks away from his thirty-sixth birthday when he received the magic call-up from the England selection committee.

It was the 1964–65 tour of South Africa and Ian Thomson (as he was known) was a late-ish replacement for Yorkshire's Tony Nicholson, who hadn't recovered from a back injury. A curious fact is that Fred Trueman (33) and Brian Statham (34) were overlooked for the tour, apparently because they were considered too old.

For the last Test, after an injury crisis, England also called up Somerset's Ken Palmer, who was coaching in South Africa at the time and was of even gentler pace than Thomson. Trueman was on a sponsored jolly in the West Indies when he read the news, and wasn't best pleased, responding with something along the lines of: 'I'm here playing for cigarette coupons while Ian Thomson and Kenny Palmer are opening the bowling for England?' Expletives deleted!

To be fair to Thomson he'd certainly been knocking on the door – knocking loudly, as it happened. In 1964, in the lead-up to his Test selection, his recent form included 10-49 against Warwickshire at Worthing – his home club ground. But soon after in South Africa he was thrust into opening England's attack and he had only modest success, taking nine wickets over five Tests. That was the extent of his international career.

Described as an archetypal English seamer, Thomson – a tall man who thrived on a green sporty track – took into competition a model medium-fast, right-arm, swing-and-seam mix. He enjoyed a rich vein of form playing for Sussex and bagged more than 100 wickets every season from 1953 to 1964. It was enough to be picked for an MCC tour to Pakistan in 1955–56, where only unofficial Tests were played.

In the latter stages of his career, Thomson played in England's first one-day competition, and in the 1964 final of the Gillette Cup at Lord's he took 4-23 to help Sussex defeat Warwickshire. He retired after the 1965 season, reappearing for two matches in 1972 when the county was suffering an injury crisis.

In the latter stages of the 20th century there were a significant number of South African cricketers who plied their trade both at home and in England. The main reason was to soften the blow that South Africa's apartheid policy was having on sport in that country.[23] Batting superstar Barry Richards was one who led the charge. He started with Hampshire in 1968, the first year counties could sign overseas players with no qualification period. Richards was followed later by the likes of Kevin Pietersen, one of several who actually went on to become qualified to play for England.

Another come-and-go South African was **Stephen Thomas Jefferies (8 December 1959 –)**, a left-arm fast-medium bowler who began his first-class career in his home country, but began the year-round summer experience with Derbyshire in 1982. He returned home to play for Western Province, who included South African Test player Peter Kirsten and English Test men Graham Gooch and John Emburey, both of whom had been banned from playing for England for three years for joining a rebel tour of South Africa.

Western Province made the Currie Cup final and Jefferies was voted one of five *South African Cricket Annual* cricketers of the year. Then it was back to England, this time to play for Lancashire, where he took 8-46 in one game, the second-best individual innings figures for the year.

---

23 South Africa's national rugby and cricket teams, for instance, were kicked out of sanctioned international competitions by their respective sport's governing bodies. The cricket team's ban lasted from 1970 to 1991.

Jefferies pushed on, and in December 1987 bagged 10-59 (off 23.5 overs) for Western Province against Orange Free State at Cape Town. The OFS line-up included classy West Indies batsman Alvin Kallicharran and South African–born England star Allan Lamb, who was the not-out batsman. Plus, OFS boasted a pretty handy opening attack: Allan Donald and Sylvester Clarke.

Then it was back to England for Jefferies who, this time, signed for Hampshire, his third county team. A highlight of that season occurred in the final of the Benson & Hedges Cup, where he won the player-of-the-match award for his return of 5-13.

Jefferies continued with Hampshire and Western Province before joining Boland for the 1993–94 season.

CHAPTER 10

AND ALL THAT

The year 1066 was a turning point in English history (and arguably its most famous date) given the events it witnessed seriously threatened national sovereignty. At the core of change was the death, in January of that year, of the childless King Edward the Confessor. A succession struggle ensued. Harold was crowned soon after Edward's death, but there were other claimants to the throne.

Battles on English soil put paid to two of three aspirants. That left France's William, Duke of Normandy. He landed troops in the south of England, bent upon taking the throne. The Battle of Hastings ended with Harold's death – and a decisive victory for the Norman-French army. The date was 14 October 1066. William the Conqueror was enthroned.

Fast-forward to the year 1930 and to the publication of a book written by WC Sellar and RJ Yeatman: *1066 and All That: A Memorable History of England, Comprising All the Parts You Can Remember, Including 103 Good Things, 5 Bad Kings and 2 Genuine Dates*. As the title suggests, this was a spoof, a tongue-in-cheek reworking of the history of England.

How, then, does all the above relate to cricket – and to the story of the individual bowling phenomenon that is covered in the pages of this book? Well, it boils down to the impish mind and sparkling humour of one of Australia's finest spin bowlers,

Arthur Mailey. You see, in 1921, playing in an Ashes tour game against Gloucestershire, Mailey posted a ten-for. Well, 10-66 to be exact.

Mailey picked up on the Sellar and Yeatman book, made a slight change to the title and in 1958 published a book of his own – *10 for 66 and All That*. The book itself is a fairly straightforward autobiographical piece that was, to me a least, in no way a parody of the game of cricket or, indeed, of cricketers. Far from it! More a dissection of bowling in general, and wrist-spin in particular, it pointed its lens on some of cricket's great players and characters of the day.

As it turns out, Mailey isn't the only first-class cricketer to return the 'historical' figures of 10-66 – there are three others, one of them Australian, two English. We'll visit their stories in due course, but we begin with the man who was a very good spin bowler, an excellent artist and a most appealing storyteller – a man who might have claimed a 'royal' title of his own, the one-time 'clown prince' of Australian cricket, **Alfred Arthur Mailey (3 January 1886 – 31 December 1967)**.

If you called Arthur Mailey 'cavalier' in his attitude you would be on the verge of being unfair to one of the great Australian bowlers – and one of the game's towering characters. After all, not many of those who have bowled leg-spin would base their craft on this premise: 'I'd rather spin and see a ball hit for four than bowl a batsman with a straight one.'

Mailey's philosophy was that he was happy to sacrifice accuracy in pursuit of turn and flight. His teammate of the Twenties Don Bradman summed it up this way: 'Someone dubbed him the man who bowled like a millionaire, and how true it was. Arthur's objective was to take wickets and the spending of runs in the process bothered him little.' Bowling for NSW against Victoria in Melbourne in 1926–27, when the home side scored the highest first-class innings total of 1107, he had figures of 4-362. Never lost for a word, he suggested to a teammate his figures would have been better had not two catches been dropped by 'a man in the pavilion wearing a bowler hat!'

Underneath the outer layer was a student of spin, one who strived to understand the variety of deliveries, the secret of flight and the sheer dynamics of the cricket ball in motion. 'The art of a spin bowler who has flight variation depends on variable spin to get that effect,' he wrote. 'It is not merely a matter of letting the ball leave the hand with more or less impetus.' Blessed with large hands, he was able to impart sizzling rotations on release. It was just a matter of making it all come together – and perfecting performance through dint of practice.

As with all bowlers, growth was incremental. 'I could always bowl an ordinary leg-break,' he wrote, 'but this new freak ball [the wrong'un], I cottoned onto it after a while and rushed home like somebody who had found a nugget of gold.'

Englishman Ian Peebles, himself a wrist-spinner at international level, said, 'When Mailey wrapped his abnormally strong fingers around a cricket ball he had one predominant object in mind – to spin it nigh to bursting point. To bamboozle the would-be striker with great leaping twist was his heart's delight.

'The enormous spin gained was the product of an ideal leg-break bowler's action. Mailey ran a few springy steps at an angle to the wicket, curled his wrist up in the region of his hip pocket and flipped the ball out with a nicely-coordinated movement of arm, wrist and fingers. He was a dangerous bowler in the air as well as off the pitch, for the fast-revolving ball dropped steeply at the end of its flight.'

One of Mailey's early jobs was in glass-blowing – and he claimed the exercise expanded and strengthened his lungs, enabling him to bowl long spells without showing signs of fatigue. He always carried a cricket ball to work and in lunch breaks, if there was a wall or a fence to bowl at, he would practise. As a youngster growing up in the Sydney beach-side suburb of Waterloo he *lived* cricket and was impatient to get involved. His idol was Victor Trumper. He would gaze for hours at a life-sized picture of the dashing batsman hanging on his bedroom wall.

Then came the day when he advanced to the Sydney first-grade competition and came up against his idol. Mailey had mixed feelings when his third ball undid the champion batsman. 'I could see a passageway through to the stumps,' he later wrote. 'The ball missed leg stump by a fraction and the bails were ripped off with the great batsman at least two yards out of his ground. As he walked past me he smiled, patted the back of his bat and said, "It was too good for me". There was no triumph in me as I watched the receding figure ... I felt like a boy who had killed a dove.'

Mailey's fame grew and his progress was rewarded with selection for the 1920–21 home series against England. He claimed three wickets in each innings in the first Test at the SCG, missed the second Test, then became a real nuisance for England with two five-wicket hauls in the third. In the fourth at the MCG he annexed a total of 13 wickets – including 9-121 in the second innings. The nine-wicket innings return remains a Test record for an Australian bowler.

He then toured England with Warwick Armstrong's 1921 team. Australia's thrust in attack was built on the pace of Jack Gregory and Ted McDonald, and Mailey played only three of the Tests for modest returns. But it was in the tour match against Gloucestershire at Cheltenham that he had the best innings of his life – at least in terms of his figures. With Gloucestershire following on after being bowled out for 127 in their first innings (chasing Australia's 438 first-innings total), Mailey put them under his spell claiming all ten wickets – with six of them bowled and two caught-and-bowled – to roll the home side for 175 and win the match for Australia. Mailey's 10-66, as we've seen, was a detail that would later give name to his autobiography.

In the early stages of that same tour another side of Arthur Mailey – the caricaturist and artist – caught the eye, and he attracted

an invitation from the chief of two London publications. He subsequently met with the editorial staff to discuss the possibility of his doing cartoons for their publications during the tour – and he walked away with a contract for £1000 a year! That was a lot of money back then and Mailey knew it. 'It was like an umpire giving me Jack Hobbs's wicket without an appeal,' he said.

Described as quiet and unassuming, with a deadpan, mock-angry style of humour, Mailey was one of cricket's most lovable and gentle characters. To him cricket was fun. He abhorred statistics, players taking themselves too seriously or 'not having a go'. Sportswriter and novelist Arunabha Sengupta said he was 'a remarkable leg-spinner and a fascinating man. He turned the ball by huge degrees, much more than his contemporaries. He tossed it up as an experiment in the science of spin, with disdain for the probable hits for boundaries and beyond.'

In retirement, Mailey continued with his love of drawing, painting in oils, writing, fishing and golf. He was a frequent visitor to England, South Africa and New Zealand with 'Arthur Mailey's touring teams'. He also made an Australian tour to North

America. He was said to be a perfect host, and one with a twinkle in the eye that made those lucky enough to be on one of his tour groups plain glad to be there.

We'll give the final word to RC Robertson-Glasgow, writing in *Wisden* in the early 1960s: 'Mailey is the greatest man I've ever met in cricket. A king without a crown.'

Disagree if you will, but for most cricket lovers the world over there has been no more dominant and enchanting figure than that of the legendary WG Grace. So what an accolade it must have been  for our next member of both the ten-for *and* 10-66 clubs to have been dubbed widely as 'Australia's WG Grace'. The comparison came after **George Giffen (27 March 1859 – 29 November 1927)** had recorded the greatest all-round performance in first-class cricket: scoring 271 and taking 16-166 for South Australia versus Victoria in 1891–92.

In his book *Cricket*, Grace said, 'He has the reputation of being the best all-round cricketer in Australia; he has certainly proved himself to be the best that has yet visited England. In bowling he was not up to Spofforth's form, or one or two of the others; nor was he so successful with the bat as Murdoch; but there can be little doubt that he combined both in a way no other Australian has yet done.'

Grace wasn't done there. 'His bowling was medium-pace right-arm, with a good break from the off varied with a fast one; and he altered both pitch and pace with great effect. He had a very high delivery and a peculiar swing of the arm which distracted the attention of the batsman. Batting, he was cool and collected on all occasions; he had great patience and watched the ball very closely; and his hitting was good all round.'

Not a bad report card from the great man himself!

Giffen was an early bloomer, first coming to notice as a 15-year-old when he bowled to WG Grace in the Adelaide Oval nets. He made his debut for South Australia at 18. A year later Giffen, showing an all-rounder's prowess, scored the first goal for the Norwood Football Club in its debut Australian Rules season in the South Australian Football Association. The match, as it happened, took place on Adelaide Oval. He was a member of its 1878 and 1879 premiership teams.

Cricket remained very much on his radar, however, and in December 1881 he lined up for the first of his 31 Tests. Curiously, he was chosen for the first Test against England at the MCG on the back of his form in club games, because South Australia had had so little interstate play at the time. In 1882 Giffen then made the first of five tours to England, though it took him a while to blossom on the international stage.

Giffen's entry into the ten-for list was secured while playing for an Australian XI against a Combined XI at the SCG in February 1884. After taking 3-62 in the Combined XI's first innings, he took all ten wickets when they were forced to follow on. Seven of his victims would at some stage play Tests for Australia. In sweeping the innings, he became the first non-English player to get a ten-for *and* the first to achieve the feat outside England.

The South Australian's international career came to full flower in the 1894–95 Ashes series. In the first Test at the SCG he scored 161 and 41 and took eight wickets. He immediately took over the captaincy for the remainder of the series in which he amassed a then Ashes series record 34 wickets, while also scoring 475 runs.

After playing his last Test in 1896, at the age of 37, Giffen pressed on with South Australia and a few days short of his forty-fourth birthday put together a stunning performance against Victoria, scoring 81 and 97 not out and taking 15 wickets. All that in a losing side!

There were times during his long career when Giffen came in for criticism – for favouring his brother Walter at the selection table; for bowling himself too often and for too long; and for the demise of CTB Turner who was Australia's leading bowler at the time (and then opening the bowling himself in a game that Australia needed to win) – but Giffen's numbers stack up. Nine times he scored a century and took ten wickets in a match. He's the only bowler in the world to snare 16 wickets in a match five times. He's the first Australian to take 1000 wickets and score 10,000 runs in first-class games, and he's the first player to notch the double of 1000 runs and 100 wickets in Tests.

In retirement Giffen coached young cricketers in a group known as 'Giffen's Early Risers'. In recognition of his contribution to the game, a grandstand at the beautiful Adelaide Oval bears his name.

If 1921 was a signature year for ten-fors, then 1956 was not far behind it. In fact, there are those who would argue that it was at least its equal, even though there were 'only' four ten-fors in 1956 to 1921's five. But 1956 was a special year. As you've read, it was the year of Jim Laker, when he notched two ten-fors in the same season, first for Surrey against the touring Australians, and then in that memorable Test at Old Trafford when he backed up his nine first-innings wickets with a Test-record ten in the second.

The third ten-for in 1956 was taken in a County Championship game by Laker's Surrey and England teammate Tony Lock. What a reign Surrey enjoyed in the Fifties, winning the Championship seven times straight from 1952 to 1958 inclusive. No surprise they dominated with a bowling attack boasting the likes of Laker, Lock, Alec Bedser and Peter Loader – not to mention with Peter May heading the batting and a great captain in Stuart Surridge.

The achievements of the Surrey spin twins are catalogued elsewhere, however. We concern ourselves here with **Kenneth 'Ken' Smales (15 September 1927 – 10 March 2015)**, who might well be described as a quiet achiever when mentioned in such august company as Laker and Lock. But he, too, was a purveyor of spin – in his case right-arm off-breaks. That his story is told in this chapter relates not to the date of his achievement, but to the commonality of his figures with those of Mailey and Giffen. Yes, another 10 for 66!

A native Yorkshireman, Smales attended the same school, Aireborough Grammar, as two of the county's all-time greats, Hedley Verity and Brian Close. Smales began with the Yorkshire second team in 1947, batting being the second arrow in his quiver, and found a way into the first team in 1948. Immediately, he settled into what was a formidable line-up.

However, Smales's tenure at Yorkshire seemed on shaky ground when he was left out of the side for the whole of the 1949 season. He was again unable to secure a regular berth in the first team through 1950, playing just three games and taking ten wickets at 22. Reading the writing on the wall, he left at the end of the 1950 season with only 13 games for the county under his belt.

Still keen to make his mark, Smales moved 70-odd miles [112 kilometres] due south after he had secured a position with the playing staff at Nottinghamshire. These were better years for him, and he remained a permanent fixture at Trent Bridge until his retirement at the end of the 1958 season. His best season with the ball was 1955, when he took 117 wickets at 24.12. He took five wickets in an innings 20 times and enjoyed five ten-wicket matches, plus a hat-trick. Over his career with the two counties, Smales took a total of 389 first-class wickets. Included in that tally was his 10-66 against Gloucestershire at Stroud. He's the only Nottinghamshire player to have achieved a ten-for.

When his cricket career ended after the 1958 season, he walked across Radcliffe Road to Nottingham Forest Football Club's ground and began employment there. He became their full-time secretary in 1961, and served during the years when manager Brian Clough took the club to great heights, having a hand in the signing of Britain's first million-pound footballer, Trevor Francis.

Tom Graveney was one of those batsmen you'd gladly pay the entrance fee to watch. For me, he was something of a right-handed David Gower, a man who caressed rather than hit the ball, who had all the shots and gave such joy to those who were fortunate enough to see him play them. He *could* bat! In Tests, 79 of them, he scored 4882 runs at 40.38; and in all first-class games, 47,793 at 44.91. But could he bowl? Nah! In all those first-class games, he took just one wicket for the cost of 167 runs.

Well, if Tom could bat, but couldn't bowl, his brother **John Kenneth Richard 'Ken' Graveney (16 December 1924 – 25 October 2015)** was his polar opposite. Like his brother (and much later, his own son, David), Ken Graveney was Gloucestershire County Cricket Club first and foremost – though both Tom and David did later ply their wares with other counties. A right-arm fast-medium who could swing it away from the right-hand bat, Graveney joined the county in 1947 – after serving in World War II with the Royal Marines and  taking part in the Normandy landings. He hit his straps two years later when he took 59 wickets and wrote his name on the ten-for list with his 10-66 in Derbyshire's second innings at Chesterfield.

It was one of those days for Graveney. Though it was a spinner's wicket, every time he was brought into the attack he would break through. Derbyshire's last pair were defiant, and his captain threatened to take him off. The trick worked, and the final wicket was his. Sadly, Graveney's career was curtailed by fitness problems and he retired with a serious back issue at the end of the 1951 season.

In 1963, after 11 years out of the game, Graveney, then 38, was coerced back into harness and agreed to captain the side. He bowled little and batted down the order that season with the team finishing eighth, falling to last in the Championship the following year. That was it.

Graveney had served as captain, chairman and president – though you could say his greatest service to the county had been introducing a new recruit: 'This is my brother, I can't get the ball past his bat.' That was his brother, Tom.

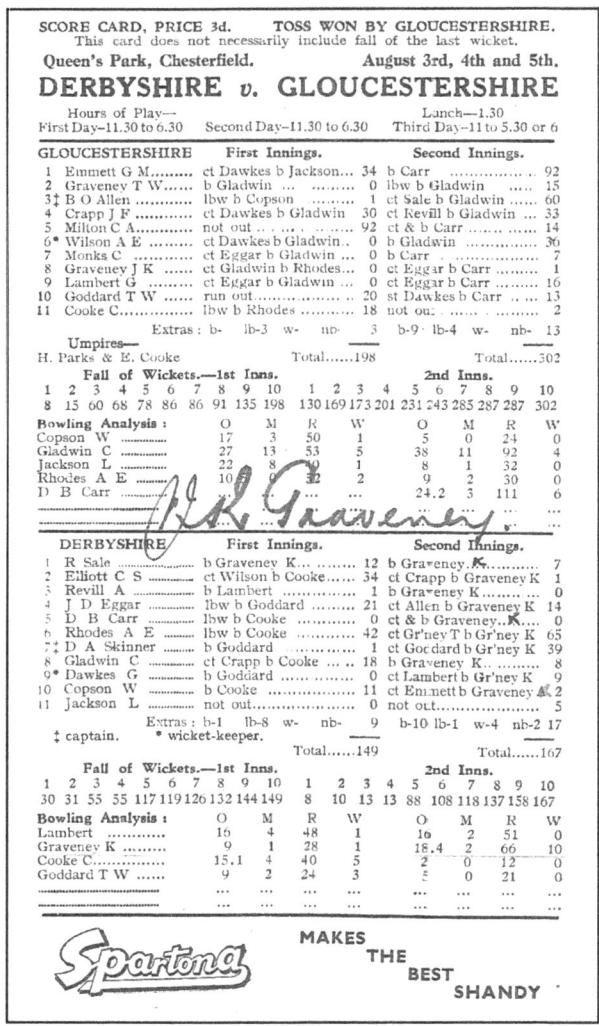

SCORE CARD, PRICE 3d.   TOSS WON BY GLOUCESTERSHIRE.
This card does not necessarily include fall of the last wicket.

Queen's Park, Chesterfield.   August 3rd, 4th and 5th.

DERBYSHIRE *v.* GLOUCESTERSHIRE

Hours of Play—   Lunch—1.30
First Day–11.30 to 6.30   Second Day–11.30 to 6.30   Third Day–11 to 5.30 or 6

GLOUCESTERSHIRE	First Innings.		Second Innings.	
1 Emmett G M	ct Dawkes b Jackson	34	b Carr	92
2 Graveney T W	b Gladwin	0	lbw b Gladwin	15
3‡ B O Allen	lbw b Copson	1	ct Sale b Gladwin	60
4 Crapp J F	ct Dawkes b Gladwin	30	ct Revill b Gladwin	33
5 Milton C A	not out	92	ct & b Carr	14
6* Wilson A E	ct Dawkes b Gladwin	0	b Gladwin	36
7 Monks C	ct Eggar b Gladwin	0	b Carr	7
8 Graveney J K	ct Gladwin b Rhodes	0	ct Eggar b Carr	1
9 Lambert G	ct Eggar b Gladwin	0	ct Eggar b Carr	16
10 Goddard T W	run out	20	st Dawkes b Carr	13
11 Cooke C	lbw b Rhodes	18	not out	2
Extras :	b- lb-3 w- nb-	3	b-9 lb-4 w- nb-	13
Umpires:—				
H. Parks & E. Cooke	Total	198	Total	302

Fall of Wickets.—1st Inns.   2nd Inns.

1	2	3	4	5	6	7	8	9	10	1	2	3	4	5	6	7	8	9	10
8	15	60	68	78	86	86	91	135	198	130	169	173	201	231	243	285	287	287	302

Bowling Analysis :	O	M	R	W	O	M	R	W
Copson W	17	3	50	1	5	0	24	0
Gladwin C	27	13	53	5	38	11	92	4
Jackson L	22	8	70	1	8	1	32	0
Rhodes A E	10	0	32	2	9	2	30	0
D B Carr					24.2	3	111	6

H.K. Graveney

DERBYSHIRE	First Innings.		Second Innings.	
1 R Sale	b Graveney K	12	b Graveney K	7
2 Elliott C S	ct Wilson b Cooke	34	ct Crapp b Graveney K	1
3 Revill A	b Lambert	1	b Graveney K	0
4 J D Eggar	lbw b Goddard	21	ct Allen b Graveney K	14
5 D B Carr	lbw b Cooke	0	ct & b Graveney K	0
6 Rhodes A E	lbw b Cooke	42	ct Gr'ney T b Gr'ney K	65
7‡ D A Skinner	b Goddard	1	ct Goddard b Gr'ney K	39
8 Gladwin C	ct Crapp b Cooke	18	b Graveney K	8
9* Dawkes G	b Goddard	0	ct Lambert b Gr'ney K	9
10 Copson W	b Cooke	11	ct Emmett b Graveney K	2
11 Jackson L	not out	0	not out	5
Extras :	b-1 lb-8 w- nb-	9	b-10 lb-1 w-4 nb-2	17
‡ captain. * wicket-keeper.				
	Total	149	Total	167

Fall of Wickets.—1st Inns.   2nd Inns.

1	2	3	4	5	6	7	8	9	10	1	2	3	4	5	6	7	8	9	10
30	31	55	55	117	119	126	132	144	149	8	10	13	13	88	108	118	137	158	167

Bowling Analysis :	O	M	R	W	O	M	R	W
Lambert	16	4	48	1	16	2	51	0
Graveney K	9	1	28	1	18.4	2	66	10
Cooke C	15.1	4	40	5	2	0	12	0
Goddard T W	9	2	24	3	5	0	21	0

Spartona MAKES THE BEST SHANDY

CHAPTER 11

PARTY POOPER

The English county of Staffordshire is famous the world over for the production of fine bone china. In cricketing circles, the county has also made its mark on the world, producing, or playing home to, a number of cricketers who have gone on to make their mark on the game.

One such cricketer was SF 'Sydney' Barnes, who many still rate as one of the finest bowlers the game has ever seen. A medium to fast-medium bowler, he could swing the ball both ways and break it from off to leg and leg to off with devastating effect. As a Test cricketer he was peerless.[24] He played 27 Tests between 1901 and 1914, his return of 189 wickets coming at the cheeseparing average of 16.43. He helped England win the Ashes in 1911–12, taking 34 wickets. In his final series, in South Africa in 1913–14, he claimed a record 49 – even though he didn't play in the final Test over a disagreement with team management!

A 15-minute drive away from Barnes's birthplace is a small town called Old Hill, a town that in its heyday was a centre of the

---

24 Almost uniquely for a regular England player, Barnes – born on 19 April 1873 in Smethwick – played little county cricket, turning out occasionally for Warwickshire and Lancashire. But he remained loyal to his home county of Staffordshire, playing in the Minor Counties Championship. He also turned out for various League cricket teams, though mainly for the Saltaire club in Yorkshire. This penchant for playing in the Leagues had financial benefits. He was paid as much for one day a week as for six at a county.

chain-making industry. In the early 20th century almost a third of Great Britain's chain works and chain shops could be found in the town.[25] And it was around this time that the town became the birthplace of *another* Staffordshire cricketer who would make the cricketing world look up from its *Wisden*s – although, unlike the well-celebrated Sydney Barnes, **William 'Eric' Hollies (5 June 1912 – 16 April 1981)** is best remembered (unfairly, given his excellent career) for a single outing against Don Bradman's touring Australians in the 1948 season.

Those touring Australians warmed up for the 1948 Ashes with a five-Test home series against an Indian team that was in its formative years after, only months earlier, the partition of India had split the subcontinent into two independent states, India and Pakistan. The Australians whizzed through the series four-nil, and Bradman, though 39, enjoyed the developing opposition by scoring a whopping 715 runs at the amazing average of 178.75.

Before the final Test he declared that he would retire after the coming Ashes tour to England. There was a feeling close to bereavement among the Australian cricketing public, understanding, all of a sudden, that they were seeing the last of the great man in full flight in international competition. However, Australian dismay became England's delight, as they welcomed The Don to their shores for a five-Test Ashes finale. He may have been a constant thorn in their side but the English fans recognised greatness when they saw it.

In his classic tour account, *Brightly Fades The Don,* former Australian player Jack Fingleton described the feeling on board the ship that would carry the Australians to England. "'He's on!" was

---

25 The practice of chain manufacture in Old Hill died out after World War II. Meantime, the town's fame, call that reflected glory, had switched to cricket. Pertinent, you might say, given that the imperial measure of a chain is 22 yards [20.12 metres] … the time-honoured length of a cricket pitch!

a cry from one (English) steward to another as the RMS *Strathaird* prepared to leave Fremantle. Bradman the Great was on his way to a fourth and final tour of the Old Country.'

From the moment the touring party stepped onto English soil the aura surrounding Bradman was almost tangible – but to be fair the rest of the team were equally lauded by the fascinated English fans. While Bradman was feted wherever he went, every training session, public appearance or county game saw massive crowds, still recovering from the ravages of war, turn out for the Australians. 'The Worcester crowds were record ones,' Fingleton wrote. 'On two successive days there were 14,000 present.'

This was typical of the way Bradman and his players were received. Clearly hundreds of thousands of fans countrywide were desperate to get a final glimpse of the greatest batsman of them all. At times there were crowd control problems with eager fans clambering over each other to get into grounds – and occasionally officials caved in under the weight of numbers and gave the all-clear for fans to sit on the grass outside the boundary.

For most of the tour Bradman was a picture of patience and courtesy. He and his team accepted the accolades with quality responses. In the meantime, there were runs to be scored, wickets to be taken and games to be won … and it was well known that Bradman was committed not only to his team claiming the Ashes, but also doing so without losing a game. It was hard work for him, off the field as much as on it. He turned 40 on 27 August (albeit after the fifth Test), and much was expected of him, both to play in as many games as was considered prudent, *and* to portray a satisfactory level of public persona. According to reports on the tour, the captain and champion batsman was given a tick in all boxes.

While Bradman's team traversed the nation, the County Championship rolled along, and for Eric Hollies – remember him? – that meant two three-day games a week, a workload that others may have felt burdensome. Hollies, though, was used to hard work. He would on one occasion send down 73 overs in a single innings! For Hollies, who began his first-class career with Warwickshire in 1932, it was a pleasant – and successful – pathway to a day at The Oval in London, where the genial wrist-spinner would spoil a going-away party in the most comprehensive manner.

Hollies absorbed a love of the game and a feeling for its finer skills from his father, who played cricket for more than 30 years and was the last lob bowler in the Birmingham League. It was a humble beginning at Warwickshire's Edgbaston home for Hollies, his meagre four wickets at 80 runs apiece no indication of what was to come. However, the following season it was 79 at 24.70 and Hollies was away, heading towards the lofty position of being regarded one of the best bowlers of his type in the world.

Fair of hair and short in stature, Hollies was not a great spinner of the ball – purveying a mix of leg-spin, top-spinners and the occasional wrong'un. But he was a craftsman who relied on high degrees of accuracy, once compared in this regard with the great

Australian leggie Clarrie Grimmett. And it was this command of line and length which was a feature of his excellent ten-for performance in 1946 against Nottinghamshire at Edgbaston. In finishing with 10-49, Hollies bowled seven, with the other three given out leg before wicket. No fielder or wicketkeeper were needed which, it could be argued, elevates the quality of a ten-for.

Hollies served the county through to 1957, notwithstanding

vital years lost to World War II. When county cricket was put on hold during the hostilities he remained at home, working for the war effort and playing as a professional in the Birmingham and District League. In five seasons there he piled up 499 wickets and his team, West Bromwich Dartmouth, won the title every time. Back with Warwickshire, the modest spin merchant played a major role in 1951, when his 145 wickets at 17.69 helped carry the team to their first County Championship in 40 years.

Apart from skill, Hollies was also blessed with loads of patience and perseverance. And a genial personality, according to cricket writer Colin Bateman. '[He was] loquacious, with a rich seam of Black Country humour ... an immensely respected and hard-working cricketer.' Another writer made this observation: 'From the boundary Hollies looks anything but a menacing bowler. He takes a few leisurely paces to the wicket and neither in action nor in demeanour is he aggressive ... He persuades his opponent out with almost an apologetic air.'

He played 13 times for England, starting by touring the West Indies in 1935. It was 12 years later that he played again for his country, a home series against South Africa. There were further Tests in 1949 (against New Zealand) and against West Indies in 1950, when he bagged 5-63 – his victims including the great Frank Worrell and Everton Weekes.

But the signature Test match appearance for the little tweaker came somewhere in between.

As the 1948 Australians set about striving to uphold their captain's mission – to not lose a game on his farewell tour – Bradman defied the law of logic, that age must tell on the international stage. He played his share of games, fought tooth and nail when it was necessary and, when the timing was right, even gave away his wicket. An earlier version of Bradman would *never* have even contemplated such an act of largesse.

Then came the game against Lancashire (26–28 May), when the master batsman looked to be human, after all …falling twice to a 19-year-old left-arm spinner. Afterwards there was some speculation about Bradman's ability to handle spin on a wicket that was helping the bowler. I refer now to Jack Fingleton's on-the-spot report. 'It was here that Malcolm Hilton took Bradman's wicket in both innings,' he wrote. 'This was a feat which sent Hilton's photograph with his family history onto the front page of all English newspapers.'

The first Test at Trent Bridge was a fortnight later. It will probably never be known if the England selectors actually considered going with the young Lancashire leftie. Instead, the spinner's job went to Jim Laker. It made no difference. The tourists won at Trent Bridge and again at Lord's in the second Test. The third Test, at Old Trafford, was drawn, before the Aussies returned to winning ways in the fourth Test in Leeds, scoring 3-404 on the last day, of which Bradman, raging against the dying of the light, you might say, contributed 173 not out.

A fortnight later the Australians turned up to play their county game against Warwickshire at Edgbaston. The home side batted first and then opened with the spin of Eric Hollies at one end. There was something of a harbinger when Hollies got one through Bradman's defences and bowled him, for 31. That prized wicket was just one of eight (for 107) from 43.5 crisp Hollies overs.

Fingleton again: 'This match turned out to be a triumph for Hollies, a blond slow bowler whose every movement in the field is greeted with the most amazing roars of appreciation by the young brigade. These teenagers had given the county committee much trouble and the result was that war was declared against the youths for the Australian game. They were told they had to behave themselves or else.

'As usual for this tour,' Fingleton continued, 'thousands queued outside the ground before the game began, but no youths were to be allowed into the ground unless accompanied by a parent. It was amazing the number of "adoptions" there were that morning in the streets outside the Edgbaston ground! But generally, the youths behaved themselves well during the Australian game.

'However, grim authority could not stop them from paying noisy tribute to Hollies every time he moved or even appeared on the field. And when he bowled Bradman I thought the ground would explode! Not even Bradman has known such youthful adulation.'[26]

Fingleton was eager to acknowledge the English spinner's talents. 'Hollies is a good bowler, that must be said at once and it must be specifically noted that Hollies clean-bowled Bradman on the only two occasions he met him – and also turned into knots one or two of the Australian heroes of the fourth Test,' he wrote.

'The Edgbaston pitch did not look a good one, but Hollies was later to show at The Oval that he would have bowled well against the Australians on any pitch. As he rolled over eight of the Australians there were sighs that a man like him had not been present at the Leeds Test [where England had failed to push home an advantage to win] – that Test will be fought over and over again for the years to come.'

Hollies, Fingleton opined, exhibited perfect control. 'He has nice flight, gives the ball plenty of air and yet is not too slow through the air. He bowls an excellent bosie [wrong'un]. I was interested to see him bowl around the stumps to Arthur Morris. Most slow bowlers dislike bowling to left-handers, but Hollies bowled exceedingly well to Morris.

---

26 Fittingly, what is now known as the Hollies Stand at Edgbaston is still occasionally noisy.

'The Australians told me that Hollies does not spin the ball very much, but, indeed, bowls many top-spinners. It was one of these which clean bowled Bradman at Edgbaston, when he offered what seemed a careless stroke and played outside the ball.'

With the fifth and final Test approaching, the England selectors now had a dilemma on their hands. Pick Hollies, and in doing concede they erred in not selecting him earlier, or leave him out and risk a public backlash? Hollies, for all that, was known to have little time for Test cricket. He was chosen for MCC in 1935, but ricked his neck and did not play. It wasn't until 1946 that he played in his first Test – though he thought little of it as he had to play second string to Doug Wright.

As the history books will show, the England selectors opted to select the Staffordshire-born offie who, on being picked, wanted to withdraw! Can you imagine? Later that year he also refused an invitation to tour South Africa. On the occasion of this fifth Test, however, he was talked around by his county committee, and so the name 'Hollies' was prepared for the scoresheet as The Oval was primed to host Bradman's final hurrah as an international cricketer.

The build-up to the Test at The Oval was intense to say the very least – and, of course, this was heightened by Hollies's success against Bradman a fortnight earlier. There were 20,000 people in the ground, most of whom were aware that Bradman had 6996 Test runs to his credit and needed just four more runs to see his Test average reach the 100 mark. While Hollies would share spin duties with the Middlesex left-armer Jack Young, Australia banked on its three-pronged pace attack of Ray Lindwall, Keith Miller and Bill Johnston. With good reason, the trio skittling England, batting first, for just 52, with Hutton's 30 the only score in double figures. With such a low total, it was now probable that Bradman's final appearance would be reduced to a single innings.

Australia's first innings began in ominous fashion for England with openers Sid Barnes and Arthur Morris putting on a stand of 117 – before Hollies had Barnes caught behind for 61. Fingleton, who had an up-and-down relationship with Bradman, tells how the final stanza in the legend's career played out. 'The Don came down the steps a lithe, athletic figure and he fingered his cap to the applause as he made his way. The reception he received must have been embarrassing for him. It lasted all the way out to the middle and then [England captain] Norman Yardley assembled his team and called for three cheers. This was given heartily. Yardley then shook Bradman by the hand.'

There has been much conjecture about the emotional toll such a welcome to the crease would have had on Bradman who, when the hubbub died down, took his guard, looked about and settled himself over his bat. Down the other end, Hollies, having just claimed Barnes's scalp, approached the wicket having in mind his recent successful outing against the best batter in cricket history.

After Bradman defended Hollies's first delivery, the leggie's next ball was pitched slightly further up and it drew Bradman forward. This time, however, Bradman missed the ball, something he was not prone to do over his long career. A fraction of a second later he would have heard the sound of the ball crashing into the stumps. Fingleton again: 'The crowd's reaction was one of the strangest experiences I've ever known on a cricket ground … one moment the crowd was acknowledging Bradman lavishly in his farewell appearance, that noise had barely died on the afternoon air when it was rent again with the crowd shrieking at Bradman's dismissal.'

Like everyone else, Bradman, who turned to observe his rearranged stumps, couldn't seem to believe what had happened. He then turned back and very slowly made his way off the ground. The crowd again made their presence known but on this occasion their applause had a sympathetic air.

As for Hollies, he'd produced the final word. He had told a Warwickshire colleague, after bowling to Bradman in the county game, that he didn't think the great Australian could pick his wrong'un. 'I know I can bowl him with it and I'll give it to him second ball,' Hollies had said. Never a truer forecast was made!

As Bradman left the field to applause acknowledging his marvellous career, Hollies turned to a teammate and said, 'Best ball I bowled all season and yet they're clapping him!'

More than his ten-for, it has to be said, this personal triumph placed little Eric Hollies from Old Hill, Staffordshire, up on a lofty pedestal. He will forever be remembered for that one magical delivery ... which robbed an icon of the perfect ending.

CHAPTER 12

AUSSIE ALL SORTS

The consensus is that the game of cricket landed in Australia with the First Fleet in 1788. In all, 11 ships arrived in what is now known as Botany Bay, carrying some 1300 people – marines, sailors, civil officers, convicts and free settlers. The idea was to establish a penal colony. Of course, the outcome was a settlement in Australia, with the Union Jack flown from every masthead lest other would-be colonists like the French and Dutch claim sovereignty over a territory the British had declared *terra nullius* (in effect, 'nobody's land') – a pronouncement that was news to the Aboriginal and Torres Strait Islander people who had lived on the continent for some 65,000 years.

Sydney was the centre of early action by the settlers, but it wasn't too long before the new arrivals, and those who followed in the wake, ventured beyond Sydney Cove. And as they spread across this great southern land they took with them their summer pastime – the game of cricket.

The first iteration of the game Down Under was essentially the same form as its English forebear, although the landscape of *Terra Australis* lacked the rustic meadows that provided a home to England's early playing fields. In time, fields were prepared for the game in Australia and it prospered accordingly, with the first recorded match taking place in Sydney in 1804, although the game is said to have been well-established before then.[27] Support for cricket came from on high. Governor Macquarie, for instance, ordered the manufacture of bats and balls in government workshops, and in 1811 he established the second Sydney Common (after Hyde Park) which, decades later, was granted to the British Army for use as a garden and cricket ground. These days, the area is known as Moore Park, the site of the Sydney Cricket Ground.

And so began the gradual development of a rich culture within Australian cricketing ranks – a culture boosted once Australian and English teams began touring each other's countries. The first sporting team to leave Australia's shores was, in fact, a cricketing one, with an Aboriginal Australian team touring England in 1868. Playing an astounding 47 matches, they won 14, drew 19, and turned many heads.

It would be fair to say the game's biggest step forward in Australia came when an English XI undertook the long sea journey to Australia and played 23 matches, including two matches against a combined Australia XI. The first of these – which was later granted first-class status and anointed the first ever Test match – took place at the Melbourne Cricket Ground in March 1877. Australia won by a margin of 45 runs. Incredibly, the result and margin of the 1977 Centenary Test, also played at the MCG, was identical.

England, of course, had a healthy head-start on Australia when it comes to cricket. It's no surprise then that when it comes to the claiming of first-class ten-fors that the first 15 players on the list – headed by William Lillywhite as you've read – were all English. But the turn of Australians and players from the other cricketing nations was to come. In Australia's case, first through the spinning

---

27 The game was first mentioned briefly in a *Sydney Gazette* report on 8 January 1804: 'The late intense weather has been very favourable to the amateurs of cricket who have scarce lost a day for the past month.'

fingers of George Giffen (in 1883), whose ten-for story has been told in a previous chapter.

The second Australian to take a ten-for was **William Peter 'Bill' Howell (29 December 1869 – 14 July 1940)**, a player who seemed to have a knack for fashioning dream-come-true scenarios for himself. In 1894–95, for instance, the touring MCC team played NSW in the annual Country Week competition. Howell, a beekeeper from the bush (as Penrith was at the time), travelled to the big smoke and ended up taking 5-44 for NSW against the MCC. How's that for a first-class debut?

Then, called into the Australian side for the third Test at Adelaide in the 1897–98 Ashes series, his first wicket was the fabled Archie MacLaren. How's that for a Test debut (which included a haul of 4-70)? And what about this? Touring with the Australian team in England in 1899, he was not picked in the first two tour games, but chosen for the third, versus Surrey at The Oval. Guess what? Howell took every Surrey wicket in the first innings, finishing with 10-28. He got 5-29 in the second innings. Not bad for your first game on English soil!

Howell was a tall, powerfully built country lad who bowled at a lively medium-pace, with tricks to burn. Making full use of strong wrists and fingers, he was able to impart sharp spin when conditions favoured, catching the inexperienced unawares as to just how much he could work the ball off the wicket. He also had a ball that he let go from a run-up of one or two paces, which served to confuse batsmen. Add to that a pleasing degree of

accuracy, plus the stamina needed for long spells, and you have a real package.

As would be expected of his type of bowler, Howell turned the ball sharply on the matting wickets when he toured South Africa in 1902–03 – taking 9-99 runs in the third Test at Cape Town and 14 wickets at 12.42 for the two Tests he played. That series aside, there were few high points in his 18 Tests. He toured England three times (1899, 1902 and 1905) and South Africa the once.

Perhaps befitting his knockabout nature, Howell loved to take the long handle to the bowling. In one innings for NSW versus the MCC in 1897–98 he scored 48 in 44 minutes in the first innings. In the second he took 59 minutes to hammer the bowling to the tune of 95 lusty runs, 76 of them coming from boundaries. In the local Penrith area, he once hit seven sixes in a seven-ball over. In another game he took 10-10.

Universally popular for his pleasant, easy-going nature, Howell was considered a great team man, and on his three tours to England he was appointed chief custodian of the team's shaving equipment because of his skill at sharpening razors.

Howell's debut Test saw him share the field with offie Hugh Trumble (141 wickets from 32 Tests), widely considered to be Australia's first truly great spinner.[28] Trumble was the second of two elite spin bowlers Australia had at their disposal in the late 19th century, the other being George Giffen (103 Test wickets from 31 matches).

Having more than one gun spinner in any given era is a real treat to selectors. So what a halcyon period it was between the wars when Australia had an embarrassment of spinning riches, players who would find their places in the 'Milky Way' of spin-bowling stardom. First came Arthur Mailey, who set things in motion in 1920. Then Clarrie Grimmett took off in 1925. Bert Ironmonger followed in 1928, and Bill O'Reilly completed a quality quartet in 1932.[29] Those were golden years for Australian captains. In a time when their pace-bowling ranks were thin – a time post McDonald and Gregory, and pre Lindwall and Miller – they had safe hands in which to place their hopes of dominating the opposition batsmen.

Of that feared spinning foursome, Mailey, as you've read, became the third Australian to record a ten-for. Nine years later, in 1930, a fourth Aussie made it onto the list, and it was another member of the fantastic four: **Clarence Victor 'Clarrie' Grimmett (25 December 1891 – 2 May 1980).**

---

28 About a century later, Shane Warne began a celebrated career (708 wickets from 145 Tests) that placed him in a class of his own among 'standard' wrist-spinners. I use the word in quotes, because the Sri Lankan tweaker Muttiah Muralitharan also was a wristy in his own right. Between 1998 and 2008, Stuart MacGill (208 wickets from 44 Tests) shared some of the limelight that favoured the great Warne – and from 2011 onwards the burden of a nation's spin load has fallen on the narrow shoulders of Nathan Lyon. He is migrating into rarefied atmosphere as one of cricket's all-time greats, *and* has done it mostly as the sole spinner in the Australian line-up.

29 'Dainty' Ironmonger was 46 years old – and spinning the ball using the stump of a forefinger mauled in a buzz-saw accident – when he first pulled on the 'baggy green' cap (his 14 Tests produced 74 wickets at 17.97). 'Tiger' O'Reilly's 32 Tests, meantime, saw him take 144 wickets at 22.59. At times both he and Grimmett opened the Australian attack.

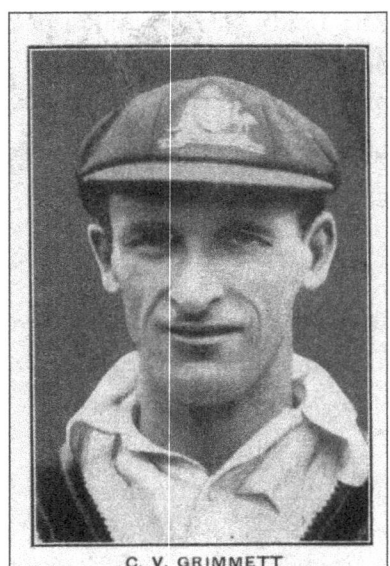

C. V. GRIMMETT

The surprise with Grimmett is that he made the ten-for list just the once. I say this because I can't help but compare him to a bowler with whom he shared both physical stature and style of delivery, Tich Freeman – a bowler who has three ten-fors to his name.

The comparisons between the two are beguiling. Grimmett stood a wiry 5 ft 7 in (1.70 m), Freeman a wispy 5 ft 2 in (1.57 m). Each was characterised by a slightly round-arm delivery, each exposed weaknesses in the best of batsmen with a full bag of the wrist-spinner's tricks, each practised assiduously (often away from prying eyes), and both desperately protected the secrets of their armoury.

Is that where we meet a fork in the road? Maybe. The fact is that while Freeman tended to shrink a little when up against the very cream, Grimmett would take out the egg-beater and whip them. Numbers tell part of the story. In all first-class games Freeman was almost without peer – totalling 3776 wickets at 18.42 apiece. In his 12 Tests, however, he had 'just' 66 wickets at 25.86. But Grimmett rose to *every* occasion. He bagged 1424 first-class wickets at 22.28, and 216 at 24.21 in 37 Tests.

The earlier review of Freeman's career in these pages underlines his constant pursuit of excellence, honing his skills, developing new deliveries and perfecting his strategies. The same must be said of Grimmett. In training he would mark a spot on a pitch and wheel away at it, bowling an eight-ball over then waiting while his well-trained dog collected the balls and brought them back to him.

Neither he nor Freeman would show a different delivery without first polishing it in practice.

Oddly enough, Grimmett, who was born and bred in New Zealand, grew up fancying his chances as a fast bowler. Better minds, who had seen him wheel down some spin, put an end to that nonsense. So began the making of a champion leggie. He was showing the ability to bowl a top-spinner at the age of ten and at 17 made his first-class debut for Wellington in the Plunket Shield. In 1914, a time when New Zealand was not yet a Test-cricketing nation, Grimmett moved to Sydney where he started playing club cricket.

After a time in Melbourne, where he took 8-86 for Victoria against South Australia, he decided to move to Adelaide in 1924. Settled and on a steep trajectory, he worked to make the world of cricket his oyster, and in February 1925 he won his first Test cap. Bill O'Reilly would later quip that Grimmett must have been 'the best Christmas present Australia ever received from [New Zealand]'.

There was a quaintness about Grimmett. Born on Christmas Day 1891, he was such a gnome-like figure, a man who would rather bowl with his cap on than hand it to the umpire. Yet there was an irrepressible urge to take the ball and wind rings around batsmen with a sizzling array of pure leggies, wrong'uns, top-spinners and, later in the piece, a devastating flipper – a delivery that hurried on and caught the man at the receiving end by surprise.

Writing in the *Barclays World of Cricket*, Ian Peebles, himself a leg-spinner, summed up the package: 'A small, prematurely bald figure, he embarked on each assault with a little lamb-like skip, trundled diagonally to the crease and swung a bony arm a little above shoulder high.' His stock ball, Peebles added, 'was the leg-break, amply spun and launched over a great range of pace and flight, ever with complete control of length and direction'.

Grimmett also bowled googlies [wrong'uns], and top-spinners. The former, said Peebles, 'was a more modest affair clearly discernible and used mostly for tactical purposes. His top-spinner was, on the other hand, a wicket-taking weapon delivered rather faster and tending to dip late in its flight. He scarcely ever bowled a loose ball. For one born on Christmas Day, he was sparing with his presents.'

Fellow Australian wrist-spinner Arthur Mailey was another to sing his praises, and he described Grimmett as responsible, self-disciplined, considerate and studious. 'This man thought a full toss was the worst form of cricket vandalism and the long hop a legacy from prehistoric days when Barbarians rolled boulders towards the enemy,' Mailey wrote with typical flair. 'Collecting a wicket was a mere incident in the game. One of the gentlest bowlers ever to lift a ball, he walked gently, picked up a cup of tea gently, arranged his tie with whispering fingers. His cap was set as though with a spirit level.

'It is true that he and I both bowled leg-breaks and wrong'uns, but there the similarity ended. My best leg-break was the top-spinner, while Grimmett's leg-break spun half laterally, half

horizontally. His round-arm delivery was mainly responsible for the amount of side-spin he put on the ball and also the secret of his immaculate length.'

Grimmett's Test career began with a bang. Chosen for the fifth Ashes Test at the SCG in March 1925, he returned figures of 5-45 and 6-37. Australia won the game and the series – and a star was on the rise. Series after series – at home and abroad, against England, West Indies and South Africa – he was a dominant force. In 1930, on Australia's tour of England, he took ten-for against Yorkshire in Sheffield, his 10-37 coming from 22.3 overs. He finished that year's Test series as the top wicket-taker from both teams with 29 at 31.89. In 1935–36, in South Africa, he was Australia's leading wicket-taker with 44 at 14.59.

And yet he was overlooked for the home Ashes series in 1936–37, which was covered for Australian and English newspapers by eminent writer Neville Cardus. 'Grimmett is the most accurate leg-spin bowler of all time. The main points of his technique are accuracy, flight and leg-spin. His greatest asset, of course, is his artfulness. He has enchanted me with his skill. I love him.'

Despite Cardus's glowing endorsement, Grimmett was also shunned for the 1938 tour to England. It made no sense – just as it made the man himself furious at the selectors. Although he was 45 at the time, Grimmett considered himself at his peak, a claim supported by his having claimed 59 wickets in his previous seven Tests. His partner in spin, Bill O'Reilly, was moved to write: 'His omission makes me boil with anger. How could the selectors have been so stupid! No better bowler ever breathed.'

Grimmett's achievements and honours give support to such a claim. Alongside his first-class and Test records (mentioned above), he took five wickets in an innings 127 times and ten in a match 33 times. Until Yasir Shah of Pakistan beat his mark in 2018, Grimmett claimed 200 Test wickets in the fewest Tests (36, to Shah's 33). His other accolades include his being awarded the *Wisden* Cricketer of the Year in 1931 and his induction into both the Australian Cricket Hall of Fame and the ICC Hall of Fame.

Not bad for a budding fast bowler who, in the end, found the right pace and, from an Australian perspective, *place.*

Scrutiny of bowling feats in first-class games has produced some stunning analyses, no better instances of that than Hedley Verity's 10-10 in a county game, or John Wisden's feat in clean bowling *all* of his ten victims.

Well, there's a story to be told about the ten-for journey of the fifth Australian member: the tall, persistent South Australian fast-medium bowler **Thomas Welbourn 'Tim' Wall (13 May 1904 –**

26 March 1981). It was 3 February 1933 and despite having made an early breakthrough with the wicket of Bill Brown, Wall was now toiling away with his fellow SA bowlers in a Sheffield Shield game in Sydney while NSW's Jack Fingleton and Don Bradman were making batting look easy.

The pair had helped NSW recover from 1-12 to 1-87 when, all of a sudden, their wall was breached – by Wall – and the innings was turned on its head. Having bowled Fingleton for 43, Wall immediately dismissed Bradman for 56 and all of a sudden NSW were 3-87. Wall then ran through the NSW batting order in extraordinary style, claiming the next seven wickets (four of them in one devastating over) to dismiss NSW for 113 – with six batsmen failing to score. Wall's final nine wickets cost him just five runs and he finished with 10-36. It's worth mentioning that, remarkably, NSW recovered to win the match, but Wall's first-innings spell was something else.

So was his run-up. Call it 'theatre', albeit probably unintentional, but Tim Wall's approach to the wicket amused most, and frustrated the rest. For all the muzzle velocity it produced, the 27 paces seemed to be extreme (unlike, for instance, West Indian speedster Michael Holding, whose long, mesmeric approach climaxed with a rocket launch). Built into the long run was a rhythmic swing of arms and body, considered to be a model action. But then as he approached the crease he performed an idiosyncratic skip. It drew this comment from the legendary broadcaster and writer Johnny Moyes: 'He had a good approach and as he reached the bowling crease kicked his feet about like a frisky colt … he could move the ball freely, and sometimes disconcertingly, had splendid stamina, was a magnificent trier and a charming companion.'

Getting back to his mark was another thing. Wall earned a reputation for perhaps the slowest walk back to his starting point – a time that seemed to get even slower when he was taking wickets.

Wall made his debut for South Australia at the age of 20 and slowly worked his way into contention for Test selection, which was hastened in the 1928–29 Ashes series when the feared Jack Gregory broke down in the first Test. Given the call-up for the fifth Test, Wall bowled a total of 75 overs and took three wickets for plenty in the first innings, but buttered up with 5-66 in the second. His match figures of 8-189 materially helped Australia to a much-needed victory. Incidentally, he claimed the wicket of England great Walter Hammond in each innings.

Subsequently, Wall was cast as leader of the Australian pace attack, where he may have been better suited to a support role. However, in those days Australia relied heavily on its spin stocks. He twice toured England (1930 and 1934), playing nine of his 18 Tests there. Wall was on duty during the 1932–33 Bodyline series, capturing a total of 16 wickets from four games, including 5-72 in the first innings of the third Test at his home ground, the Adelaide Oval.

The amiable Wall was roundly applauded for his reliability and earnest endeavour, three times taking five wickets in an innings in

Tests, including 5-14 against South Africa at Brisbane in 1931–32. Rich reward for constantly attacking the stumps. He rarely let one go down leg side, or outside off – and possessed a good bouncer, which caused problems for the very good England batsman Herbert Sutcliffe, whom he dismissed four times in 1932–33.

A schoolteacher away from the cricket field, after retirement Tim Wall was a prominent junior coach and became involved in cricket administration. He died in 1981 after a long battle with Parkinson's Disease.

There was a close connect between me and the sixth Australian to add his name to the ten-for list. For starters, we joined the list two seasons apart in the mid-Sixties: him in January 1966, me in October 1967. Second, we both completed our ten-fors against the same team, Victoria! In fact, seven of his victims were later mine too: Redpath, Watson, Potter, Stackpole, Jordon, Grant and Connolly.

A bond, call it a friendship, developed from the moment **Peter John Allan (31 December 1935 – 22 June 2023)** sent me a congratulatory telegram, welcoming me to the ten-for club. And that bond extended to a rare bit of inter-team socialising. When Queensland were playing in Perth, 'Piccolo' would come to our place for dinner, and vice versa when I was in Brisbane with the WA team. After our playing days were over, there remained occasional contact as our lives moved in different directions.

One thing about my old mate was that he could make the Kookaburra just about go around corners. Tall, lithe and with a graceful approach and sizeable leap into the side-on delivery position, Allan mainly operated downwind – and usually swung it away from the right-hander.

In January 1966, at the MCG, he wheeled down those swingers like a magician. It was day two of a Sheffield Shield clash – and I take my hat off to him, because often wickets at the 'G' were so bare that there was no shine left on the ball after the first ten overs. Dennis Lillie, Queensland's leg-spinner, recalled that the weather was fine and the pitch was a little trickier than usual. 'He was bowling his usual fast-medium and the ball was moving around a bit – typical of Peter,' said Lillie. 'It was late swing, and a number of them were caught behind the wicket. In my opinion he bowled well and they batted badly.'

At the end of the day's play the Victorian Cricket Association had a small presentation when they handed the ball to Allan after a small speech of congratulations. 'His response,' Lillie said, 'perhaps reflected the fact that he had been enticed to come to Melbourne earlier to play club cricket with the hope of playing for Victoria but was overlooked. He couldn't resist the opportunity and in response  quipped, "Of all the teams you would want to take all ten against, Victoria easily heads the list."'

So the name Peter Allan went into the record books, 10-61 written next to it. He became one of only three players to take ten-for in a Sheffield Shield game, and the only man to complete the feat at the MCG. Incredibly, in gathering the ten dismissals he bowled unchanged for 15.6 eight-ball overs, the equivalent of 21 overs on the trot nowadays. Such a workload would be unheard-of in today's age of micro-management of a pace bowler's output.

Allan hovered around the Australian team, first touring the West Indies in 1965. However, he got ill early on and was not selected for any of the Tests. He got his chance in the first Ashes clash of 1965–66, taking two wickets. Twelfth man for the second Test, he was omitted for the third in Sydney, later admitting this was a blessing in disguise, 'because that was when I played the Shield match against Victoria and took the ten wickets in one innings'. He was recalled for the fourth Test but withdrew late through injury – and that was that.

He capped off the 1965–66 season in grand fashion, taking all ten wickets in an innings for the South Brisbane club (though it wasn't a first-class match). Can you imagine that? Twice in the one season; two mounted balls sitting on the mantel shelf. Allan's best season for Queensland was 1968–69, when he captured 46 wickets at the miserly cost of 16.36, after which he announced his retirement.

The quietly spoken Queenslander spent the last decade of his working life on Hamilton Island, off the Queensland coast, where he worked as a civil celebrant. He claimed to have married almost 3000 couples – seven of them on one particular Valentine's Day. 'That to me was just great,' he said. 'Nobody is sad at a wedding, but I often wonder how many of them are still married.'

The seventh – and most recent – Australian member of the ten-for club is yours truly. And with that, I'll return to my story presently.

CHAPTER 13

10 FOR 44

continued

As my inswinger did for Jack Potter, and he departed the scene with Victoria precariously placed at 4-37, I couldn't help thinking, 'We're a silly chance here.' Knowing I had alongside me two highly rated Test bowlers in Graham McKenzie and Tony Lock, plus left-arm pacer Jim Hubble, recovered enough from the previous day's foot injury, there would be any amount of opportunities for us to go through the back half of the Victorian batting. But we still had to negotiate the straight bat of Bill Lawry – and we would not want to be wasteful if and when a chance came along!

The situation was tailor-made for Lawry. He *loved* a fight. Was renowned for it the cricket world over. No, we would have to chisel him out. And with Potter's departure, Lawry was joined by a player who was something of his antithesis. Keith Stackpole was one of those see-ball, hit-ball batsmen, a pugnacious back-foot player – from which position he pulled, hooked and cut with great power.

Stacky was a tough competitor, who always looked to take on the bowling. He was an ideal man to fill a middle-order slot. He played 43 Tests between 1966 and 1974 and averaged 37.4 over 2807 runs. He was a bit of a 'Captain Grumpy', and we used to say of him that he wouldn't acknowledge that he was out unless all three stumps were lying on the ground!

One could understand him being grumpy about the extraordinary way he lost his wicket this day, however. It was another of my inswingers, this one pitched up to the point that the ball actually landed on the toe of Stackpole's front foot. He offered a drive, but the ball rebounded off his boot, hit the bat and bobbled high in the air to mid-off. Fielding there and taking a simple catch was Jock Irvine, a fine, aggressive middle-order batsman, lost to WA cricket in 1970 when he moved to Melbourne for work purposes.[30] I can still see the look of disbelief after he had accepted the simple catch off Stacky.

Five-for:

Keith Stackpole, caught Jock Irvine, bowled Brayshaw, 0
Victoria – 5-37

Victoria's much-vaunted batting order was in disarray. They'd just lost three wickets for no runs and I had figures of 5-5! Realising that, I nodded towards the players' dressing-room, where coach Wally Langdon was a more than interested spectator. 'Get to 5-5 and I'll ask Todge to take a photo of the scoreboard,' I remember he'd said the previous evening. I don't know if he ever followed through on that.

I'd love to have known just what was going through Bill Lawry's mind as he watched Stacky disappear up the players' race and Graeme Watson emerge with his typically jaunty stride. Known to all as Beatle, because of his not-so-fashionable (at the time) long hair, Watson was a very talented all-rounder. A hard-hitting batsman who, if he got going, could really move the game forward. He was also a fine gully fielder and a very capable medium-fast bowler who in his days playing for Western Australia in Perth

---

30 He made three centuries and eight half-centuries for WA and toured India and South Africa in 1969–70, but didn't play a Test.

could generate enormous pace with the sea breeze at his back. If the Indian Premier League had been around in those days, Beatle possessed all the weaponry required to blitz his way through it. He was a good bloke, too.

Six-for

Graeme Watson, caught John Inverarity, bowled Brayshaw, 37
Victoria 6-104

With Watson joining his captain at the crease, the pair went about righting the ship. By now the sea breeze had pushed the morning easterly back and I had changed to operating from the northern end. But for a while the batsmen kept us at bay and the pair carried the score to 104 before Watson edged my outswinger and was caught at slip, John Inverarity accepting the chance.

Now *there* was an all-round package as a cricketer! With bat in hand Inverarity displayed wonderful technique and concentration, and he could score all around the wicket. He bowled canny left-arm orthodox, too, which got better over the years. Plus, he was a born leader – following Tony Lock as WA captain and displaying a great tactical approach. Inverarity toured England in 1968 and 1972 and finished his career with South Australia, having moved to Adelaide with his work in education. He later served as a national selector.

The wicket of Watson left the game evenly poised. Though Victoria were six down they were just 58 runs away from overhauling our first dig of 161, so first-innings points were hanging tantalisingly close to both teams.

Further developments shortly.

CHAPTER 14

EXTRAS

The applause that rang around Lord's Cricket Ground in July 2024 as James Anderson left the field for the final time in his celebrated Test career will never be forgotten by those fortunate enough to have been present for the shining moment. A walking advertisement for everything that is right about the game, Anderson left the Test match arena having become the first pace bowler to go past 700 wickets. His record 704 dismissals placed him exactly 100 wickets ahead of his long-time new-ball partner, Stuart Broad.

Bowling and batting milestones like this have been part of Test cricket's fabric since it began its long and fascinating journey at the MCG in 1877. And as the numbers began totting up from that day onwards, a race commenced to see who would be the first to reach the 100-wicket milestone. Eighteen years later (the race being more of a distance affair than a sprint[31]), that honour went to English left-arm spin bowler **Johnny Briggs (3 October 1862 – 11 January 1902)** – but only just. Going into the fourth Test at the SCG in 1895, three players – Briggs, his England teammate Bobby Peel, and Australia's Charles 'The Terror' Turner – were vying for the honour. On 1 February, Briggs won the race. Three days later

---

31 Until 1889, when South Africa became the third Test-playing nation, the only way to collect Test scalps was in matches between Australia and England. It was, then, slow going.

Turner followed suit in what proved to be his last Test match appearance.

Shortish (standing 5 ft 5 in – 165 cm) and stocky of build, Briggs spent a deal of time playing league cricket and rugby before landing at Lancashire in 1879 – in his eighteenth year. In his book *Cricket*, WG Grace said of him, 'His bowling is above medium-pace, round-arm, left-hand, and he breaks both ways; but he is most destructive with his leg-breaks. In batting, bowling and fielding he is quite first-class and no English representative eleven would be complete without him.'

Briggs's spin became prodigious turn on helpful pitches, backed by skilful variations of pace and flight. And he was rated one of the finest all-rounders of his day. He was a regular for Lancashire from 1883. Chosen for the 1884–85 Ashes tour on the back of his form with the bat, he made his debut in the first Test at Adelaide, but didn't bowl and batted down the list. Batting at number seven in the first innings of the second Test at the MCG, he made a career-defining 121 and helped England to a ten-wicket victory.

Eleven wickets for 73 in the second Test of the return series in 1886 at Lord's, followed by six at The Oval, helped England win the series three-nil and established Briggs as a permanent member of the team. And 1888 was a high point playing for Lancashire. Making the most of some deadly pitches that summer he posted 160 wickets at only 10.49 each.

Briggs was in the spotlight again in the second Test against South Africa at Cape Town in 1889, with match figures of 15-28! On his fourth tour to Australia, in 1891–92, he did the hat-trick in

Adelaide, sealing victory for England with match figures of 12-136. That feat with the ball – in what was his eighteenth Test – made him the first player to achieve a century, a ten-wicket match and a hat-trick.

Of course, over time, others have joined this exclusive club, namely India's Irfan Pathan (26 matches), England's Moeen Ali (40) and Stuart Broad (46), Wasim Akram of Pakistan (87), and India's Harbhajan Singh (88 games). Briggs remained

the fastest to have posted the 'treble' until England's Gus Atkinson, playing in just his tenth Test, put his name forward with a hat-trick against New Zealand in Wellington in November 2024. This moment, which would have been memorable on its own, followed his 12 wickets on debut against the West Indies at Lord's in July 2024, and his 118 against Sri Lanka, also at Lord's, a few weeks later.

Briggs continued to be a major contributor with Lancashire, helping the county to its first official championship title in 1897. He then missed a lot of cricket through a chest injury, but on his return in 1900 joined the ten-for club with his 10-55 against Worcestershire at Old Trafford. It would take a herculean effort for anybody to trump Briggs's quartet – of completing the Test match treble *and* taking the lot in a first-class game!

Throughout his time with Lancashire, being a professional among a number of amateurs, he was called upon to bear the heavy burden of not only opening the bowling but sometimes bowling all day in tandem with other professionals. Following his retirement after the 1900 season, Briggs was diagnosed with mental illness and admitted to an asylum. He died in 1902 aged just 39.

What more could a bowler do to attract the attention of the national selectors? You'd think a return of 14-119 against a touring side – in this case, South Africa in 1929 – might have done the trick. But when the likes of Harold Larwood and Maurice Tate are leading the England attack, little room is left (in the selectors' eyes at least) for a medium-pacer.

As has been so often the case down the years for many an athlete, **John 'Jack' Mercer (22 April 1893 – 31 August 1987)** was literally born at the wrong time. He could get late swing both ways, and obtain sharp off-spin on a rain-affected wicket. And when the shine was off the ball he could turn to off-breaks. Yet he was always overlooked by the England selectors. Good judges pondered why. In the words of legendary commentator-writer John Arlott, 'He bowled more overs, conceded more runs, took more wickets, scored the fastest fifty, made more ducks and was not out more times than anyone else in Glamorgan's history.'

Mercer began his cricket journey when he joined the staff at Sussex in 1913 but no sooner had he done so than World War I intervened. Mercer picked up again with Sussex after the war but a lack of opportunity led him, in 1921, to join newly promoted Glamorgan. Such circumstances made for a slow start, but in 1924 he created a sensation by hitting the great Wilfred Rhodes for four sixes in an innings of 57 at Bradford. The following year he had his first 100-wicket season. He really blossomed in the 1926 season. Figures of 8-39 against Gloucestershire and a hand in the rout of Somerset for 59 and 77 earned him second place in the national averages and a *Wisden* Cricketer of the Year nomination.

The 1929 season saw him take 145 wickets, but he was hampered by injury in the ensuing years and it wasn't until 1936, at the age of 41, that he returned to fitness and form. That year, as well as taking 12 wickets in a match against Leicestershire, Mercer – swinging the ball 'lavishly' – put his name on the ten-for list, with 10-51 against Worcestershire at New Road, Worcester. The Association of Cricket Statisticians and Historians' book on Mercer, *A Bowler of Magical Spells* by Andrew Hignell, recounts that in the ten-for game he had a bit of a wait for the tenth wicket, after  claiming the ninth. 'It looked as if the record might elude him. But Peter Jackson then skied a ball high into the outfield and George Lavis set off to try and get underneath it,' Hignell wrote.

'Jack [Mercer] responded by standing at the end of his follow through with his hands raised up, praying to the heavens. As the ball swirled around, Jack also turned to umpire Ernie Cooke and said: "It's six bob to four that George will drop it." Ernie took the odds, but Jack was happy to settle his debts as George, after juggling with the ball for a few heart-stopping seconds, held on to it with an audible sigh of relief echoing all around the ground.'

For all his efforts and success with Glamorgan – who did not renew Mercer's contract after 1939 – a Test cap remained elusive. His one flirtation with representative competition had come in 1926–27 when he was a late call-up to join the MCC's tour of India before they had Test status. He didn't get a game but his characteristic cheerfulness was proof against anything. To Mercer – who was a magician in his down time, and a member of the magicians' club, Magic Circle – his tribulations and misfortunes were simply an endless cause of laughter and jesting.

After World War II, Mercer took up the role of coach of Northamptonshire – and even turned out for them at the age of 54. He opened the bowling and took two wickets. His personal innings had reached 94 when he died in 1987.

How players in cricket's first-class cohort must have rued the onset of the two world wars – privately, that is, for to have spoken out about how it was affecting their careers would have been viewed as unpatriotic or at least selfish. In earlier chapters we noted the prime examples of two who paid the ultimate penalty (Charlie Blythe and Hedley Verity), but we have also paid lip service to the many whose time in the game came to a full stop, never to be resumed after the conflagration had died down.

One of the many was **Arthur Fielder (19 July 1877 – 30 August 1949)**, who had been a nailed-down fast bowler for Kent in the golden years when they won the County Championship four times from 1906 to 1913. And he was the leading wicket-taker for the

team in the first of those years with 158 victims, this earning him the honour of *Wisden*'s Cricketer of the Year. One fine day that summer he bagged 10-90 (five of them bowled) for the Players versus the Gentlemen at Lord's. He was the first to achieve the feat in this high-profile annual match.

Fielder's game was built on a controlled line just outside off stump, complemented by an ability to swing the ball away from the right-hander. To confuse the best bats, he could also break the ball back. He was able to bowl long spells, but had an interesting run-up. A contemporary account described it thus: 'Fielder has three different paces when running to the wicket and at each change he bobs his head as if to avoid something hurled at him.'

Fielder remained a solid contributor with the ball for Kent, in 1906 taking 172 wickets, and becoming one of only four men to take more than 150 in a season for the county. He claimed over 100 wickets again in 1909, 1911 and 1913, and was also part of the Kent Championship–winning sides of 1909, 1910 and 1913.

Though Fielder was strictly a tail-end batsman, he is recognised in the Kent annals for one contribution with the bat in most extraordinary circumstances. On one special Wednesday in July 1909, Fielder, coming in at his customary number 11, joined Frank Woolley at the crease with their team 40 runs in arrears of Worcestershire's first innings. Facing a hat-trick ball, Fielder managed to stave that off before he and Woolley went to town. They carved up the Worcestershire attack in a lightning partnership of 235, setting a new world record for the tenth wicket. Fielder's undefeated 112 was his only first-class century. The partnership remains the highest last-wicket stand in the County Championship. Almost inconceivably, Kent went on to win the game by an innings.

Arthur Fielder played six Tests, four of them on the 1907–08 tour to Australia, when he claimed 25 wickets at 25.08. He was also batting when England pinched a one-wicket victory in the second Test in Melbourne. He would have been run out if Gerry Hazlitt's throw had hit the stumps.

Sadly for him, the advent of World War I ended his cricketing safari. You could say a very good career was nipped in the bud.

No review of the ten-for cohort would be complete without a thorough examination of a man who stood tall over the game, both as a player and an administrator: **Sir George Oswald Browning 'Gubby' Allen (31 July 1902 – 29 November 1989).** Let us deal first with the player.

Allen was recognised as a serious fast bowler, with a rhythmical run-up of moderate length and a side-on action that saw his left shoulder almost thrusting at the batsman. He finished off with a strong rotation of the bowling arm and a full follow-through – in short, a classical side-on action. A description that could very easily be applied to the great Dennis Lillee. Testimony from RC Robertson-Glasgow reads, 'His bowling, though it varies from piercing accuracy to almost ludicrous irrelevance, has often touched greatness.'

Born in Sydney, Australia, Allen grew up in England and played for Middlesex before touring Down Under for the infamous Bodyline series of 1932–33. There was some debate over his selection but, as the tour advanced, Allen's skills with ball and bat were appreciated by his teammates.

Of course, this was the Ashes series that was dominated by the controversial aggression of the England bowlers who – encouraged by England's captain, Douglas Jardine, and spearheaded by Harold Larwood – would target the bodies of the Australians. For his part, Allen refused to apply his pace to these tactics. He was able to do this as he was an amateur like Jardine, compared to the professional Larwood, who had little option but to do what he was told.

However, it was said at a time after the tour that Don Bradman had been intimidated by Allen's all-out speed.

Allen captained England in 11 Test matches but, often because of work commitments, played only sporadically for Middlesex. In a county match against Lancashire in 1929 he notched up figures of 10-40 to join the ten-for club, becoming only the second man to record the feat in a first-class game at Lord's. On the way he claimed the last seven wickets for 13 runs in 69 deliveries. Not bad, when you consider he hadn't arrived at the ground till 11.50 am as he'd been working that morning! So he came on first change.

As fine a cricketer as he was, Allen's contribution to the game had only just begun. Allen made the transition into administration, playing many influential roles in the MCC. A shrewd, though not always visible, figure at Lord's, his leadership and acumen would be felt throughout the cricketing world. Among many posts, he served as chairman of England selectors. Plus, in 1963, he had a stint as MCC president.

Another who went on the Bodyline tour was **Thomas Bignall 'Tommy' Mitchell (4 September 1902 – 27 January 1996)**. A highly skilled leg-spin merchant, he was barely sighted Down Under as the England quicks created a maelstrom. He reserved his best for Derbyshire, for whom he played ten full seasons – and took more than 100 wickets each time.

Mitchell was spied as a burgeoning talent in 1926, when Derbyshire's captain, Guy Jackson, took a county team to play the local colliery where Mitchell was a worker. A prodigious spinner of the ball, he used a lively whirling action, making full use of his body, arm and very strong wrists

and fingers. Reports of the day suggest that he learnt to spin the ball while at the snooker table, finger-spinning the white ball from the centre spot, around the stacked reds and into the bottom left-hand pocket.

In Mitchell's day, Derbyshire relied mainly on their pace bowlers, and most home pitches were made to suit them. But Mitchell was able to adapt his manifest talents to whatever the conditions, in 1935 bagging a club-record 168 wickets. He wore dark-rimmed spectacles, and the fabled writer Neville Cardus said of his bowling, 'The ball had only to see those spectacles and it began spinning madly.' While not a batsman of note, he loved to dance down the wicket and hit sixes back over the bowler's head.

Mitchell played two of his five Tests on the Bodyline tour, his main distinction being dismissing the great Bill Woodfull in both innings of the fourth Test. This was a fast bowler's tour and subsequently he was unable to hold a place in the England team.

However, for Derbyshire, Mitchell went from strength to strength in the dry summers of 1933 and 1934 – at times bowling with sensational skill, such as when he helped dismiss Worcestershire for 48 on a good pitch in 1934. The following year he put his name on the ten-for list (10-64) against Leicestershire at Leicester.

Tommy Mitchell was well liked and renowned for having a real zest for life, a generosity of spirit and a wry sense of humour. That countenance was combined with fierce pride, independence and loyalty.

The advent of World War II in August 1939 played havoc with cricket worldwide, the one exception being the continuation of the first-class game in India. Cricket struggled on in Australia before any decision was taken to cancel – and there was no interstate competition from seasons 1942–43 to 1944–45. In fact, the Melbourne Cricket Ground was commandeered for service until 1946–47. In the meantime, any important games were played at Princes Park in Carlton.

The 1939 county season was almost over when war was declared. Both London grounds were commandeered and it wasn't until the so-called Victory Tests, played between May and August 1945, that cricket of any real standard was played again in England.[32] Naturally a great number of professional cricketers ended up in the armed forces, many of them, including Hedley Verity, losing their lives in the conflict.

Given the heavy atmosphere hanging over Britain it was a coincidence that two players in county cricket were able to find the form to record their ten-for performances in the 1939 season. Let us first look at **Thomas Francis 'Frank' Smailes (27 March 1910 – 1 December 1970).**

Smailes was a mainstay of the Yorkshire attack during a golden period when the county won eight championships out of ten. Though that side boasted luminaries like Verity, Len Hutton and Bill Bowes, Smailes was a valued contributor because of his versatility. He bowled swingers with the new ball but switched to off-spin in suitable conditions, such as a rain-affected strip. Smailes could also bat. In

---

32 The Victory Tests consisted of five matches contested between a combined Australian Services XI and an English national side. Despite the name, they were never accorded Test status.

the 1938 season he posted two centuries in scoring more than 1000 runs.

Smailes showed very good form through that year. Match figures of 10-137 against the Australians in Sheffield earned him selection in a squad for the third Test at Old Trafford but the game was washed out. Those rainy days in July 1938 delayed his Test debut by eight years! That moment came after the war, against India, at Lord's in 1946. In what would prove to be his only Test, Smailes took 3-44 in India's second innings.

Smailes's ability to move the ball, both through the air and off the pitch, could make him a real handful – and that's how he made the ten-for club. In a game against Derbyshire at Sheffield in 1939 he followed first-innings figures of 4-11 – when Derbyshire were dismissed for just 20 – with 10-47. He was only the third Yorkshire player after Alonzo Drake and Verity (twice) to achieve the feat.

When war broke out Smailes enlisted and rose to the rank of captain. He fought Rommel's Afrika Korps and, later, joined the Allied offensive in Sicily and Italy – where he learned of the death of his teammate, Hedley Verity. He and fellow Yorkshire player Phil King visited the cemetery at Caserta, where their comrade was buried, and erected a simple cross on the grave.

The other man to grab a ten-for as the clouds of war gathered over county grounds across Britain was **Edward Alfred 'Eddie' Watts (1 August 1912 – 3 May 1982)**. Cast in very much a similar mould to Smailes, he was a strongly built right-arm fast bowler who could swing the ball both ways and got plenty off the wicket. He also made regular contributions with the bat in the middle order.

Watts began with Surrey as an amateur in 1933, showing promise from the start, scoring 318 runs at 39.75 and taking 28 wickets. It was natural, then, that he joined the staff full time in 1934, and he made a mark with 928 runs and 91 wickets. Against the potent Yorkshire attack he went on a rampage, scoring 123 in less than two hours – with four sixes and 14 fours.

Known for a 'shrewd cricket brain', Watts often opened the Surrey attack with his uncle, Alf Gover, who later became a noted coach.[33] In 1939, Watts's pace at Edgbaston proved too much for Warwickshire's best, and in the second innings he posted 10-67 off 24.1 overs. Eight of his wickets were caught, two fell lbw. Curiously, he only bowled four overs in Warwickshire's first innings, failing to take a wicket.

Watts's career with Surrey spanned from 1933 to 1949 and, like many others, he was robbed of some of his best years by the war. At the end of 1949 he retired and for a time ran a sports shop in Cheam, Surrey.

There was a very good reason why the preponderance of successful county bowlers – in particular those who appear in this book – were finger-spinners: so many pitches provided a very happy hunting ground for them. The word 'unplayable' springs to mind when considering the relative merits of a spinner when compared with a seamer.

---

33 When fielding at short leg for Surrey at Kingston in 1946, Gover took a catch from Rodney Exton (Combined Services) by closing his legs on the ball. Gover could see nothing as he was in the act of putting his sweater over his head. It was Jim Laker's first wicket in first-class cricket.

During my time as director of cricket and first-team coach at Kent (2002–03) I had the chance to break bread with Mike Denness, the former England captain, and I took the opportunity to ask him about playing on pitches left open to the elements. 'It was simple,' he said. 'We could be out of a game at stumps on day two, but if it had rained overnight we just knew "Deadly" [Derek Underwood] would win it for us.'

Right-arm, left-arm, it didn't make a difference. If you could land them and put a bit of work on the ball, you were going to be too much for even the best of the batters. These men of spin were also more than a handful on dry and dusty strips. Remember Jim Laker at Old Trafford in 1956? With that in mind, let's take a look at another two spinners who made the most of the wickets of the day, starting with **Edward 'George' Dennett (27 April 1879 – 15 September 1937)**, a left-arm orthodox bowler who plied his trade for Gloucestershire from 1903 to 1926.

Dennett, who was considered one of the best bowlers never to play Test cricket, was spotted by Gilbert Jessop (a giant of a batsman for Gloucestershire), batting and bowling with great promise in a club game in Bristol. He endured a tough start, against Middlesex at Lord's, but Jessop stood by his man. 'Despite the rare pasting he received, Dennett neither lost his head nor his length, nor did he seem the slightest bit dismayed by our infernally bad fielding.'

Possessed of the spinner's cunning, combined with deceptive flight, Dennett was almost as effective on firm wickets as he was on rain-affected surfaces. Testament to that, in the years 1904 to 1914, he never failed to top 100 wickets for the season.

In 1906 Dennett had a moment, taking 10-40 off 19.4 overs against Essex at Bristol. Gloucestershire used only two bowlers over Essex's first innings. Illustrating perfectly the vagaries of cricket, Dennett's fellow opening bowler, FB Roberts, a right-arm quick, bowled 19 overs of his own and conceded a similar amount of runs – but of course he went wicketless with 0-42.[34]

The following year Dennett was the leading wicket-taker in all first-class matches with 201. In the game against Northamptonshire at Gloucester, the visitors were dismissed for 12 runs – equalling the lowest total in first-class cricket – and Dennett took 8-9, including a hat-trick.

Recognised as a consistently hard-working and earnest cricketer, Dennett also had fun in a game against Kent at Dover in 1912. It was a day when 30 wickets fell for 268 runs, and in one spell he dismissed the last six Kent wickets without conceding a run.

After missing vital years through World War I, Dennett returned to county cricket but never regained his best form. Nevertheless, he was one of relatively few who could look back on a career total of more than 2000 wickets.

From Dennett we move on to a quality all-rounder who started out bowling at slightly above medium-pace and was a bold striker of the ball. **Vallance William Crisp Jupp (27 March 1891 – 9 July 1960)** was once declared the best amateur cricketer

---

34 Roberts was another victim of the Great War. He was killed in action in Flanders in 1916.

in England. Like many others, the true depth of his game was seriously dented by the arrival of World War I when he was in his mid-twenties.

He started out in 1909 with Sussex and enjoyed great form in 1914, heading the bowling and scoring more than 1500 runs, including a highest innings of 217 not out. He joined the war effort with the Royal Engineers, serving in France, Salonika and Palestine. After the war, Jupp picked up where he had left off, and at the end of the 1920 season was picked to tour Australia but had to decline – a decision almost unthinkable these days.

He did play two Tests against Warwick Armstrong's Australians in England in 1921 – a season in which he enjoyed sparkling form, with almost 2000 runs at 47 and 93 wickets at less than 23 apiece. Jupp remained in the selectors' eyes and toured South Africa in 1922–23, where he played four Tests. Plus, there were two Tests against the West Indies in 1928, a season in which he took 166 wickets at 20.15.

In the meantime, Jupp had moved to Northamptonshire as honorary secretary, which enabled him to play out his career as an amateur. As the years went by his bowling became more of a slow medium-pace, which morphed into off-spin, when he would turn it as much as anybody.

Jupp's byword might have been *adaptability*: with batting he would strike a medium between enterprise and caution; with bowling he would cleverly settle into the best pace for the conditions. In 1928, his bowling powers peaked and he took 166 wickets at 20.15. His star-studded story shows that he achieved the double of 1000 runs and 100 wickets in ten seasons.

If there was a blot on Jupp's copybook it was that he had to miss the 1934 and 1935 seasons when he was imprisoned for manslaughter after the car he was driving was involved in a fatal accident.

CHAPTER 15

IN TESTS

It is well documented in these pages that in late July 1956 – in the fourth Ashes Test against Australia at Old Trafford – the genial England off-spinner Jim Laker broke new ground by becoming the first bowler to take ten-for in a Test match. Since then, the feat has been achieved twice more. That's just three Test ten-fors in 148 years.

You get an even better sense of the degree of difficulty when you absorb statistician Steven Lynch's analysis. At the time of writing there had been 2573 Tests contested since Australia played England at the MCG in 1877, the game later recognised as the first-ever Test match. Steven extrapolates this figure out to almost 9500 innings. So that's about 3166 innings per ten-for.

So after Laker's ten-for in 1956, it wasn't until 1999 that he had to make room on his pedestal for the second man to achieve a Test ten-for – in this case, Indian bowling great **Anil Kumble (17 October 1970 –)** who retired in 2008 rightly satisfied with his lot. 'I have no regrets,' he said. 'Whatever happens, happens for good. I have done everything I could on a [Test] cricket field: ten wickets [in an innings], a century, 600 wickets, captaincy. I have done everything.'

Kumble, the fourth-highest wicket-taker in Test history (with 619 wickets), cast a long shadow on a cricket field. Standing at 1.85 metres (6 ft 1 in) he had a build more likely to have carried

a pace bowler than a spin merchant (for students of the hierarchy of Australian spinners, his physique was far more reminiscent of Bill O'Reilly than of O'Reilly's teammate Clarrie Grimmett). Kumble was a wrist-spinner who wasn't a big turner of the ball. Rather, he built his deadly potion on over-spin, side-spin, a late-developed wrong'un, hidebound accuracy, great durability and the knack of using his height to full advantage in deriving whatever lift that was available on a given surface.

Kumble was nicknamed 'Jumbo', apparently in reference to the jumbo jet—speed of his bowling, though the name might equally have referred to his memory. After his retirement he recalled former Indian captain Mansur Ali Khan Pataudi saying, early in Kumble's career, 'This lad, I don't see him winning a Test match for India either at home or abroad. He rarely turns the ball, at best he can be restrictive.' To that, came this fitting Kumble riposte: 'The first question that I was asked post-retirement was how does it feel to finish with 619 wickets [in Tests] without spinning the ball? I said it is nice that I took eighteen years to realise that.'

Indian writer Rahul Bhattacharya reckoned that no bowler in Indian cricket history won India more Test matches. 'And there probably hasn't been a harder trier, either,' Bhattacharya wrote. 'Kumble, like the great tall wrist-spinners – Bill O'Reilly and his own idol BS Chandrasekhar – traded the leg-spinner's proverbial yo-yo for a spear as the ball hacked through the air rather than hanging in it and came off the pitch with a kick rather than a kink.'

Sambit Bal, the editor of ESPNcricinfo, praised Kumble's mastering of the craft when reflecting on the bowler's impact on the game. 'That Kumble has been an unusual spinner has been said many times before,' he wrote. 'It has also been said, a trifle unfairly, that he was a unidimensional bowler. Probably he lacked the turn of [Shane] Warne and Murali [Muttiah Muralitharan], but his variety was more subtle. He has shown that not only turn and flight can deceive the batsman, but also changes of length and pace. He has been a cultural practitioner of his unique craft and a master of nuances.'

Kumble certainly found the right formula after becoming yet another individual who turned to the mysteries of spin after setting out as a fast bowler. From that point he worked assiduously at his game to become widely regarded as one of the best leg-spinners in Test cricket history.

After making his first-class debut for Karnataka in November 1989, at the age of 19, Kumble was chosen first in the Indian one-day international team in April 1990. He made his Test debut when India toured England later that year.

It was on the 1992–93 tour of South Africa that he first made the cricket world stand up and take notice, claiming eight wickets in the second Test, and 18 at 25.94 over the three-Test series. He backed that up later in the year when England toured India. Before you knew it the Bengaluru-born bowler had reached 50 wickets in ten matches – then 100 in 21, the second-fastest Indian to reach this milestone after the 1960s off-spinner Erapalli Prasanna. In

1995, Kumble then showed a liking for English conditions when he played the season for Northamptonshire and was the leading wicket-taker with 105 at 20.40 – the only player in the County Championship to top the 100 mark.

And so we come to Pakistan's 1999 tour of India when Kumble's momentous ten-for moment arrived – with the help of some minor collusion by his teammates. It was the second Test at Delhi where India, batting first, posted 252. Pakistan could only muster 172 in response in part due to Kumble's 4-75 which included his bowling of Inzamam-ul-Haq. India's second dig of 339 left Pakistan needing an unlikely 420 to win.

They made a great start, with Saeed Anwar and Shahid Afridi combining for an opening partnership of 101 before Kumble claimed his first wicket, Afridi, caught behind for 41. The new man Ijaz Ahmed went first ball, trapped in front by Kumble. When Kumble bowled Inzamam for the second time in the match it was 3-115 and the rot set in. Kumble made hay. When Kumble had Saqlain Mushtaq lbw for another golden duck, the rangy spinner had nine wickets to his name and Pakistan were 9-198.

With Mushtaq falling on the last ball of a Kumble over, Javagal Srinath, bowling at the other end, did all he could to ensure his teammate had the chance to make history, avoiding taking the final wicket by sending down an over of deliveries out of the batsman's reach. On the third ball of his next over Kumble duly got his ten-for – and in doing so carried India to victory – with Wasim Akram out, caught by VVS Laxman.

Five years later the durable Indian passed 400 wickets in Tests, doing so in 30 fewer games than Kapil Dev and seven fewer than Shane Warne. And the records continued to tumble. During the 2006 England tour of India he claimed his 500th Test wicket, and in the West Indies later that year he became only the second player after Warne to score 2000 runs and take more than 500 wickets in Tests.

And still there was more! On 10 August 2007, against England at The Oval, Kumble scored his maiden Test century. It was his 118th Test – no player has taken longer to score a maiden Test hundred. And then, five months later, on 17 January 2008 at the WACA Ground in Perth, Kumble had Andrew Symonds caught at slip to raise his 600th wicket in Tests.

But there was even more to Anil Kumble than milestones, numbers and records. Those who saw a lot of him talk about his perseverance, his hunger to learn, even his courage – such as when he bandaged a fractured jaw to deliver a stirring spell in a Test in Antigua in 2002, taking the wicket of the great Brian Lara.

In closing, we'll recall Indian journalist Rahul Bhattacharya's serious tribute to a seriously good cricketer: 'More than one modern-day batsman remarked that there was no more difficult challenge in cricket than handling Kumble on a wearing surface.'

A quirky circumstance surrounds the cricket career of the third man to claim ten-for a Test match. For starters he was born in Mumbai, and it was *in* Mumbai that he joined the club – but he was playing for New Zealand *against* his native India.

Ajaz Yunus Patel (21 October 1988 –) was the fifth cricketer of Indian origin to play for New Zealand – but he was no late recruit, having moved to the Land of the

Long White Cloud with his family at the age of eight. In his youth he tried to make his way as a pace bowler, but soon realised that his short stature (5 ft 6 in – 1.67 m) would make it very difficult for him to reach the top. So he made the change and emerged as a left-arm orthodox spin bowler.

It worked a treat! The *new* Ajaz hit form in 2015–16, taking 43 wickets in the Plunket Shield season for Central Districts. Indeed, Patel was the highest wicket-taker in the domestic competition for three years running – peaking with 48 at 21.52 in 2017–18. After that he was named New Zealand's domestic player of the year, then won selection for the Black Caps at the age of 30.

That was for a T20 international, but his Test debut came soon after when New Zealand played three Tests against Pakistan in the United Arab Emirates. In the first he claimed five second-innings wickets – a rare feat on debut. New Zealand won by four runs and Patel was named man of the match.

Fast forward to November 2021, and Patel was chosen for a two-Test tour of India. He had unremarkable returns in the first Test, which was drawn, but in the second he had the match of his life – though funnily enough he *wasn't* named man of the match, probably due to the fact India won the game by 372 runs.

Having won the toss India batted first at Mumbai's Wankhede Stadium. Openers Mayank Agarwal and Shubman Gill had put on 80 before Patel dismissed Gill for 44. In his next over Patel picked up the new man, Cheteshwar Pujara, for a duck. Four balls later he sent a groan around the ground when he trapped Virat Kohli in front before the champion batsman had opened his account. While India would recover from being 3-80 to score 325, Patel kept taking wickets as he bowled over after over. Indeed, by the time he bowled India out with his tenth wicket of the innings he'd sent down a marathon 47.5 overs. This puts the seemingly expensive figures of 10-119 into perspective.

After taking four wickets in India's second innings, Patel finished the match with 14-225, the best return in a Test match against India.

As the accolades poured in – from the likes of Anil Kumble, Sir Richard Hadlee and Nathan Lyon – he found time to contemplate just what had happened. 'One of the biggest dreams when it came to a cricketing journey for me was to be able to play cricket in Mumbai,' he said. 'To do it in such emphatic fashion is something I'd never dreamed of … just playing there was almost fulfilling a dream. To leave my name on the honours board is quite special.'

In an article published in *The New Zealand Herald* Patel expounded on what made his ten-for feat that much more memorable. 'At the ground I had a lot of family, like cousins and sisters-in-law, and it was quite cool to see them and play in front of them. They all knew I was a cricketer and played international cricket, but none of them had actually had the opportunity to watch me play.

'I think even if you were writing your own script, you probably wouldn't write something like that because it was too far-fetched and ridiculous to comprehend. Because cricket is such a superstitious game, nobody on the team really mentioned it until the ninth wicket … before that everyone was just carrying on as usual.

'It never really crossed my mind until the ninth. I hadn't even thought about the record, I just thought how cool it would be. When the ninth wicket fell I was like, "Oh I've got four balls and I've got to use these four balls otherwise it might happen quickly at the other end." Obviously afterwards when I was told I was the third person ever I thought that was very cool. After walking off I had a text from Sir Richard Hadlee, which *was* cool.'

Perhaps an added measure of satisfaction for Patel stemmed from an incident years earlier when the spinner was given the cold shoulder at the Wankhede Stadium practice pitches. At the time he hadn't yet played a Test, but he was a seasoned first-class player back in New Zealand and he was keen to turn his arm over. 'I saw people at a cricket net so I went there and asked these guys if I could come have a bowl and they're like "No it's for only people in the club" – so I got turned down.'

In recent times Patel has been a campaigner for pitches in New Zealand to be made more favourable to spin bowlers – a topic close to his heart due to his struggles on home pitches. Of the 21 Tests he had played by the end of 2024, only three were in New Zealand (two at Wellington and the other at Christchurch). And he failed to take a wicket in those three, meaning all of his 85 Test wickets have come in matches outside New Zealand.[35] 'I'd love to see a few more wickets that offer something,' he said. 'Even in domestic cricket there is space for groundsmen to experiment a little bit and give players a different challenge. Even from a batting perspective, it allows players to learn how to cope.'

---

35 It's a stark home-and-away record in Tests for Patel, but not an isolated case. For instance, Willie Bates, playing for England in the late 19th century, ended his career suddenly through a freakish injury with 50 Test wickets to his name – all taken in Australia. The current Indian speedster Jasprit Bumrah, meantime, had 79 in Tests before taking his first on home soil.

CHAPTER 16
AN ODD ONE

In 1908, a man who was born and bred in the United States – and whose home base for cricket was *in* the United States – once topped the first-class bowling averages in England. If that's not hard enough to get your head around, he would be declared by no lesser authority than an England captain, Sir Pelham Warner, as 'one of the finest bowlers of all time'!

John Barton 'Bart' King (19 October 1873 – 1 October 1965), born in Philadelphia in 1873, competed with the best cricketers from England and Australia around the turn of the 20th century and stood shoulder-to-shoulder with all of them. In his heyday, King's feats with bat and ball earned him the epithet of 'the best-known American in England', a badge of honour doubtless assisted by the fact that he was well known as one who didn't take things too seriously out in the middle. In fact, he was once dubbed 'the Bob Hope of cricket', in reference to his quips and stories.

He was forever chiding opposition players and umpires, though it must be said that most of it was delivered with tongue firmly in cheek. He once spoke for 90 minutes at a dinner in England and the guests kept laughing all the way – even though King spoke with a dead-pan expression. One guest suggested the audience were 'always in doubt when to take him seriously'.

But why cricket for this very American fellow? Well, one of the earliest mentions of cricket being played in the American

colonies dates back to 1737. William Stephens, a planter living in Georgia, wrote, 'Many of our townsmen, freeholders, inmates and servants were assembled in the principal square at cricket and various other athletick *(sic)* sports.' A match was reported in a New York paper in 1751, and eight years later a team of English players sailed across the Atlantic and played five games.

Cricket later flourished in New York, Chicago and California, mostly played by expat Englishmen. However, one outcome was the growing popularity of cricket in Philadelphia. Hence the connection with Bart King, who almost unbelievably grew to be regarded as one of the world's greatest bowlers.

Not surprisingly, King began his sporting life in the game of baseball, an experience which many good judges would say was the grounding of his exquisite skill at moving the cricket ball through the air. He perfected this ability to such a degree that in 1909 he took 10-53 (including seven bowled and two lbw) in a first-class game at Haverford, near Philadelphia, playing for The Gentlemen of Philadelphia against The Gentlemen of Ireland. He followed this by taking a hat-trick in the second innings.

In King's time cricket in the United States was largely dominated by 'gentleman' players. He, too, played strictly as an amateur, helped with employment by wealthy teammates and patrons. A tall, muscular right-hander, he intimidated rival batsmen with raw pace. But, as mentioned, there was much more than that to his game. Playing for the Belmont Cricket Club in Philadelphia, he developed a high degree of skill at swinging the ball. He regularly dismissed quality batsmen with his unique delivery, which he called the 'angler', which swung from off to leg to a right-hand bat.

However, in favourable conditions, King could also swing it the other way – much to the dismay of England's CB Fry, who, according to legend, was so bamboozled by the devastating inswinger that he asked King to bowl a few at him in the nets. King agreed do so, to the point that Fry eventually felt comfortable against the angler. But when he came to the crease, prepared for that delivery, King gave him one that swung the other way first ball and had him caught in the slips!

This ability to go both ways through the air – at pace – made King more than a handful when pitted against an Australian team that stopped off in Philadelphia on the way home after a tour of England in 1893. His five first-innings wickets helped the Americans to an innings win. After which the Australian captain, Jack Blackham, said to the victors, 'You have better players here than we have been led to believe. They class with England's best.'

While King continued to dominate what might be called lesser competition in America – for instance, topping his wicket-taking by scoring two triple-centuries – it was in the more serious locale of cricket in England that he established a reputation that placed him in the highest ranks. He made three tours of England with the Philadelphia team – in 1897, 1903 and 1908. Initially there was lukewarm interest in the interlopers from across the Atlantic – until, that is, they met a full-strength Sussex side. King's pace and swinging deliveries brought him figures of 7-13 and 6-102 in the game, and the result was outright victory for the

tourists. Against Warwickshire he again dominated with a total of 12 wickets. Another win for Philadelphia.

King played in 13 of the 15 matches when the Americans toured again in 1903. The highlight, for him, was at Old Trafford. After bagging five wickets in Lancashire's first innings, he set the ground alight in the second. In his first over after lunch on the second day, he yorked one of the openers, and then his replacement with the next ball. He clean bowled two more in his second over, before ripping a stump out of the ground in his next. In three overs he had taken five wickets for seven runs. A batsman was run out, then King returned to take the remaining wickets for figures of 9-62.

Against Surrey, King had scores of 98 and 113 not out, adding two three-wicket hauls in what must still rank as one of the great all-round performances in first-class cricket. His return from the first-class games on that tour was 653 runs at 28.89 and 93 wickets at the miserly rate of 14.91. No longer a surprise package, it was plain that county clubs were eager to gain his signature. He declined, however, returning for a final tour in 1908. Though now 35 years old, King's bowling average over 87 wickets was 11.01, tops for the entire England season – and a record low figure for English cricket which stood until 1958.

King fronted up to an Australian team in Philadelphia in 1912. Now nearing his fortieth year, he took 9-78 in game one, which the locals won by two runs, and 8-74 in the return bout. In all first-class matches this Goliath of American cricket scored 2134 runs at 20.52, with one century, and took 415 wickets. What a player! On his passing, aged 91, he was dubbed one of the greatest cricketers of all time.

Further praise came from on high. In his book *10 for 66 and All That*, Australian spin legend Arthur Mailey spoke unstintingly of the American, having seen him in action in Philadelphia in 1913. 'It was then that I was convinced of his amazing mastery of curve and swerve,' Mailey wrote. 'He was one of the few pace bowlers I've ever met who knew *why* the ball swerved in the air and could explain it better than any expert on ballistics.'

Mailey later included King in his World XI. 'Perhaps I should have chosen either Jack Gregory, Ted McDonald or Harold Larwood, but I feel that Bart King, the Philadelphian, was the greatest and most versatile fast bowler of all time.'

Fitting, perhaps, to end this tribute with a story about a club game in Philly between King's Belmont and Trenton from New Jersey. The Trenton team had so many players short for the start because of travel hiccups that, by arrangement, they were allowed to bat first. King effortlessly rattled through the order and watched as the last man in was the recently arrived captain, who observed that if he'd been present at the start of the game it would have been a different story.

Whereupon King, who had claimed the nine wickets that had fallen, sent all ten of his team from the field. On second thought, following some heckling from the other side of the boundary, he recalled one, and placed him near the square-leg umpire. When it was just himself and his teammate, plus the Trenton captain and two umpires, King bowled one of his anglers, which knocked back the leg stump, the ball rolling to rest at the feet of his sole fieldsman.

In spectacular fashion befitting the master showman, King had taken all ten wickets to fall – which he did on three occasions in all.

CHAPTER 17

WHAT A YEAR

In 1921 the world was still coming to terms with life after war, the cataclysmic Great War, also known as World War I, having ended three years before. Since then the population of Britain had put its collective shoulders to the wheel in the task of mopping up and resuming normal life. Sport, and cricket in particular, played a big part in that.

County cricket in England resumed in 1919. Test cricket got back on track in 1920, with England touring Australia late that year for a five-test series won 5-0 by the home side. The following year, 1921, 'The Big Ship', Warwick Armstrong, brought the fifteenth Australian team to England for another five-Test Ashes series.

While the home side continued to pick up the pieces of what was left of its cricket-playing stocks – and tried to rekindle in those who remained a sense of passion for the game – Armstrong's travelling party sailed on relatively calmer seas. As evidence of that, the Australians deployed only 13 players across the five Tests, winning three and drawing the other two. England, meanwhile, in trying desperately to find the talent to match their marauding visitors, used no fewer than 30 players.

England were led by the doughty JWHT Douglas whose initials, according to wags, stood for 'Johnny Won't Hit Today'. After losing the first Test by ten wickets, the second by eight wickets and the third by 219 runs, Douglas must have heaved a sigh of relief at drawing both the fourth and fifth Tests. Those draws, however, hardly undermined the dominance of Australia, particularly their pace attack of Ted McDonald, who had 27 wickets, and Jack Gregory, with 19. And if that dynamic duo – arguably the first great Test new-ball fast bowlers – ever tired, or there was anything in the pitch, there was always the spin of Arthur Mailey, who captured 12 wickets for the series.

Mailey, the classy wrist-spinner and prime comedian of every team that was fortunate enough to have him aboard, qualifies for special mention in this chapter because he was one of five players who recorded ten-fors in 1921. Considering the all-time ten-for list has 91 names on it and it dates back to 1837, five ten-fors in a single year is quite something – even more so when you consider that all five took place over a span of just 52 days. And there were other remarkable oddities, too. Somerset, for instance, suffered the indignity of being twice on the receiving end. And on 20 June, the tenpins tumbled twice on the one day. Incredible.

Mailey's 10-66, coming for the Australians against Gloucestershire

at Cheltenham in August, has of course already been dealt with in these pages, so to the other four 1921 ten-fors we go, starting with **William 'Billy' Bestwick (24 February 1875 – 2 May 1938)**, who was one of those two who hit the jackpot on 20 June.

Bestwick was a right-arm medium-fast bowler and a colourful character, to say the least. On his way to playing his final game of county cricket at the ripe age of 50, he experienced many ups and plenty of downs. His predilection for bouts of drinking, for instance, gave one headache after another to the Derbyshire officialdom. In 1909 they suspended him before sacking him at the end of the season.

Bestwick had an off-season job in the mines, an occupation that brought him into each season bounding with energy and endurance. Add to that, he operated off a short run, and he was able to sustain brisk pace for long periods. His high arm action produced awkward lift from the pitch – and, despite his night-time proclivities, he was able to maintain excellent levels of accuracy.

Bestwick's ten-for performance came against Glamorgan at Cardiff. On the first day he had figures of 4-71, but he had such a bout with the bottle on the Sunday rest day that it seemed unlikely that he could participate on the final day. His captain took the bit between his teeth, threw Bestwick the ball and told him to open the bowling.

He rose to the occasion, taking a wicket with his fifth ball and finishing the Glamorgan innings with three wickets in four balls. He had bowled throughout the innings to register 10-40. Seven of his victims were clean bowled. This was his best season with the ball, totalling 147 wickets at 16.72. All that at the age of 44!

It was considered that Bestwick's off-field habits and unpredictable nature cost him the chance of gaining a Test cap. He had suffered badly when, in 1906, his wife died and left him with a young child. And matters worsened in early 1909 when he was involved in a pub brawl that ended in the death of one of the participants. Billy was charged with unlawful killing, but was acquitted by a jury.

Bestwick had the joy of playing two games for Derbyshire in 1922 with his son, Robert. In the first of those they bowled together against another father and son, Willie and Bernard Quaife of Warwickshire. After his retirement Bestwick became an umpire, standing in 238 first-class games and three Tests, in 1929 and 1930.

Known to all and sundry as 'Farmer', **John Cornish 'Jack' White (19 February 1891 – 2 May 1961)** stepped out for his native county, Somerset, for 28 years. He was described as 'unique', in that his slow left-armers didn't spin sharply. Instead, White relied on a great variety of flight and subtle changes of pace. His action was simple and economical, a few paces leading to an unhurried swing of his fully extended left arm. An uncanny degree of accuracy made him a handful for the best of batsmen, even on good wickets.

White was one of the outstanding successes of England's 1928–29 tour of Australia. On the faster pitches there he was able to adopt a shorter length that, in turn, opened up a fuller scope for his tricks of flight and length. He was the workhorse of the England attack on that tour. To wit, he braved scorching temperatures in the Adelaide Test to register match figures of 13-256 from a marathon 124.5 overs. In all, White played 15 Tests, 14 of them after he had turned 37. He captained England in four of them.

There was more to White's game than those nagging tweakers. For Somerset he captured 100 wickets in a season 14 times, and on two of those occasions scored more than 1000 runs, thus twice completing the 'cricketer's double'. His total number of wickets for Somerset, 2156, remains the county record. His ten-for performance came against Worcestershire at Worcester, at the cost of 76 runs. Two years earlier he had wrecked Worcestershire with 16 wickets for 83.

The epithet 'Farmer' related not only to his profession, but also to the fact that in presence and character he epitomised the popular idea of England's West Country yeomen. Of medium height and sturdy build, his apple cheeks and bright blue eyes radiated well-being. A man of attractive character, White was said to be 'imperturbable and cheerful in all circumstances – and, when the day's play was done, he loved nothing more than a game of poker, which he played as he bowled, with a fine, bland shrewdness.'

White captained Somerset from 1927 to 1931, during that period also acting as an England selector. His Somerset teammate RC Robertson-Glasgow later wrote of his bowling, 'Besides the length and direction and the variety of flight, he made the ball do a little each way on the truest pitch without any advertisement from his fingers; and he made the ball bounce high even on a wet slow surface.'

Thomas 'Tom' Rushby (6 September 1880 – 13 July 1962) was a fast-medium bowler for Surrey between 1903 and 1921. In his prime Rushby was ranked among the best in his craft. Twice he headed the Surrey averages; in 1914 with 103 wickets at 19.14 and in his last season, 1921, when he dismissed 59 batsmen at 18.84.

The best performance of a bowler who never lost his enthusiasm for the job at hand came in that last season, when he took all ten Somerset first-innings wickets for 43 runs in 17.5

overs at Taunton. Rushby bowled unchanged in that innings, a feat occasionally performed in the day. His ten-for innings analysis remains a record for Surrey. His name rests alongside that of Tom Richardson, Eddie Watts, Laker and Lock as the only Surrey players to take them all in a first-class innings.

A tribute to Rushby's endurance was the fact that this feat was achieved in his final season, at the age of 40. Earlier, in the 1907 season, he had teamed up at The Oval with the bespectacled Jack Crawford in bowling unchanged over both Sussex innings. Rushby's six wickets for 67 runs and Crawford's 11 for 63 cleaned out Sussex – victory for Surrey by an innings and 94 runs.

Rushby dropped out of the game after a stellar 1921 season, through illness. He may have had his differences with the club's administration, but he never lost his enthusiasm for bowling his medium-pacers for however often and however long it was required. There were many times when he and Bill Hitch carried the Surrey attack. Never highly regarded as a batsman, Rushby hit 1227 runs at the tailender's average of 7.90.

Completing the incredible list of five in 1921 is **Charles Warrington Leonard 'Charlie' Parker (14 October 1882 – 11 July 1959)**. A left-arm spinner whose long fingers enabled him to extract biting turn from even the most docile of surfaces, Charlie Parker remains the third most prolific wicket-taker in first-class cricket – only Wilfred Rhodes and Tich Freeman lie ahead of him. This from a man who was more attracted to golf than cricket before the legendary WG Grace recommended him to Gloucestershire.

Parker's storied career contained many highlights. In 1921 he put his name on the ten-for list by dismissing, in Bristol, the whole

Somerset line-up at a personal cost of 79 runs. He chipped in with three second-innings wickets too. Three years later he became the first man to capture three hat-tricks in a single season – a feat later equalled by the Indian medium-pacer Joginder Singh Rao (in 1963–64) and the future England fast-medium bowler Dean Headley, then playing for Kent (in 1996). Parker also took 9-36 for Gloucestershire versus Yorkshire at Bristol in 1922. In doing so he hit the stumps five times in successive deliveries (though the second ball was called a no-ball).

In 1931, at the grand old age of 48, Parker equalled Jack Hearne's record of reaching the 100-wicket mark by 12 June. A late bloomer, he found his best form from the age of 35, claiming 100 wickets in a season in 16 successive seasons, on five of those occasions exceeding 200.

Parker had struggled to win a berth for Gloucestershire until cricket resumed after World War I. He benefited significantly from a technical change, bringing his medium pace back to a slower style, and from 1920 he rose to be one of the best left-arm spinners in England. With a high arm action and acute power of spin – and slightly quicker than most spin bowlers – he was able in favourable conditions to hit off stump from outside leg. Almost unplayable on rain-affected or crumbling pitches, Parker commanded every batsman's respect.

It remains one of cricket's mysteries that Parker made only one Test match appearance, against Australia in 1921, when he took two wickets. It was considered that Australian wickets would be unsuited to his type of bowling. But it was known that he had a famous altercation with the influential Pelham Warner, which didn't help his Test prospects. After he retired in 1935 Parker became a first-class umpire.

CHAPTER 18
AROUND THE WORLD

It is acknowledged, beyond any doubt, that the genesis of the game we now know as 'cricket' began in the fields of rural England as far back as the 13th century. Taking a natural impetus from that nation's far-reaching fancy for colonisation, a refined version – something akin to the game we now recognise – travelled across the seas to far-reaching outposts.

The book *Barclays World of Cricket* says that 'stumps were first pitched in India as early as 1721 but that must have been an impromptu game, among sailors off a trading ship. Then, in 1792, the Calcutta Cricket Club was established on the site where Eden Gardens now stands.'

So, the first record of cricket being played outside England placed India at the top of the order. Drawing a rough line through the history of the Home Country's passion for colonisation, Australia was the third country where cricket began to flourish.

Next to show a liking for the summer game was South Africa, soldiers bringing it with them to the southern tip of the African continent. It is thought the game there dated back to 1795. Meantime, cricket was taking root among the Caribbean countries now known as the West Indies, there being knowledge of the formation of a club in 1806.

In 1832 the first cricket club was formed in Ceylon, later to be renamed Sri Lanka. New Zealand followed; records indicate that the first games there were contested in 1842. In earlier pages, there are reports of a surprisingly buoyant cricket fraternity in the United States, particularly around Philadelphia. Of course, Pakistan was created in 1947 by the event of the partition of India – where cricket was already well organised within its boundaries.

Each of those cricketing nations has produced at least one member of the ten-for list. In chronological order – starting with England and ending with Pakistan – we look into the credentials of the first ten-for candidate from each constituency, excepting those who have already been documented in earlier chapters.

ENGLAND

The first player to take all ten wickets in a first-class game in England, or anywhere else for that matter, was William Lillywhite, whose exploits are recounted in the chapter 'Trailblazers'.

INDIA

It is high praise indeed when such luminaries of the game as Jim Laker, Sir Everton Weekes and Erapalli Prasanna pronounce you as the best leg-spin bowler they had seen. But Sir Garry Sobers went one better, declaring he was 'better than Shane Warne'. Those are some of the accolades that fell on the shoulders of India's **Subhash Pandharinath 'Fergie' Gupte (11 December 1929 – 31 May 2002).** And close examination reveals that the career numbers back up such a golden reference.

Having seen Muttiah Muralitharan at close quarters, the term 'he could spin it on glass' resonates. But that's what the West Indians who toured India in 1958–59 said of Gupte's work with the ball. A little man, he had a high arm action and the classical wrist-spinner's predilection for experimenting with flight and ball rotation.

He spun the ball sharply, further confusing the best bats with a fizzing top-spinner and two wrong'uns: one, which a good batsman could pick, came at a low trajectory, the other, from his customary high trajectory, came laced with overspin and dipped and bounced deceptively.

Gupte, who inherited the nickname 'Fergie' from the West Indies leg-spinner Wilfred Ferguson, should have been the second, after Laker, to take all ten wickets in a Test match. Playing against West Indies on jute matting at Kanpur in 1958–59, he had seven wickets to his name when wicketkeeper Naren Tamhane dropped a chance off Lance Gibbs. He had to be satisfied with figures of 9-102. He had already put his name on the list in 1954 (10-78), playing for Bombay against a Pakistan Combined Services and Bahawalpur XI at Bombay.

He was in devastating form when New Zealand toured in 1955–56, bagging 34 wickets in four Tests. On a radically different stage, playing for Rishton in the Lancashire League, he registered a second ten-wicket haul. He also claimed two hat-tricks in one innings of another game.

Sadly, Gupte's outstanding international career ended in controversy. During England's 1961–62 tour of India, he and a teammate were accused of inviting a receptionist from the hotel in which the team were staying up to their room. Though they both denied the allegation, they were dropped – and Gupte never played for India again.

Bitter at this outcome, he quit India for good at the age of 33 and emigrated to Trinidad. His career haul in Test matches was 149 wickets – at that time only Richie Benaud and Clarrie Grimmett, among leg-spinners, had taken more. In Tests he had five in an innings 12 times and ten in a match once.

AUSTRALIA
The first Australian to claim a first-class ten-for, and the first to take all ten in a game held outside of England, was '10 for 66er' George Giffen (see 'And All That'). Bill Howell was the first Australian in England ('Aussie All Sorts') to achieve the feat, while Tim Wall ('Aussie All Sorts') was the first to do so in the Sheffield Shield competition.

SOUTH AFRICA
The best wrist-spin bowlers, Shane Warne being a shining example, have a full bag of tricks: a variety of deliveries designed to confuse the man at the other end. Like Subhash Gupte, who paraded two different wrong'uns. Just when the world's best batsmen think they've worked out what's coming, bang! – a new delivery – like the doosra Muralitharan and Ravichandran Ashwin introduced

well into their careers. Like the deadly flipper Warne produced.

For the wrist-spin merchant, variety is one thing – but greatness comes to those who can land the fizzing delivery in the danger spot. For South African tweaker **Albert Edward Ernest Vogler (28 November 1876 – 9 August 1946)** it was a bit of everything. At his best one of the very best, his special trick was delivering the off-break with a leg-break action. Done with such deception that no batsman claimed he could pick what was coming down the 22 yards.

This was a huge advantage. Ernie Vogler mixed the off-break with one that came straight through at a greater pace. Was this the forerunner of the flipper? Born in South Africa, Vogler plied his trade for Natal, switching to Transvaal before moving to England in 1905 in the hope of making cricket a profession.

In between two seasons for the MCC he played for South Africa in the 1905–06 series against England. It was back to England, then back home again where he had a stellar season for his third domestic team, Eastern Province, tallying 505 runs at 36 and 55 wickets in nine games at just 10.54.

His best game return came in 1906–07 at Johannesburg, against Griqualand West: a true all-round performance. Eastern Province batted first and Vogler top-scored with 79 to help his team reach 403. He then took 6-12 from ten overs and when the Griquas followed on he captured a brilliant 10-26 in the second innings, for match figures of 16-38! Eastern Province won by an innings and 301 runs. Vogler's 10-26 remains the best first-class innings return ever achieved in South Africa.

Vogler proved a real handful on the matting wickets when England toured in 1909–10, bagging 36 wickets at 21.75 in the five Tests. Named as a *Wisden* Cricketer of the Year in 1908, he was once rated by RE 'Tip' Foster, a former captain of England, as the 'most difficult bowler in the world'. That was no understatement. For his bag of tricks knew no peer at the time – and scarcely any batsman who faced him could detect the difference in his delivery of the leg-break and the wrong'un.

Ernie Vogler quietly faded from the scene after a disappointing tour to Australia in 1910–11, when he played only the first and fourth Tests, taking just four wickets. Put simply, the hard wickets offered him little spin – and the Australian bats responded to captain Warwick Armstrong's exhortation to 'hit the googly bowlers off their length'. In all first-class matches on the tour he had only a paltry 21 wickets at nearly 39 apiece.

WEST INDIES

Cricket in the West Indies has produced some fabulously talented players – Learie Constantine, the 'Three Ws' (Frank Worrell, Everton Weekes and Clyde Walcott), Wes Hall, Charlie Griffith, Garry Sobers, Vivian Richards, Curtly Ambrose, the list goes on.

Unlike this elite crew, **Delmont Cameron St Clair 'Fitz' Hinds (1 June 1880 – details of death unknown)** is far from a household name in Caribbean sporting circles – but he *does* have a first-class ten-for to his name. If that *is*, in fact, his name. It should be mentioned here that some historians dispute whether the Delmont Cameron St Clair Hinds listed on ESPNcricinfo and CricketArchive is the cricketer known as 'Fitz' Hinds – and as such the date of birth listed above may not be accurate.

'Fitz Hinds' did exist, however, and the Barbados-born cricketer came out of virtual obscurity in 1900 to be chosen in the first West Indies touring side to England. Hinds had not played a single important game before his selection, which was clouded in controversy because he was coloured – and rated as a professional. In those days the Caribbean nations were very British, and cricket there was very much the white man's game. They were the amateurs, while coloured players were professionals, worthy only for bowling to white players in the nets.

So, at the time, Hinds's selection for the 1900 tour certainly was controversial. He was coloured *and* a professional. His pre-tour biographical note read: 'Good all-round cricketer. Bowls well, with a peculiar action. Member of Spartan Cricket Club.'

Given the controversy surrounding his selection, it was no surprise that Hinds struggled on the tour. He scored two fifties but averaged only 20 with the bat. Bowled sparingly, he took only six wickets. Sometimes he filled in as a wicketkeeper and in one game took six catches. Even so, the luminary Pelham Warner, writing in the 1901 *Wisden*, said he was 'often useful in his peculiar style, and was a keen hard-working cricketer'.

On his return from England, Hinds played for AB St Hill's XI in the summer of 1900–01 – and in a 12-a-side match against Trinidad at Port of Spain in January 1901 he bowled 19.1 overs in taking 10-36. Eventually he was picked for Barbados and was chosen for combined West Indies teams in 1901–02 and 1904–05.

Hinds later moved to live in the United States – and played against the 1913 Australians on their way home from an Ashes tour, in New York. And yet still, all these years later, learned debate continues over the fundamental matter of his real identity.

SRI LANKA

One of the latecomers to the world cricket stage, Sri Lanka was awarded Test-match status in 1981 and played its first Test in February, 1982 – against England in Colombo, which the visitors won by seven wickets. At that point, **Gallage Pramodya Wickramasinghe (14 August 1971 –)** was 11 years old and likely playing knock-up games with friends and a bit of junior cricket.

A right-arm medium-fast bowler, Wickramasinghe made his first-class debut six years later in 1988, playing for the Sinhalese Sports Club. He put his name up for consideration by the national selectors a year later at the Youth Asia Cup Championship. After making his one-day international (ODI) debut in December 1990, he further laid claims for Test selection in November 1991, when he scooped 10-41 for the Sinhalese Sports Club against Kalutara in Colombo – and in doing so becoming the first Sri Lankan to take all ten.

His selection in the Test team followed shortly after, and Wickramasinghe did his best work at that level, taking eight wickets in helping Sri Lanka win its first away Test series, in Pakistan. Meantime, he was performing creditably in the ODI field, a contributor in the 1992, 1996 and 1999 World Cup campaigns – particularly 1996 when Sri Lanka won the Cup for the first and so far only time. He played four matches in that campaign, and although he didn't take a wicket, he did have the figures of seven overs for 38 runs in the final against Australia. He claimed his 100th ODI wicket in 1999, dismissing Zimbabwe's Andy Flower.

Wickramasinghe's career came to a virtual standstill in 2000 when he had shoulder surgery in Australia. He made a futile attempt two years later to regain his form in ODI clashes with England and India.

He then morphed into other roles in cricket – as a national selector, for a period chairman of the panel. These years were shaded by controversy when he made corruption claims against certain Sri Lankan players – and in taking a strong stand by dropping senior players in a bid to bring on young talent for the 2023 World Cup, a move that backfired.

Having said all that, Wickramasinghe had a fine all-round career with perhaps his best work done in the ODI format: 134 games for 109 wickets at 39.64.

NEW ZEALAND

We have read stories in these pages of players whose durability has astounded us. Men like 'Tich' Freeman – who was in his forty-fourth year when he claimed his *third* ten-for. Others, particularly in the early years, played first-class cricket well into their fifties, piling up a stunning number of games, runs, wickets and catches.

At the other end of the scale are those players who were gone from the first-class ranks no sooner than they'd arrived. Most didn't have time to leave a mark – although **Albert Edward Moss (3 October 1863 – 11 December 1945)** was a notable exception. Moss came into first-class cricket aged 26 and departed the scene after playing only four games, all in the same season. By that stage, however, he'd already joined the ten-for list, achieving the feat on his first-class debut no less. He remains the only player to get ten-for on debut in an eleven-a-side match, and the only person to have taken a ten-for in New Zealand.

Moss was born in England, but moved with his family to live in New Zealand when his father sought relief from tuberculosis. He developed as a fast bowler, and indeed was once described as 'the fastest bowler ever seen in New Zealand'. He made his debut for Canterbury against Wellington at Christchurch on 27 December 1889 – and the following day bagged ten-for, 10-28 off 21.3 overs. He also took three wickets in the second innings.

Moss is said to have taken great pride in his achievement, having the match ball mounted. However, his was a career destined to be short. After taking 13 wickets in his next three games his cricketing career came to a screeching halt when, in 1891, he was tried in the Supreme Court, charged with 'wounding his wife with intent to murder'. He was found not guilty on the grounds of insanity but jailed until his release in early 1896, when he was deported to South America.

He then moved to South Africa. Hearing of his charitable work there, his wife joined him and they later remarried. In a touching gesture his wife returned the ball commemorating his ten-wicket game – and it now resides in the museum at Lancaster Park, home of the Canterbury club.

The couple moved to live in England in 1918. Moss died at their home in Essex in 1945 at the age of 82. Has there ever been a career span so short – and yet so fruitful?

USA

Perhaps not surprisingly, only one American has taken a first-class ten-for. As explored in 'An Odd One', that was the rather brilliant Bart King.

PAKISTAN

Good all-rounders are worth their weight in gold. We West Australians, for instance, were spoilt by the presence in more recent times of two outstanding all-rounders in Rod Marsh and Adam Gilchrist. Excellent wicketkeepers, both held down middle-order batting slots in Test matches and could turn a game with their audacious strokeplay – though, for obvious reasons, not so much with the ball.[36]

Of course, when we think of all-rounders we tend not to picture wicketkeeper-batters but bowlers who can bat (such as Kapil Dev,

---

36 To give him his due, Marsh bowled a little, and he even has a first-class wicket to his name. He also bowled seven overs in Test cricket. Gilchrist, however, never rolled his arm over in a first-class match – but he did manage a single delivery in an Indian Premier League T20 match in 2014. Incredibly, he took a wicket, that of Harbhajan Singh. Singh, Gilchrist's main tormentor in the epic 2001 Border–Gavaskar Test series in India, was caught in the deep after slogging. Gilchrist's celebration is worth looking up.

Richard Hadlee, Imran Khan, Ravindra Jadeja), batters who can bowl (Frank Worrell, Wally Hammond, Shane Watson), or players who seem equally adept at both (like Garry Sobers, Ian Botham, Keith Miller, Jacques Kallis, Ben Stokes).

Shahid Mahmood (17 March 1939 – 13 December 2020), the first Pakistani to join the ten-for list, was arguably more of the middle variety, the batter who could bowl. Better recognised as a left-hand opening bat than as a bowler, he played first-class cricket in Pakistan from 1957 to 1969. His big day came in what turned out to be his final season. Playing for Karachi Whites against Khairpur at the National Stadium, Mahmood etched his name into history, and helped win the game for the Whites, with a haul of 10-58 from 25 overs. Three other Pakistani bowlers have since repeated the feat: Imran Adil (1989), Naeem Akhtar (1995) and Zulfiqar Babar (2009).

Seven years earlier, Mahmood had made his only Test match appearance, playing at Nottingham on Pakistan's 1962 tour of England. He fared poorly, but back home he continued to play well in the domestic Quaid-e-Azam Trophy competition. With the bat he was a regular run-maker, ending his first-class career with 3117 runs at the healthy average of 31.80 – including five hundreds and 15 half-centuries.

He was born in Lucknow, India, but moved to Pakistan after partition in 1947. Following his cricket days, Mahmood moved to live in the United States, where he died in 2020. PCB chairman Ehsan Mani said of his career, 'He was a seasoned first-class player who made his mark in domestic cricket.'

CHAPTER 19
OTHERS

Turn over enough stones and you are bound to uncover hitherto hidden gems in the world of cricket. And within the cohort of those who captured ten-for in a first-class innings – 84 in all, when you account for the six who achieved the feat more than once – is a treasure trove of stories. Like the one with which I choose to begin this chapter: the man who in Melbourne, on 15 March 1877, faced Australia's Dave Gregory at the toss of a coin for what turned out to be the first Test match ever contested.

For all that he will be known for this unique fact, **James Lillywhite (23 February 1842 – 25 October 1929)** had little in the way of personal performance in the game. First, he lost the toss. Australia chose to bat, which did at least mean that Lillywhite was the first person in Test history to lead their team onto the field. The glory stopped there for Lillywhite. He scored ten in the first innings and four in the second, and Australia won the historic encounter by 45 runs. England took the second match, but Lillywhite never captained England again.

Lillywhite came from a great cricketing family, of whom the best known was his uncle, William (the great bowler who stands as the first man to record ten-for in a first-class game – see 'Trailblazers'). He bowled as he batted, left-handed, was rather slow with a high delivery and, like others of his ilk, was exceptionally accurate.

He was in his twenty-first year when he first appeared at Lord's, playing for Sussex against the MCC. In that game he took 14 wickets for 57 – nine of them in the second innings for just 29 runs. According to WG Grace, he 'improved every year afterwards and very soon was acknowledged as one of the best bowlers of the day, in accuracy of pitch, straightness and ease of delivery. He bowled slow left-arm and never seemed to tire.'

Doing his bit to maintain the high standards of the Lillywhites, James recorded his own ten-wicket haul, at the cost of 129 runs, in a game between North versus South at Canterbury in 1872. Lillywhite made numerous tours, to Australia (four times) and once to North America. In Australia in 1873–74, he had some remarkable performances, including taking 18-72 against a 15-man NSW in Sydney and 12-61 against an 18-man Victoria in Melbourne.

After his playing days he stood as an efficient umpire, from 1883 to 1901 – and adjudicated in six Test matches.

Now to the man who sent down the first ball in Test cricket: **Alfred Shaw (28 August 1842 – 16 January 1907)**. Short, but powerfully built, Shaw was a mere spectator that day at the MCG, while Australian opener Charles Bannerman dominated the England attack. Bannerman scored 165 (before retiring hurt) in Australia's match-winning first innings of 245. But Shaw's return of 3-51 from 55.3 overs was followed by 5-38 in the second innings. His efforts in the second innings saw him become the first Englishman to reap a five-wicket haul in a Test match, Australia's Billy Midwinter having beaten him to the overall honour with 5-78 in England's first innings.

WG Grace claimed Shaw was one of the best round-arm bowlers of the 19th century, though oddly he was thought of more as a batsman, at least at first. But after 1870, when he began to bowl about medium-pace, his success with the ball was so great that his batting excellence was lost sight of by the general public.

'The great power of his bowling lay in its good length and unvaried precision,' Grace wrote. 'He could break both ways, but got more work on the ball from the off, and he was one of the few bowlers who could very quickly cause a batsman to make a mistake if he was too eager to hit. An impatient batsman might make two spanking hits in succession off him but he would not make a third.

'On a good wicket when batting against him I did not find it difficult to play the ball, but I had to watch him carefully and wait patiently before I could score. Some days he was irresistible and there can be little doubt that for the MCC and his county few bowlers have done such good service. He also had wonderful stamina.'

Shaw's endurance is underscored by the fact that he played first-class cricket from 1864 to 1897, during that time captaining Nottinghamshire to four successive unofficial championships. His own ten-for haul came while playing for MCC against the North, at Lord's in 1874. His 10-73 included two wickets taken with the help of the safe hands of WG Grace himself.

Underlining Grace's claims of his durability, in an 1875 match between Notts and MCC at Lord's, Shaw sent down 41 overs and two balls for seven runs and seven wickets. And his dismissals included Grace.

Shaw played in the England team that met Australia in 1880 at The Oval in the first Test played on English soil. That season he took 177 wickets in first-class matches for less than nine runs apiece. Two years earlier he had played for MCC at Lord's in a sensational match against the First Australian Eleven. He and Fred Morley dismissed the Australians for a total of 41, though the touring team ended up the victors.

However, this corpulent medium-pacer was equally well known for a matter of technical significance in the development of the game. It was Shaw who suggested that creases defining the pitch layout should be made by using whitewash – thus doing away with the practice of scratching the marks.

In the first years of cricket in Australia, the game was, naturally enough, a pastime for Englishmen who had come to live Down Under by various means, and for a variety of reasons. It took years before this fact was literally 'bred out' and Australian-born players began to emerge and develop their own styles. So it wasn't completely off the page that in the interim period there would be the odd occasion when mix-and-match would take on a whole new meaning – with two of the ten-for family bearing testament to that.

Albert Edwin Trott (6 February 1873 – 30 July 1914) was born in the Melbourne suburb of Abbotsford and, with his older brother Harry, played for Victoria. It raised eyebrows when, after just three games, Albert was chosen to play for Australia. It was

the third Test against England at
Adelaide in 1894–95 and he made
a big noise, taking 8-43 with his
slinging, round-arm action, and
scoring 38 and 72, both not out. He
added an unbeaten 85 in the Fourth
Test but, oddly, was not chosen for
the 1896 tour to England that his
brother captained.

Instead of staying at home and
rueing his misfortune, Trott sailed
to England independently and soon joined the ground staff at
Lord's. Two years later he found himself a spot with Middlesex.
Shortly after that he toured South Africa with an England side,
playing two games that were later given Test-match status. It made
him the last cricketer so far to have played for both Australia and
England.

Trott enjoyed huge success in county games. He began for
Middlesex in 1898. Overcoming a hand injury he finished the
season with a flurry, helping Middlesex to win eight matches of
nine, drawing the other. In the whole season he took 102 wickets
for the county. He went to the top of the tree as an all-rounder over
the next two seasons. He scored 1175 runs and took 239 wickets
in 1899, and in 1900 his figures came out at 1337 runs and 211
wickets.

At his best, Trott's bowling was extraordinarily good and quite
idiosyncratic – with an appreciably lower delivery style. He had
plenty of spin, but he depended less on break than on an endless
variety of pace, rarely bowling two balls alike. He could whip in a
yorker at tremendous speed.

Trott was also renowned for big hitting – he remains the only
man ever to hit a ball over the Lord's Pavilion. He was also one

of only two to take two hat-tricks in a first-class innings, the feat occurring in his own benefit match – which may have ironically reduced his chances of making money from the game. Trott was recognised as a *Wisden* cricketer of the year in 1899, and the following year took his own ten-for (10-42) against Somerset at Taunton. For all his stout performances at the end of the century, suddenly his game started to fall apart after the 1901 season, when he took 176 wickets.

A colourful character, Trott would think nothing of sharing an ale with a spectator while fielding on the boundary. Tragically, he took his life at the age of 41.

Another with 'dual nationality' in cricket was **Samuel Moses James 'Sammy' Woods (13 April 1867 – 30 April 1931)**. If ever there was an all-round sportsman it was Woods. A classy cricketer, he also

played rugby union for England and county-level soccer and hockey. As we shall see, in cricket he was a true all-rounder.

Woods moved from his birthplace of Australia to England at the age of 16, with a view to completing his education. While doing so at Cambridge University in 1888 he was given a call-up to the Australian squad to face England and played three Tests. And it was while playing for Cambridge University in 1890 that he claimed 10-69 against CI Thornton's XI.

Woods was at one stage considered one of the finest bowlers in England. In the words of Sir Pelham Warner, he was 'the most artistic and subtle fast bowler there has ever been'. High praise indeed! AA Thomson, meanwhile, said 'Sammy radiated such elemental force in hard hitting, fast bowling and electrical fielding that he might have been a forerunner to Sir Learie Constantine.'

Strongly built, with a cheery disposition and unflinching courage, he was generally at his best against the better bats. He was fast and accurate, commanding not only a deadly yorker but also a slower ball that was as formidable and deceptive as any that he sent down.

Woods was a fine batsman. In fact, over his first-class career he scored 19 centuries, 18 of them for Somerset. He was chosen in a privately raised team that toured South Africa in 1895–96, where his performance with the ball was beginning to lose its potency. Fortunately for him, his batting blossomed. He made several tours abroad – to America in 1891, South Africa, the West Indies and again to the United States. Curiously, he never played a senior match in his native Australia.

A well-reputed leader, too, he captained Cambridge University and the Gentlemen, while for 12 years the Somerset county side benefited from his positive leadership.

Yet another born in Australia who made his name playing overseas (mainly in England) was **Francis Alfred 'Frank' Tarrant (11 December 1880 – 29 January 1951)**. Tarrant played for Victoria, then headed to England where he qualified to play for Middlesex as a left-arm spinner and middle-order batsman.

Though not a real threat on hard wickets, he was almost unplayable on rain-affected surfaces. This was most evident the day

he returned figures of 9-59 against Nottinghamshire at Lord's – one of his victims saying he had 'never seen a finer piece of bowling'.

Tarrant's all-round talents were reflected by his achievement, eight times, of county cricket's all-round 'double' – a season in which 1000 runs and 100 wickets are achieved. In 1907 he bagged 183 wickets and scored 1552 runs. Four years later he did even better, scoring more than 2000 runs and taking more than 100 wickets. Yet, he was forever overlooked by the England selectors.

It was during World War I, in 1918–19, when playing cricket in India, that he claimed his ten-for. Playing for Lord Willingdon's XI against the Maharaja of Cooch-Behar's XI in Poona, he returned figures of 10-90. In the same game he scored 182 not out. After the war he played mostly in India, appearing for the Europeans in the Bombay Quadrangular tournament.

Tarrant played his last first-class game at the age of 56. On retirement as a player he turned his hand to umpiring, standing in two Tests, when England toured India in 1933–34 – the first Tests played on Indian soil. He later shared umpiring duties with his son Louis, a rare occasion when a father and son stood together in a first-class match.

Australian author Mike Coward's 2020 book about Tarrant is subtitled *Cricket's Forgotten Pioneer*. Coward argues that Tarrant's record 'validates argument that he is the greatest all-rounder not to have played Test cricket'.

It is almost certain that this would not happen in the frantic world of sport these days – that a man could play both professional cricket *and* football of any code.[37] But that was the case for two members of the ten-for club, albeit a long time ago.

Though a promising cricketer, **Alonzo Robson Drake (16 April 1884 – 14 February 1919)** first concentrated on football (soccer), playing for Doncaster Rovers, then Sheffield United. He also had periods with Birmingham, Queens Park Rangers, Huddersfield Town and, finally, Rotherham Town.

Drake's cricket career began in earnest in 1911 when he was first chosen for Yorkshire. In that season he returned a batting average of 35 and took 61 wickets. A left-arm medium-pacer, he was a handful when on song. Probably linked to his participation in the winter code, he was renowned for his fitness, enabling long spells at the crease. He combined this precious asset with deadly accuracy, making him a real threat when operating on rain-affected wickets.

It is an extraordinary fact that he needed only 53 deliveries (8.5 overs) to claim 10-35 against Somerset at Weston-super-Mare in

---

37 A woman could, though. Australian cricketer Ellyse Perry is one of the best female cricketers of all time and continues to star for her country with both bat and ball. She made her international debut in all three formats in the summer of 2007–08 and to date has played 13 Tests, 155 ODIs and 165 T20Is. A few months before her ODI debut she played her first match for the Matildas, Australia's national football (soccer) team. Until 2014, when she chose to concentrate on cricket, she played both cricket and football at the highest levels. By then Perry, who played variously for the Central Coast Mariners, Canberra United and Sydney FC, had won 18 caps for the Matildas.

1914. He bowled unchanged through the game and took a total of 15 wickets for 51 runs. In fact, 1914 was a stellar season for Drake. Among his returns were five wickets for six runs against Derbyshire (at Leeds) and four wickets in four balls in the return match at Chesterfield. Twice that summer Drake bowled unchanged through both innings of a game, something that happened in consecutive matches – against Gloucestershire (at Bristol) and in his ten-for game against Somerset.

Drake was a vital part of the Yorkshire team in the seasons leading up to World War I – but the end of the 1914 season brought down the curtain on his cricketing days. He was a heavy smoker and was twice rejected by the army when he tried to enlist at the outbreak of war. He subsequently fell into ill health, and died aged only 34 in February 1919.

Another who mixed a career in cricket with one in football was **Henry 'Harry' Howell (29 November 1890 – 9 July 1932)**. However, unlike Drake, his right-arm fast bowling for Warwickshire was perceived as good enough to lift him into the ranks of Test cricket. He made five appearances for England between 1920 and 1924, in matches against Australia and South Africa.

Howell first played for Warwickshire in 1913, at the age of 22. A year later he was fully established as a member of the team. Taking a fairly long run and bowling with a nice easy action, he was distinctly a fast bowler without, however, possessing the special gift of extra pace off the pitch.

After World War I he met with real success. In 1920 he had 161 wickets in all matches, and in 1923 secured 152, that season taking 10-51 against Yorkshire at Edgbaston, the first Warwickshire player to achieve a ten-for. A year later on the same ground he was involved in the dismissal of Hampshire for 15. In the course of four overs and five balls Howell took six wickets for seven runs. This was a truly amazing match: Hampshire, after following on 218 in arrears, hit up a total of 521 and in the end won by 155 runs. Howell's career finished in 1929.

In the winter game Howell played for Wolverhampton Wanderers, Stoke and Port Vale. He made himself more than welcome with hat-tricks for Stoke in 1917 (against Manchester City) and 1918 (against Burnley). What this says about Howell, or the respective games he played, who can say, but he never managed a cricket hat-trick – not first-class anyway.

And now to two English bowlers whose reputations precede them – and whose raw figures over long careers for county and country place them in rare air. A pair of giants of the game.

A man who embodied all that is potent about pace bowling, **Thomas 'Tom' Richardson (11 August 1870 – 2 July 1912)**

possessed the ability to produce considerable pace from a long and vigorous approach, with a high arm action that gave sharp lift off a good length. He was renowned – and feared – for what today would be recognised as an off-cutter, but in his heyday was known as a 'break-back'.

Richardson overcame suggestions that his action was illegal and played a total of 358 first-class matches, including 14 Tests. He was one of the premier bowlers of his time, with numbers to back that up. In one devastating period of four seasons from 1894 he collected 1005 wickets – a figure surpassed over such a period only by the Kent leg-spinner Tich Freeman.

During his amazing 1894 season for Surrey he claimed 10-45 against Essex at The Oval, his return for that summer coming at the stunning average of 10.23, and a strike rate of a wicket every 23 deliveries. If anything, 1895 was even better: 290 wickets, a more than decent figure for a season's work (though it was again surpassed only by Freeman).

In his prime Richardson had every good quality a fast bowler can possess. He was lithe and supple, which combined with a splendid physique and inexhaustible energy. For sustained pace through a long innings, he perhaps had no equal. It was his pronounced off-break, in combination with great speed, that made him an irresistible package.

This was borne out in the last innings of the Ashes match at Manchester in 1896. Having made England follow on, the Australians were left with 125 to win. They crept home by three wickets, but with Richardson piling on the pressure it took them three hours to get the runs. In the Test at Lord's in the same season he and George Lohmann fired the Australians out for 53 on a perfect pitch. In that innings Richardson bowled 11 overs and three balls for 39 runs and six wickets.

Richardson's game went into a serious decline at the age of 28. He had put on a lot of weight, and lost the brilliance and zest that had made him one of the best of his time. After his playing days his health declined and he died of a heart attack at the age of 41.

Another Tom – **Thomas William John 'Tom' Goddard (1 October 1901 – 22 May 1966)** – was just as potent a force. A right-arm finger-spinner, Goddard remains the fifth-highest wicket-taker in all first-class cricket and is regarded as one of the greatest bowlers of his style ever to step on the green sward.

A giant of a man, with massive hands, Goddard was a prodigious spinner of the ball. He operated mainly around the wicket and his height enabled awkward bounce on even the easiest of batting surfaces. On a helpful pitch he was almost unplayable. His combination at Gloucestershire with the left-handed Charlie Parker was formidable – much along the lines of Laker and Lock for Surrey and England.

Amazingly, when Goddard first played for Gloucestershire in 1922 it was as a fast bowler. However, he gained little traction with this mode of delivery and decided to leave the county cricket scene in order to work on the switch to off-spin. He made the transition with such success that he was re-engaged by Gloucestershire and was an instant success. In 1929 he bagged 184 wickets at 16.

Among the sparkling years that produced 2979 scalps in first-class games was a total of six hat-tricks, the same as his spin partner Parker – only one short of the all-time record set by Kent's Doug Wright. One of the hat-tricks came in a Test, against South Africa at Johannesburg in 1938–39.

Goddard played in only eight Tests, but by the end of a truly illustrious career had produced 16 occasions when he took more than 100 wickets in a season. Four of those times he topped

200 – and in 1937 he peaked at 248 victims. Included in that thunderstorm of wickets was his epic 10-113 against Worcestershire at Cheltenham.

Two years after that Goddard achieved the feat of taking 17 wickets in a day – 9-38 and 8-68 – against Kent at Bristol. His final total of first-class wickets places him at fifth on the all-time list, behind Rhodes, Freeman, Parker and JT Hearne.

Some are well recognised in the lengthy pantheon of cricket. Mention the name WG Grace and everybody – that is *everybody* – puts their hand up and says, 'Yes, of course I've heard of *him* … he's that big bloke with a bushy black beard and a healthy stomach.' Others are not so well known, and the list of those who have taken the magical ten-for bears a few of this ilk.

Take **Edward D'Oyley 'Ted' Barratt (April 21, 1844 – February 27, 1891),** who was a left-arm slow round-arm bowler. Let your imagination make something of that description in the fairly rigid parameters of today's bowlers. He played for Surrey from 1872 to 1886, and right in the middle of that he gained fame for claiming 10-43 for the Players against Australians at The Oval in 1878.

Short in stature and powerful of build, Barratt's best deliveries would drift through the air and spin sharply from leg. The aforementioned Grace saw 'many an impatient or thoughtless batsman' spoon the ball while trying to hit, even slash, wildly at a Barratt floater. 'A little thought,' the great man added, 'would have produced a step back and cut.' Helping Barratt's cause, though, was a deadly variation of a quicker ball that went on with the arm.

However, against Grace and the great man's brother, EM, Barratt acknowledged he was virtually powerless. Said Grace: 'Against EM and me he seldom bowled the floater – EM ran yards out of his ground and pulled him to the boundary so often that Barratt was frightened to bowl a good length to him, and his short ones were just as mercilessly thrashed.' Barratt admitted that he was completely at their mercy, stating, 'It's no use now; my little game is over. Help yourselves, gentlemen.'

His *Wisden* obituary noted that, 'At his best, Barratt was certainly a very fine slow bowler, being able on certain wickets to get more work on the ball than almost any other cricketer of his generation.' Barratt enjoyed a rewarding season in 1878, when he claimed 135 wickets at 14.04. He bettered that in 1883, with 148 at 15.90 – including 18 five-wicket innings and six ten-wicket matches.

The injection of George Lohmann and John Beaumont into the Surrey attack cost Barratt opportunity, and he dropped out of county cricket after 1884.

CHAPTER 20

10 FOR 44

continued

For Shield cricketers in the late 1960s there was no more prized scalp than that of Bill Lawry. I recall one game in Perth when he batted through the whole day, reaching his century shortly before stumps. He defied WA's powerful pace attack on a very bouncy wicket and was literally black and blue from the body blows he withstood. We all knew that for a fact, from a newspaper photograph the next day.

That innings was painful to watch. But it was testament to the man's courage and resolve. His really *was* a prized scalp. I was living in England, near Manchester, in 1968. When the Ashes tour took the Aussies to a Test at Old Trafford I was invited into our dressing-room. The Australian second innings began, and when England dismissed Lawry for 17, the crowd's reaction almost brought the grandstand down. Such was the value of his wicket.

Now this great fighter was standing between us and a pathway to an unexpected bonus: first-innings points and a chance to redeem ourselves when it came to batting again.

Seven-for:
Bill Lawry, caught Gordon Becker, bowled Brayshaw, 47
Victoria 7-138

I'd been swinging the ball nicely through the Victorian innings but this time it was a wayward delivery down leg side that claimed a wicket, and the prized wicket at that. Lawry attempted a leg glance but only succeeded in getting a fine edge, which was taken, diving to his right, by our wicketkeeper Gordon Becker, better known to all and sundry as 'Crunch'. This related to the fact that with bat in hand he looked to *crunch* the bowling to all points of the compass – and there was no better example of this than his sizzling 195 (one of his three first-class centuries) against the touring Indians in Perth in November 1967 – a knock that set us up for a win by an innings and 20 runs. A sound gloveman, Crunch toured South Africa in 1966–67, but didn't play a Test.

After Crunch's diving catch did for Lawry, the Victorian was silent, but I later – *much* later – learnt that he wasn't happy with the dismissal. In 2006 my family moved to Victoria and I was doing some bowling coaching at the Prahran club in Melbourne. The president told me one training day that he would be seeing Bill at a meeting that night, would I like him to give him my best wishes? Of course, I said. Next time I saw the president he said he'd passed on my message. Then he reported verbatim Bill's response: 'Tell Braysh I didn't hit it!'

All those years later, eh! But he had been given out and had to walk off, with his team now seven down, but still 24 runs short of first-innings points.

Over my career, at all levels, I found that wicketkeepers were a breed of their own. In my experience they would invariably choose to change in the back of the dressing-room, where their gear would be strewn haphazardly all over the floor. They didn't mind being a bit grubby, and I'll give you an example. If Rod Marsh had a good day of it on the first day of a game he would then wear the same shirt, trousers and jock strap for the remainder of the game – and I can tell you from personal experience that standing next to him in the slips on a hot day could be a fairly smelly affair. Wherever possible I would stand upwind of him.

Similarly, probably because of their position – and duties – in the field, wicketkeepers often had a lot to say out there. They saw it as one of their tasks to do all they could to maintain a high standard of activity and enthusiasm. Some, however, would tend to go over the top. One who filled these roles to the fullest extent was Victoria's Ray Jordon. Commonly known as 'Slug', he must have had the most raucous and mouthy voice of all out in the middle.

In fact, the only time under Bill Lawry's rule that we were welcomed into the Victorian rooms was at the end of a day's play in Perth during which Jordon had taken a blow to the face and been rushed to hospital. Well, after being discharged, Slug later arrived in the rather sedate atmosphere of the rooms with his face literally held together by some elastic wrapping.

The situation of the game at that time had Victoria needing to survive the final day to save defeat. It was all hands on deck. Well, Slug was trying to indicate to his captain that, if needed in this cause, he'd be prepared to pad up – broken jaw notwithstanding. 'Okay, but first you have to pass a fitness test,' Bill said. Slug nodded. 'Can you say f**k?' Bill asked. Slug knew the word very well and, as we watched on with piqued interest, he gave it his best shot. The only sound forthcoming, however, was a low guttural growl. 'Sorry, pal,' said Bill, 'fitness test failed.'

Having said all of the above, Jordon was a good competitor and a handy batsman, with one first-class century to his name.

Eight-for:
Ray Jordon, caught Gordon Becker, bowled Brayshaw, 9
Victoria 8-151

Jordon and John Grant advanced Victoria's score bit by bit, adding 13 to carry the total to 151, close to the target of 162. Then Jordon succumbed to my outswinger, nibbling it to 'keeper Becker. Victoria were now eight down and still 11 runs away from a lead. It was one of those days when not many scoring shots penetrated the infield – and if any looked like doing so, WA could boast one of the best 'ring' fieldsmen in the business. True, Tony Mann – who played four Tests against India during the World Series Cricket years, and scored a century as a nightwatchman in the Perth match – was a handy bat and a very smart leg-spinner. More than that, he was a gun in one-saving positions in the WA infield. Helping him in this endeavour was his rocket of a throwing arm – which explained his nickname, 'Rocket'.

John Grant was a real cricketer's cricketer. He was a bit short in stature to be a really damaging fast bowler, but he gave everything to every delivery and produced a very lively ball, even though he was unable to get the menacing lift that most pace bowlers thrive on. A year after this game I ran into the 'General' as an opposition professional in the Lancashire League. It was a competition made to order for his type of cricket.

I rated him as a batsman, too, a very handy number eight who never gave his wicket away. So there was no way I thought the battle for first-innings points was over while he was still at the crease, and the target so close at hand.

Nine-for:
John Grant, bowled Brayshaw, 24
Victoria 9-152

Just one run later, however, the General missed a straight one and was bowled for 24, the third-highest score in the Victorian innings. Now nerves were jangling in both camps, with WA needing one wicket, the Vics just ten runs.

I did of course realise that having dismissed Grant I had all nine wickets to have fallen, but I promise you I was so flushed with the thought that we could defend our miserable total against the Old Foe that all I wanted was for somebody – *anybody* – to take that last, vital wicket. Looking back, I think that I *and* my ten teammates out there were in a state of shock, realising that all of a sudden first-innings points were in the offing. To my knowledge nothing was said by anybody about my being on the verge of a ten-for as we perched on the brink of the mighty unexpected! We did have a dressing-room rule not to speak, or even move position, when a particularly tight play was unfolding. It seems we took the same attitude out in the middle!

CHAPTER 21
SUNDRIES

There have been many quaint traditions handed down over the years in English cricket. One has been the matter of issuing a player his county cap. On being admitted, a player is given a cap bearing a small replica of the insignia of the county. For instance, a Lancashire player is first given a cap that is adorned by the bud of a red rose. The cap given to a Lancashire player who has earned promotion through good service and performance shows a red rose in full bloom.

Another long-standing tradition in county cricket is the granting of a benefit season, which is a method of financially rewarding a player who has given long and good service to the club. The system originated in the 19th century and was designed to help out professional players who were paid low wages and generally could not afford to play on after the age of 40.

This so-called 'benefit' in the early days usually amounted to offering the gate receipts of a designated match to the beneficiary. Nowadays a benefit *year* is granted to a player who the club decides has deserved it – usually, but not necessarily, after about ten years as a capped player. This gives the player a whole year to summon up a committee to help him plan and implement events aimed at raising money, like special dinners, a designated game, raffles, auctions and the like.

Though most players who give good service to a club will receive the highly valued cap and be granted a benefit year, it is not automatic. In fact, a player can have quite a significant career in first-class cricket without ever winning his cap or being granted a benefit year.

One who would know all about becoming a capped player is **Robert 'Bob' Berry (29 January 1926 – 2 December 2006)**. He

R. BERRY
Derbyshire

was the first to be capped by three different counties. An orthodox left-arm spinner, Berry grew up near Manchester and landed on the Lancashire staff in 1948, but that was just the start of a varied journey.

After claiming five wickets in a Test trial in 1950 Berry was a surprise selection for the first Test against the West Indies at his home ground, Old Trafford. It was a pitch made for spinners and Berry had match figures of 9-116. Another left-armer making his debut (for the opposition), Alf Valentine, claimed 11 for the match, including the first eight – a unique start to an international career.

Berry then toured Australia and New Zealand with MCC in 1950–51. He had little luck, however, and when he returned to Lancashire he found himself behind Malcolm Hilton in the pecking order of the county's spin stocks.

In 1953 Hilton suffered a form slump and Berry rose to the challenge, taking 98 wickets at 18.97, including 10-102 against Worcestershire at Blackpool. After touring India with a Commonwealth Eleven in 1953–54, he again became second fiddle to Hilton and eventually made a move to play for Worcestershire.

Berry had four good years for the club, taking 5-60 against the South Africans in his first match for them. He ended up taking a total of 250 wickets with Worcestershire before continuing his journey by joining Derbyshire, where he spun the ball until his first-class career came to an end after the 1962 season. He was an excellent outfielder, but a true rabbit with the bat at the end of an innings.

There have been few Scots who have made a mark in English cricket, but **Alexander Stuart 'Alex' Kennedy (24 January 1891 – 15 November 1959)** was a notable exception. Born in Edinburgh, he landed in first-class cricket with Hampshire at the age of 16 and ended a wonderful career as one of the most prolific bowlers the game has seen. Strongly built and bowling at medium-pace, he swung the ball both ways, with a deadly third delivery that cut from leg. And he could go all day.

Again, it all could have added up to more, for Kennedy's career was interrupted by World War I. The year hostilities began he claimed 164 wickets at 20. Back in action after the war, in 1921, he hit the high spots with 205 wickets and 1129 runs. Surprisingly, despite his many talents he made only five Test appearances, in South Africa in 1922–23, where he enjoyed bowling on the mats and took 31 wickets at 28.74.

Kennedy's batting had humble beginnings. He worked his way up from tailender through every number in the order up to opening, and when he made 101 against Kent in 1923, he was said to be 'caution itself up to a point'. Between 1921 and 1932 Kennedy was rated one of the most effective all-rounders in the game.

Kennedy could look back on a career that produced a ten-for (10-37) for Players against Gentlemen, at The Oval in 1927 – and more than 100 wickets in a season 15 times. Plus, he completed the 'cricketer's double' – 1000 runs and 100 wickets in a season – five times.

Along the way he posted some stunning innings figures: 9-33 v Lancashire at Liverpool in 1920; 9-46 v Derbyshire at Portsmouth, 1929; 8-11 v Glamorgan at Cardiff, 1921; and 7-8 v Warwickshire at Portsmouth, 1927, when he disposed of six men in 14 balls while conceding four runs.

In the annals of first-class cricket the list of players who have taken ten-fors encompasses an age range of nearly 38 years. The oldest player on the list (see 'What a Year') is Billy Bestwick, who secured his ten-for aged 46 years and 116 days.

The youngest to have claimed all ten is Pakistan's **Mohammad Imran Adil (20 November 1970 –)** who added his name to the list when he was just 18 years old (well, 18 and 344 days, to be exact). This cricket game's not so tough, he must have thought when, on 30 October 1989, while playing for Bahawalpur against Faisalabad at the Iqbal Stadium, Faisalabad, he knocked the home team flying, taking 10-92 from 22.5 overs.

A right-arm fast-medium, Adil opened up with the new ball and set the stadium on fire, having the first three back in the pavilion with just one run on the board. A partnership of 85 followed, and Faisalabad was 6-209 and well back in the game before Adil cleaned up the back half – all out for 226. He then picked up 5-66 in Faisalabad's second innings.

Adil was something of a child prodigy. He was seven days short of his fifteenth birthday when he made his first-class debut. But there was no real fairytale beginning for the young tyro as wickets were hard come by early in his career. This was in part a testament to the docile nature of playing surfaces regularly provided. Such pitches once prompted Imran Khan to stand down from a Test match while in his prime, and in 1979–80 they gave Dennis Lillee his worst series wicket haul, just three wickets in three Tests. It is an odd fact that for the remainder of that season's Patron's Trophy, Adil took only seven more wickets (in six games).

Adil remains the youngest player to have taken a first-class ten-for, nudging out Middlesex-born medium pacer Tony Pearson, who was 19 when he took 10-78 in 1961 playing for Leicestershire against Cambridge University in Loughborough.

One who began his first-class career at the same age Adil took his ten-for was burly fast bowler **Richard Leonard Johnson (29 December 1974 –)**. Johnson was 18 when, in 1992, he made

his first-class debut as an opening bowler for Middlesex. Two years later, after ending Brian Lara's run of five consecutive first-class centuries that summer, he added his name to the ten-for list with a return of 10-45 against Derbyshire at Derby, the best innings figures in the County Championship since Eric Hollies took all ten in 1946.

After the 1995 season Johnson was picked to tour South Africa, but had to pull out with a back injury. He was back in the calculations in 2001 – picked in a squad for the final three Tests against the Aussies. However, it wasn't until England played Zimbabwe two years later that he finally won a Test cap. He made the most of it, picking up a 6-33, including two in his first over. Recalled for the winter tour of Bangladesh, he came in for the second Test at Chittagong and promptly took another five-for. He added ten ODIs in 2003, which was his only year of representative cricket.

By this time Johnson had switched to play for Somerset for the 2001 season, helping them to a one-day title that year. He returned to Middlesex in 2007, retiring as a player at the end of that season – and embarking on a coaching career that eventually landed him the job of Middlesex's head coach in 2022.

The Hurlingham Club, which opened in 1869, is one of those quaint, exclusive premises that upper-class Londoners would have been proud to claim their own. It is set on 42 acres of superb grounds, one of the features of which is a lovely cricket field – in which, around about where a square-leg umpire might plant his feet, stands a massive tree. Before a game starts a voice emanates from the ether, informing the uninitiated that they shouldn't worry about the tree, nobody had ever been caught out of it.

In 1969 I got a good look at the place, having been paid to be part of a cricket match to celebrate the centenary of the august institution. The captain of the side for which I was playing was none other than **Trevor Edward Bailey (3 December 1923 – 10 February 2011),** a cricket writer, broadcaster and former England Test cricketer. I recall his very pleasant demeanour as he changed his position between overs, quietly marshalling his forces.

I also recall the moment when, having decided it was time for me to have a trundle, he walked by and gently asked, 'Would you come down?' That unmistakable voice, heard so often on BBC coverage of Ashes Tests. There was a warmth, even civility, about it. Which we grew to enjoy, along with the likes of John Arlott and Brian Johnston.

But Bailey was a cricketer, too. And a very good one! In his day he was regarded as one of the best all-rounders in the world. Playing for England he was perhaps best remembered for his doggedness at the crease, which earned him the nickname 'Barnacle'. In a BBC obituary it was said, 'His stubborn refusal to be out, normally brought more pleasure to the team than to the spectators. But he was a good enough cricketer to be judged retrospectively as the leading all-rounder in the world for most of his international career.'

Bailey was a right-arm fast-medium bowler, whose ability to swing the ball made him a natural fit with the likes of Alec Bedser, Fred Trueman, Brian Statham and Frank Tyson. His first-class career began with Essex in 1946 and lasted 21 achieving years. One of many high points came in a game against Lancashire at Clacton-on-Sea in 1949, when he joined the ten-for club with his 10-90 off 39.4 overs. His overall body of work – 28,641 runs and 2082 wickets – places him in elite company in first-class cricket.

Bailey captained Essex from 1961 to 1966 and held administrative positions that enabled him to be paid by the club, but still remain an amateur player (it was considered the done thing in those days for the captain of a county team to be an amateur). Teammate and fellow England player Keith Fletcher said this arrangement was fine: 'He was a better cricketer than the pros ... and someone instrumental in taking Essex County Cricket Club into the modern era.'

Bailey played 61 Tests between 1949 and 1959. He enjoyed a day out in the fifth Test against the West Indies at Kingston, Jamaica, in 1953–54. His figures of 7-34 helped England win the match and share the series two-all. He played his final Test on the 1958–59 Ashes tour. After retiring he became a fixture on the BBC's *Test Match Special* radio program, and is remembered very fondly for his droll delivery and humour over a 26-year involvement.

Radio broadcasting of cricket matches in both Australia and England dates back to the 1920s. Ever since, it has been usual practice for a commentary team to be led by a professional broadcaster – but always with support from what became known as 'expert summarisers'. And down the years there have been many, many examples of former first-class players lining up for the latter role. It makes sense – they have been out there in the cauldron of competition, they can bring knowledge and experience to the product.

One of those to make the short stride from wearing the creams to talking about what's actually going on out there in the middle was **John David 'Jack' Bannister (23 August 1930 – 23 January 2016).** A fast-medium bowler, he played for Warwickshire from 1950 to 1969 and enjoyed good form with the ball.

A solid career peaked in 1959 when he took 10-41 for Warwickshire at Birmingham against a Combined Services team that included several players with first-class experience. These remain the best figures in an innings for the county.

Bannister played a pivotal role in 1967 in setting up the Professional Cricketers' Association, a sort of trade union for county players, in which he served in various capacities for 20 years. He was a driver in forming the players' pension scheme. At one stage he worked as a bookmaker in Wolverhampton, but moved on when his media career took off.

He joined the BBC's TV cricket coverage in 1984, first as an expert then, from 1988, as a lead commentator. He continued to call NatWest Trophy and Sunday League games until 1999, then had a full role in the BBC's coverage of the 1999 World Cup. His bright personality behind the microphone came to the fore during England's tour of South Africa in 1995–96, when he threatened to eat a newspaper if South Africa won the Test series. They did … and *he* did!

Whenever I talk with a young bowler who has 'I-want-to-succeed' written all over their face, one of my first questions is, 'How do you go with batting?' Sadly, most will admit they don't think that much of this *other* part of the game. My response is to almost beg them to change this line of thinking; to tell them that a quality all-rounder is worth his weight in gold to a team. Just look at Mitchell Marsh and how he projected himself up the ladder by growing both sides of his game.

There have been a number in the ten-for club who, as has been explored, have fitted the all-rounder description and **Naeem Akhtar (2 December 1967 –)** is another. A right-hand batsman and pace bowler who played for Rawalpindi from 1990–2004 he did equally well with bat and ball. In first-class games he totted up 3013 runs at 21.99, with ten half-centuries and two three-figure scores.

These were invaluable runs on top of his efforts with the ball, which included 17 five-wicket hauls and two ten-wicket games.

The second of those occurred in a first-class match in December 1995 at Peshawar, when Akhtar claimed a ten-for representing Rawalpindi B against Peshawar. Even more impressively, his ten wickets, from 21.3 overs, cost only 28 runs – the equal fifth-most miserly ten-for on our list.

Between 1999 and 2002 he travelled to England and played many games in the Derbyshire League. At home and in England he appeared in a total of 99 List A matches, scoring 1430 runs at 21.34 and taking 123 wickets at 23.83 – including one five-wicket haul.

Despite a commendable career in domestic cricket, Akhtar never represented Pakistan, though he did make a single ODI appearance for Pakistan A in December 1995, against England A. On the face of it, a pretty good all-round career.

As mentioned above, Naeem Akhtar's ten-for in 1995 came at the expense of just 28 runs. The most miserly ten-for on our list was, however, Hedley Verity's stunning 10-10 at Leeds in 1932. Verity's exploits were, evidently, worth a chapter of their own (see 'Verity').

But what of the most *expensive* ten-for in first-class cricket? Let me get to that by way of a story.

When England toured Down Under in 1982–83 my wife and I were invited to a cocktail party at the home of the British Consul General in the leafy Perth suburb of Claremont. Of course, the whole England party was in attendance, and all were obviously well-schooled in the ethics and general standards of behaviour as befitting their station on such an occasion.

We were standing with another couple, enjoying a glorious view of the Swan River and a glass of Swan Valley chablis, when a short, stocky, you could say untidy-looking, chap in a team blazer approached us. Before any of us could utter so much as a 'How do you do', the other lady (not my wife!) among the group said, 'Oh, hello, you must be the physio – or are you the baggage manager?' Another pause, this time a quite awkward pause. 'And hello to you, too, ma'am,' the stocky man said, 'actually I'm one of the players!'

That short, stocky figure belonged to **Edward Ernest 'Eddie' Hemmings (February 20, 1949 –)**. And that chunky physique was to precipitate an incident at the Brisbane Cricket Ground when a group of home fans smuggled into the ground a small pig – daubed on one flank with 'Eddie' and on the other, 'Botham' (referring to the outstanding all-rounder's equally impressive girth). The pig was released on to the playing area, much to the amusement of the crowd, though *not* the England party and their supporters.

Revenge can be sweet. In the fifth Test at the SCG of that 1982–83 Ashes tour Hemmings made 95 as a nightwatchman and took six wickets – efforts that helped England draw the match.

Hemmings, who peddled right-arm off-spinners after starting as a seam bowler, had been forced to wait until he was 33 before he was given a Test-match call-up – which came against Pakistan in 1982 when he took three wickets in the match. He was never able to nail down a spot in the Test team, however, what with his having to compete with the likes of Ray Illingworth, Tony Greig (temporarily in a spinner's guise), Geoff Miller, John Emburey and Vic Marks.

Hemmings did play 16 Tests – though it wasn't all cakes and ale for the burly tweaker. In the Lord's Test against India in 1990 he was hit for four successive sixes by Kapil Dev when India needed 24 to save the follow-on with the last man at the other end. Hemmings had a day out of his own at Kingston, Jamaica, however, in 1982 – claiming ten-for in a rain-marred match between an International XI and a West Indies XI. In doing so he conceded 175 runs, the most conceded by any player in achieving the rare feat, though I don't imagine that would have spoiled his delight. And why would it? His victims that day included batting greats like Gordon Greenidge, Desmond Haynes, Clive Lloyd and wicketkeeping all-rounder Jeff Dujon.

After helping Nottinghamshire to a Championship–NatWest Trophy double in 1987, he had a day out in the 1987 World Cup semifinal against India, his return of 4-52 (which included the wickets of Mohammad Azharuddin, Kapil Dev, Ravi Shastri and Chetan Sharma) playing a big role in England's win. He was, with figures of 2-48, the best of England's bowlers in the final against Australia at Eden Gardens in Kolkata, but Australia's 5-253 proved a tad too good as England finished their 50-over chase on 8-246.

In county games for Nottinghamshire, Hemmings made his only first-class century, 127 not out against Yorkshire in 1982. Before retiring from first-class cricket at 46, Hemmings suited up for a few seasons with Sussex.

Not a bad career for a man once mistaken for a baggage manager.

CHAPTER 22

A GOLDEN SUMMER

Western Australia were admitted to the Sheffield Shield competition in time for the 1947–48 season. Recognising the difficulty of taking the state's group of players from 'casual' competition to really serious stuff in the Shield, the WA Cricket Association went looking for someone to captain the team in its first campaign. They came up with Keith Carmody, a seasoned veteran from New South Wales.

Western Australia couldn't have made a better start. Nor could have Carmody, leading the side to the title in their first season – albeit with WA playing their rivals just once each, instead of twice. While Carmody continued to captain beyond that first season things got tougher, and these were mostly years of mediocrity for the WA side. However, during the Fifties and into the Sixties, several quality players made the trip to the West, some through recruitment and others simply seeking greater opportunities. Players like Ken Meuleman, Bob Simpson, Neil Hawke, Rohan Kanhai. Then, in time for the 1962–63 season, came the recruitment of Surrey and England spinner **Graham Anthony Richard 'Tony' Lock (5 July 1929 – 30 March 1995)**.

Lock signed up after he was left out of England's tour of Australia that same season despite his playing regularly in 1962. This move turned out to be an outstanding success for WA, as Lock – who'd play every season up to and including 1970–71 –

would go on to be a premier wicket-taker in the competition *and* lead WA to its second Sheffield Shield victory in 1967–68.

I have a particularly clear memory of Lock's arrival in Perth, mainly because he was farmed out to play for my club, Claremont-Cottesloe, whenever the first-class schedule permitted. I had captained Claremont-Cottesloe the previous season, but happily stood aside for the Test-playing champion. He arrived in WA on the eve of the first club game of the season and was brought straight to our ground to meet the players at a team gathering after training. It was a chance for us to get to know him and him to get to know us. I was introduced to him personally and he immediately took me to one side, out of hearing from the others.

The purpose was soon evident, when he made the following comment: 'Now Ian, you may call me Tony, but I want you to instruct the others to call me either Mr Lock or Sir ... definitely not Tony or Skipper.'

I knew how well this would go down, particularly with the more experienced among the troops, and when I duly informed them of this request, Ron Elliott, who had appointed himself as spokesman, said, 'Mr Lock be buggered. He'll be Locky to me!' The request came to rest then and there, and 'Locky' soon became accustomed to the Australian way.

It was in a lot of ways a privilege to play with a man of his stature, and one thing I do recall is just how big a man he was physically. For whatever reason, I had him pictured as being much smaller. I soon learned that he was a bit of a mixture as a person, drifting in and out of a Cockney accent and one with a bit of a plum in his mouth.

He did, however, possess a sense of humour, telling us, for instance, that his initials GAR stood for Great All Rounder. Great bowler and great close-in fielder, yes, but great batsman? Nah! He *could* bat, though, but only when the team needed him to hold up an end for an established batsman. And not when he occasionally offered his wicket to an opposition bowler, as part of a tit-for-tat arrangement to follow when he himself was bowling to the tail.

In fact, Locky made an art form of this ploy, in a day and age when not a lot was expected of nine, ten and jack in the batting order. His strategy was simple. Stick long-on and long-off out, bowl two or three quicker ones and then a floaty pie which, often enough, resulted in a wild slog – and there was another wicket to his name. I was fielding at mid-off in Perth one day when a tailie walked by, stopped and said to Locky, 'Well, Tony, you've got me with the slower one, the faster one, the one from behind the umpire … What's it going to be today?' The reply: 'I think I'll bounce you out.' Blow me down, Locky raised a half-tracker shoulder-high and the fellow was caught at square leg, attempting the hook shot.

Locky was an old man in the company of much younger WA players, and he did all he could to preserve his energy – and his body. He very rarely bowled in the nets and if he did it was for no more than one delivery which, of course, landed dead on the spot. He barely ever spun one on our hard wickets, but did all his damage with flight, angles and deadly accuracy. On match days he pulled bandages from his kit bag and thoroughly bound up both knees. Having said all of that, Lock was an extraordinary success for WA.

On one of our four-game eastern states tours I shared a motel room with him and it was there that I really got to know the man.

Given his age compared with mine, he was inclined to get plenty of bed rest, while the rest of us might go out for a feed. I would leave him lying on his bed in his pyjamas watching television and come back a couple of hours later, TV still going and him still lying on his bed in his pyjamas. The following morning he would be up before I was, and every morning without fail he would present me with a cup of tea in bed.

He and I often talked about cricket and I remember raising the subject of his action, it being well documented that early in his time in county cricket he had been no-balled for throwing. Locky didn't resile from talking about this phase in his long and celebrated career. He quite frankly told me that the problem had stemmed from his faster ball. He went on to say that he had generated the extra pace through what he called a 'double whirl' – in other words, rotating his bowling arm not once, but twice before releasing the ball. I later saw at first hand how this had worked for the Victorian speedster Alan 'Froggy' Thomson, whose frantic, whirling action earned him four Test appearances.

Locky admitted that he had been no-balled more than once and had been placed in a position where he had to take steps to change his action. 'It was all to do with a double whirl in my wind-up,' he said, 'and when I really let one fly there was nobody quicker than me.' As I said, Tony was a big, strong fellow.

This question over Lock's action occurred a long time ago – and in today's more relaxed times maybe it wouldn't even have caused the raising of any eyebrow – but more than once his career was punctuated by serious questions over the matter. Having made his first-class debut for Surrey in 1946 (a week after his seventeenth birthday), he looked to have the world at his feet. He was tall for a spin bowler, well built – and from an early stage a mop of red hair matched a burgeoning reputation as an aggressive, attacking tweaker who spun it sharply when conditions were at all favourable.

Playing for Surrey in the County Championship, his left-arm delivery style was a perfect foil for teammate Jim Laker's right-arm off-spin. However, as his promising career progressed, it was felt by those of influence that he would not really make it at the next level without being able to impart more spin on the ball. That set Lock to thinking. He embarked on an off-season technical change. The result was a lower trajectory that produced prodigious spin at something more akin to medium-pace.

It looked like a great idea, but there was a downside – an undercurrent about his action, and concern that the occasional delivery was outside the laws. This came to a head in 1952. Playing for Surrey at The Oval against the touring Indian team, he was no-balled three times. This was a massive setback just one week after Lock had made his Test debut. The young up-and-comer backed off immediately and went into the off-season trying to iron out the problem. The heart of it was his faster ball, which really menaced any batsman who was already battling to cope with Lock's spin and guile.

Countless hours were spent in the nets, restoring something of his original action, but Lock was again called for throwing in the West Indies in 1953–54. As a temporary measure he stopped using the faster ball, a delivery that once drew the legendary lament from Doug Insole, the Essex captain, to the square-leg umpire when he was bowled by Lock in fading light: 'I know I'm out – but bowled or run out?'

It was on a tour of New Zealand in 1958–59, where he took 13 Test wickets at less than nine apiece, that Lock actually *saw* himself bowling on film. He was genuinely shocked by the imperfection of his action and later said, 'Had I known I was throwing I wouldn't have bowled that way.' So it was back to the drawing board, and he remodelled his action once more.

Bear all of that in mind and consider the mindset of Norm O'Neill after he'd been mysteriously left out of the Australian team for the 1966–67 tour of South Africa. A very fine batsman, O'Neill was on a mission to prove the selectors wrong – and he took a particular toll on Lock, who returned the unflattering figures of 2-124 as the New South Welshman made his own arrangements with a century on his home turf.

Fast forward a month to the return game in Perth where O'Neill was once more in full flight. That is, until right out of the blue, his stumps were splayed all over the place. I was fielding at mid-off, amazed at the dismissal, which had come out of nowhere. In fact, I was just as surprised as Norm but rather enlightened when, as he passed me on the way back to the pavilion, he muttered, 'The bastard. He chucked it!' Enter the Locky double whirl; exit Norm O'Neill for a very well-made 78.

Of course, Lock was, on paper at least, the villain of sorts in the 1956 Ashes Test at Old Trafford, the match in which Jim Laker famously took 19 wickets. Locky's crime? Having the temerity to dismiss an Australian batsman! But the one wicket Laker didn't capture in that amazing game was that of opener Jim Burke, the third to fall in Australia's *first* innings. From the point of view of history being made, it would have been a tragedy of Shakespearian proportions had Locky's only wicket been the twentieth Aussie to fall.

The tall left-arm finger-spinner had played in the drawn first Test at Trent Bridge, taking a total of four wickets to Laker's six. He was omitted for the Lord's Test which, played on a pitch that favoured pace, the Australians won comfortably. The Headingley track was made for spin and the 'Two Ls' ran riot – Laker with 11 and Lock seven as England levelled the series.

This paved the way for another spin bowler's paradise at Old Trafford, after which the tourists found themselves 2-1 down with just one match remaining. With England already holding the Ashes, a win at The Oval would not have seen Australia wrestle back the old urn. In any case, the match was drawn and Australia, though exhausted, had some ways to go before returning home – heading off to Pakistan for a single Test and then India for three. Not surprisingly, Laker dominated the Ashes series bowling averages (taking a still-standing Ashes record 46 wickets at 9.60), while Lock was the second-most prolific wicket-taker for the home team with 15 wickets.

The 1956 season in England abounded with one outstanding performance after another by the homespun purveyors of finger spin. In one extraordinary summer Laker had become the first man to complete a ten-for in a Test match, he'd posted the yet-unequalled match total of 19 wickets in a Test match, *and* he'd become the only man to complete two ten-fors in the same season (the Australian bats  having fallen victim to his peerless guile when bowling for Surrey at The Oval ahead of the first Test).

You'd be excused for thinking that that amazing summer would be content with two ten-fors – but you'd be wrong. That man Tony Lock stole some of the limelight when playing for Surrey against Kent at Blackheath three weeks before the Old Trafford debacle. He bagged the lot for figures of 10-54 from 29.1

overs, having claimed 6-29 in Kent's first innings. Game figures of 16-83. Not bad!

Though standing in his teammate's shadow for most of that phenomenal summer, Lock actually took more first-class wickets than anyone else in 1956. His 155 wickets came at the outstanding average of 12.6. So, between them, the Surrey spin twins had done ten-for three times in one season. And Lock would be my captain in October 1967 when I surprisingly found myself going for a ten-for of my very own against Victoria at the WACA Ground.

CHAPTER 23
THE MODERNS

Two personal experiences – one in a Sheffield Shield game in Melbourne, the other a club game in Perth, both involving Tony Lock – served to underline to me how very difficult it must have been to be a batsman in the game's early days; days when uncovered wickets were the accepted norm, and bowlers of all types, though mainly finger-spinners, often had field days.

In the first instance, WA caught Victoria on a wicket at the MCG that was slightly soft on the surface. In other words, very difficult conditions for batting. The scoreboard showed the figures of 4-11 against my name when Tony Lock came up to me and said, 'That'll do for now, son,' and took the ball himself.

Playing for WA, Lock toiled almost all the time on hard wickets that offered him no opportunity to spin the ball. In fact, I recall one day our wicketkeeper Gordon Becker at the close of play back in the dressing-room saying with a grin to Tony, 'Mate, you *actually* spun one that session!' To which one of us called out, 'Must have hit a pebble.' Still, such was his mastery of flight and variation of pace that he was still one of the best bowlers in the whole competition year after year.

But we could tell from watching him in action that day in Melbourne that the old fella was rejuvenated. He was like a cat pouncing on a mouse – then toying with that mouse as a cat will do. He cleaned up the tail like I'm sure I never could have, and WA went on to win the game.

On the other occasion, I was actually playing *against* Tony in a club game at Midland Oval, where he was on another one-year secondment. Now it was *my* turn to try to make some sense of a wicket that was a little bit soft on the top. Locky was nigh-on unplayable. Bowling around the wicket, he could pitch the ball outside leg stump and threaten the middle and off. Only one of us, former New Zealand batsman Bill Playle, had the experience and technique to handle Lock's work. The rest of us were like lambs to the slaughter.

Looking back at so many of the accounts in these pages it's clear that many of the players in the ten-for club benefited from bowling on uncovered wickets – and some remarkable analysis bears that out. Since the move to fully cover pitches in England in the late 1960s, I'd suggest it has become so much more difficult for players to join the list, and that going forward there will be fewer and fewer players adding their names.

Since the turn of the Millennium, for instance, only eight bowlers have registered ten-fors. And the two most recent occurrences – by New Zealand spinner Ajaz Patel in a Test, and Haryana pace bowler Anshul Kamboj in a Ranji Trophy match (of whom more in a moment) – took place in India. This indicates to me that perhaps only on the Indian sub-continent, where pitches favourable to spin bowlers are a regular occurrence, will we see too many more players join the list.

If protected wickets make ten-for hauls less likely, perhaps too have developments in sports science. I'm thinking here about the biomechanists and physiotherapists who are convincing coaches that pace bowlers should not be overworked either in practice or in match situations. How times have changed in this regard! If you're not bowling, you're not taking wickets.

I can only hark back to the days when the great Dennis Lillee trained so thoroughly that he could push himself on match days to bowl as many as 25 eight-ball overs in one day. That's the equivalent of 33 six-ball overs. Nowadays pace bowlers are 'managed' to a total more in the vicinity of 18 to 20 in one day. Dennis worked a match-day output that would be completely unacceptable to the scientists today. But even after all that he could produce a wicket ball in the shadow of stumps. Ask Viv Richards.

But I digress. Let us salute, in chronological order, the eight players who have put their name on the ten-for list since the turn of the century.

For a very obvious reason (rarely favourable conditions), top-class Indian swing bowlers have been few and far between. The great Kapil Dev is an obvious exception – but his time was 40 years ago. In more recent years Zaheer Khan and RP Singh have admirably flown the flag for the craft.

But every now and then one pops up. **Debasis Sarbeswar Mohanty (20 July 1976 –)**, a gangly, right-arm medium-pacer, moved the ball significantly through the air, and off the wicket, when conditions suited. And he achieved something his highly rated predecessors did not. When playing for East Zone versus South Zone at Agartala in January 2001, he claimed 10-46 – his wickets including Indian cricketing royalty VVS Laxman and Rahul Dravid.

Mohanty played two Tests and 45 ODIs but in a sense Mohanty bucked the odds even to be chosen for national teams. He came up through India A ranks, and though his style wasn't universally suited to Indian conditions, he impressed coach Kris Srikkanth, who pushed for him to be given a chance. It was said of him that his bowling action promised more than the speed he was able to find. The truth of the matter is, perhaps only Kolkata and Mohali would produce the sort of wicket his type of bowling needed. In fact, on flat pitches elsewhere, he would sometimes conserve energy by bowling off-spin.

Mohanty took just two wickets across his two Tests but he rose to greater heights in ODIs where he took a total of 57 wickets at 29.15. At one stage he resided in the top 20 of the ICC world rankings for the format. At the 1999 World Cup he was the second-highest Indian wicket-taker, though he played four games fewer than the leader, Javagal Srinath (another of his victims in his ten-for haul, as it happens).

A very capable lower-order batsman, Mohanty loved to hit the ball out of the park. There was a brief period when No. 11 Mohanty, along with No. 10 Rahul Sanghvi, entertained crowds with monster sixes, though most often in losing causes.

There was a school of thought that the Indian selectors didn't quite know what to do with Mohanty's game, perhaps erring by not trying him in the more favourable English conditions. In latter times he has served as a national selector.

In the second half of the 20th century the fortunes of West Indies cricket at the Test match–level rested on a treasure trove of fast bowlers. Turn a corner and there'd be another quality quickie glittering in the sunshine.

The first iteration was Wesley Hall and Charlie Griffith, rampant in the Fifties and Sixties. Then came the battering ram of the following two decades comprising Andy Roberts, Michael Holding, Joel Garner and Colin Croft. And just when you thought it had to get better for the world's batters, along came Malcolm Marshall, Courtney Walsh, Curtly Ambrose and Ian Bishop.

Such was the depth of talent, a fringe West Indian pace bowler who would walk into almost any other country's Test team was often unable to win a regular berth for their own. In that category, I'm thinking Franklyn Stephenson, Wayne Daniel, Sylvester Clarke, Patrick Patterson and, a little later, **Ottis Delroy Gibson (16 March 1969 –)**. Gibson, like those mentioned above, was capable of producing genuine pace. Tall, powerfully built and, typically for a West Indian, very athletic, he managed only two Test appearances without distinction – one against England in 1995, the other against South Africa four years later.

It turned out that this journeyman of world cricket was pointed more in the direction of the one-day format, where his explosive batting in the middle order and his cunning with the ball in the closing overs made him a valued selection. Gibson played 15 one-day internationals, top-scoring with 52 against Australia and taking 5-42 against Sri Lanka. He claimed another five-wicket haul against the Sri Lankans and finished this facet of his career with an impressive bowling average of 18.26.

As a journeyman, Gibson parlayed his wares to any eager buyer the cricket world over. It was in his time with Durham, in 2007, that he claimed his ten-for, his figures of 10-47 coming against a Shane Warne–captained Hampshire at Chester-le-Street. This was a golden season for Gibson. He finished with a record number of wickets in any season for Durham, and was voted the player of the year for the whole County Championship.

Soon after, he began a storybook career in coaching. He coached the West Indies to victory in the 2012 T20 World Cup, he was a bowling coach for both Bangladesh and England at various times, he was head coach of South Africa from 2017 to 2019, he coached in the Indian Premier League, and most recently he was at the helm of Yorkshire.

When examining the circumstances of each of the 91 instances of ten-fors, you uncover many variations on the same theme. However, in the case of **Mario Wickus Olivier (3 November 1982 –)**, his 10-65 for the Warriors against the Eagles at Bloemfontein on 1 December 2007 made for novel reading.

For a start, five of the right-arm seamer's wickets were given out leg before wicket, a far-from-normal occurrence. Then, just when the 25-year-old had bagged the first eight wickets to fall in a tidy 12-over spell, his captain, Zander de Bruyn, took him out of the attack. Olivier and his team-mates sat on the razor's edge, hoping no other bowler would take a wicket.

The lunch break was taken and Olivier was philosophical. 'Zander knew I wanted to get the ten,' he said. 'He is the captain and I respect his decisions, but he did say this was my day and I would bowl again after lunch. It was probably not a nice thing to do, but I prayed that no-one else would take a wicket.'

On his return, the job was completed and the name Mario Olivier was added to the list – making him the third South African to achieve the feat, after Bert Vogler (1906–07) and Stephen Jefferies (1987–88).

Another distinctive feature of Olivier's ten-for is that despite his grand efforts with the ball in the first innings, the Eagles went on to win by ten wickets … meaning he actually took all the opposition's wickets to fall in the match. Of the experience, he said 'I can't describe my feelings, I'm on cloud nine.'

In cricket, as in many other sports and walks of life, progress doesn't always come easily. Sometimes it's a matter of patiently plugging away, hoping that sooner, rather than later, your talents will be recognised with selection for higher honours.

I'll give you two examples of just how patience can pay off if you keep knocking loudly enough on the door. First is batsman Michael Hussey, who had scored a whopping 15,313 first-class runs before he was given a Test call-up at the age of 28. Second is Chris Rogers, who also had a pile of runs to his credit before being chosen at 30 years old for one Test. And he then waited five more years before being offered another cap!

Both had done a long apprenticeship in state and county cricket. Both were finally rewarded for their personal patience and stickability. And, in due course, both repaid the selectors' ultimate confidence in the finished product.

Like Hussey and Rogers, Pakistani slow left-armer **Zulfiqar Babar (10 December 1978 –)** endured a long wait – more than ten years from his debut in first-class ranks in 2002 – before the national selectors listed his name for a Test appearance, against South Africa in a series in the United Arab Emirates

in 2013. By then he had already taken 309 first-class wickets at an average of 20.36. Talk about having to knock the door down!

Hailing from a small town near Lahore, Babar had to work extra hard to be noticed. It all began to come together for him in 2009–10, when he claimed 69 wickets at 16.42. And in December 2009 he joined the ten-for ranks (10-143) for Multan against Islamabad in Multan. He came into the attack first change, after Ansar Javed and Tahir Maqsood had first use of the ball. At the end of day two – his birthday, as it happened – he had five wickets to his name. He came out on day three and took the other five. His analysis – 39.4-3-143-10, the second-most expensive ten-for on the list – underlines the effort Babar laid down in becoming the fourth Pakistani to notch up the magical number.

Three seasons later he claimed headlines in Pakistan with 93 wickets in 13 first-class games at the pleasing average of 17.04. And in October 2013 Babar made an auspicious Test debut, claiming the wickets of South African bats JP Duminy, Faf du Plessis and Robin Peterson in the first innings and following up with two in the second innings, materially helping Pakistan win the match.

Again, another wait. Babar had made a successful move to T20 and on 27 July 2013, at 34 years and 229 days, he finally played his first international game in the format. He picked up three wickets and hit a six off the last delivery to win the game.

At the T20 World Cup in 2014 Babar stopped Australia in its tracks, claiming David Warner and Shane Watson in the first over – helping Pakistan win by 16 runs. In the end, patience did pay off for Babar, who reflected on the times when progress wasn't all he had hoped for. 'I always leave such matters in the hands of Allah,' he said. 'Perhaps it was my destiny to be playing for Pakistan at a time when people would be seriously considering other options in life.'

Sri Lankan cricket fans have had a number of bowlers over the years who are worth toasting, either with tea – preferably of the Ceylon variety – or what the locals call a toddy, an alcoholic drink made from the sap of the coconut flower. Chief among them, of course, is Muttiah Muralitharan.

The first – and to date, only – man to have reached 800 wickets in Tests, Murali, who began his first-class career in 1992, stands head and shoulders above his country's best bowling stocks. Looking down from the peak, however, there are many others worth celebrating, including some who have been half forgotten by the passing of time.

For instance, historians remind us of a left-armer named Tommy Kelaart who was highly regarded on the cricketing scene some 100 years before Murali began casting his spells. Kelaart stands out as a man who dismissed the legendary WG Grace for a duck in October 1891, when the England team had a stopover in Ceylon (now Sri Lanka) on their way to Australia for an Ashes series.

In January 2019, another bowler put his name up in lights when he became the second Sri Lankan bowler (after Pramodya Wickramasinghe) to take a ten-for. Playing for Colombo Cricket Club against Saracens at Moratuwa, **Pawuluge Malinda Pushpakumara (March 24, 1987 –)**, a slow left-armer relying on high degrees of accuracy, grabbed 10-37 in the second innings. This followed a six-wicket return from the first

innings, giving him match figures of 16-110. He took the new ball in the second innings and bowled unchanged for 18.4 overs. Included in that haul was his 700th first-class wicket.

It's worth noting that there might well have been *two* ten-fors in the same match. In Colombo's first innings, slow left-armer Chamikara Edirisinghe had 9-87 to his name when Ashen Bandara, very much a part-time bowler, spoiled the party by taking the last wicket.

Pushpakumara, meanwhile, found his way into all formats of the game, though his Test debut in 2017 was truly hard work. He was one of an attack that was flayed mercilessly by the Indians whose first innings ended on 619, before going on to win by an innings and 53 runs.

But there were good times, too, for Pushpakumara. In the 2019–20 SLC T20 Tournament (contested by 26 Sri Lankan domestic teams) he was the leading wicket-taker, with 18 wickets from nine matches.

Take a dive into the history of cricket in South Africa and mount a search for champion bowlers and you're likely to come up with a collection of quicks, the likes of Shaun Pollock, Allan Donald, Dale Steyn, Jacques Kallis and Fanie de Villiers. The name I would put forward is that of Donald, in his prime the most feared fast bowler in the world. He put the frighteners on batsmen from three angles: one, sustained blistering pace; two, devastating late movement through the air and off the wicket; and, three, withering competitive juices (reminiscent, for me, of the fire that burned in Dennis Lillee's belly).

But what about South African spin bowlers? I put up three. Ernie Vogler played his cricket early in the 20th century, converting from pace to wrist-spin with great success. Half a century later

Hugh Tayfield's right-arm orthodox spinners had him ranked among the world's best. Then there was Paul Adams – his action perhaps best described as a 'frog in a blender' – who enjoyed a very successful career.

As excellent as those mentioned were, only Vogler could match **Sean Andre Whitehead (7 March 1997 –)** in taking all ten wickets in an innings. The young left-arm orthodox bowler put his name on the list when taking 10-36 in November 2021 in a Division 2 match between South Western Districts and Easterns at Oudtshoorn – so becoming the fourth South African after Vogler, and pacemen Steve Jefferies and Mario Olivier, to achieve the feat.

Whitehead made his first-class debut for Free State in 2016–17. In September 2018, having represented South Africa at the Under-19 World Cup, he was drafted by Free State into their T20 program. He is a more than handy batsman, having scored two centuries among 868 first-class runs at an average of 37.73.

Skipping over the seventh member of the modern brigade – the aforementioned Ajaz Patel, whose ten-for came in a Test match for New Zealand against India in Mumbai in 2021 – brings us to the eighth and final (at the time of writing) 'moderns' candidate.

Plying his lively fast-mediums for Haryana against Kerala at Chaudhary Bansi Lal Cricket Stadium in Lahli in November 2024, **Anshul Kamboj (6 December 2000 –)** became just the sixth Indian to achieve a ten-for, and only the third player to bag the lot in the history of the Ranji Trophy.[38]

---

38 The other Indian ten-for bowlers were, to refresh your memory, Chatterjee, Sunderam, Subhash Gupte (1954–55), Anil Kumble (1998–99) and Debasis Mohanty. Chatterjee (1956–57) and Pradeep Sunderam (1985–86) were the other two bowlers whose ten-fors came in Ranji Trophy matches.

Kamboj claimed eight of his 10-49 on day two, taking only 30.1 overs to complete the job on day three – six caught, three bowled and one leg-before-wicket. It was a leap to prominence in Indian cricket, following a return of 8-69 earlier in the Duleep Trophy and a total of 16 wickets in five innings for India C.

He climbed up the ladder with a debut for the Mumbai Indians in the 2024 IPL season, picking up two wickets from three games played.

CHAPTER 24
10 FOR 44

continued

With the fall of John Grant's wicket Victoria were nine down, though just ten runs short of a first-innings lead. For my part, I had nine wickets to my name and you're going to have to believe me when I say I didn't care who took the tenth, as long as we did so before the Vics got those ten runs!

My WA teammate John Inverarity recalls the state of play as though it were yesterday. 'Ian's prospects for taking all ten were looking rather rosy, because in came Alan Connolly – who was a very good bowler but whose batting was of a very modest standard.'

'Al Pal' was, indeed, a fine bowler for Victoria and Australia over many years. He started as a really fast bowler, running in hard from a long run-up, but after suffering some back injuries he remodelled himself as a medium-fast with a basketful of variations and great accuracy. When you were facing him, especially on the rather questionable early-season MCG tracks, he was a real handful. Now everything rested both on his broad shoulders (but with bat, not ball, in hand) and those of the man down the other end, Bob Bitmead – a left-arm spinner who bowled off his wrong foot, actually releasing the ball off his left leg.

Ten-for:

Alan Connolly, caught Inverarity, bowled Brayshaw, 0
Victoria all out 152
Brayshaw 10-44

Like me, Inverarity was excited by the chance of WA getting first-innings points, particularly after a disappointing batting performance – Inverarity aside, it should be said. And he recalls he had a feeling he would play a part in what turned out to be a very special day for me.

'I remember being very excited at the prospect of my long-standing mate getting all ten wickets,' he says. 'I was fielding at second slip and I recall taking a further step forward and hoping that Connolly would be good enough to get an edge. I remember thinking, "If he nicks it, I will catch it." In fact, I had this intuitive feeling that it was going to come and that I would take it. Sure enough it came and I smothered the ball with both hands.'

The Victorian innings ended close enough to the afternoon tea interval that the break was taken forthwith. At that time, the premier ABC commentator in Perth was a fellow called Jim Fitzmaurice, a man with a nimble sense of humour whom we all loved. Well, Jim followed us into the dressing-room, and when we had settled down he said, 'Make sure you're listening to the radio when we go live on air shortly for a summary of the day's play so far.' Jim then took me with him to the broadcast position, situated at the back of the members' stand.

We both donned a pair of headphones and at the appropriate time the studio announcer said, 'We now cross to the WACA Ground and Jim Fitzmaurice, for a summary of the Sheffield

Shield match between Western Australia and Victoria.' The cross was made, and Jim's crisp voice took over. Straight to the point and with a wicked grin on his face just away to my right he began, 'Welcome to the WACA Ground, in particular to listeners in Victoria – with the news that the star-studded Victorian batting line-up, in their quest for the world innings record of one thousand, one hundred and seven runs, have fallen approximately one thousand runs short.'

I am told that the screams of laughter from the WA room would have been heard in the heart of the city, and most certainly would have penetrated the single brick wall that separated our dressing-room from that of the visitors, where the mood would have been very different from ours.

When I returned to the dressing-room, some strangers were present. One of them was Sir Donald Bradman, then a national selector. I was unsure what to do. I had met the great man. We all had. He made a practice of entering the visiting team's rooms at the Adelaide Oval, where the captain of the day would introduce all his players. Still, on this occasion, I hesitated. He solved the problem. He walked up, shook my hand and said quietly, 'Enjoy it, sonny … it won't last long.'

Those were prophetic words indeed. I took two second-innings wickets (one of them Bill Lawry's, this time bowled!), for a match total of 12. In the remaining seven games of the campaign, however, I managed only 12 more! I have reflected, not too often, on The Don's rather parsimonious comment – and wondered that he hadn't been a little more effusive. No 'well done', no smile, just 'Enjoy it'.

The other side of the coin came a day after the game, when I received a telegram from Peter Allan, who had taken his ten-for, also against Victoria, two seasons prior. The message read: 'Congratulations Ian stop Welcome to the club stop Thank God for the Vics stop.' Classic! No wonder Piccolo and I struck up a friendship that lasted beyond our playing days.

With first innings points in the bag, it was now over to our openers – Bill Playle and Ross Edwards – to do their bit and set up a chance for outright points. Bill had played eight Tests for New Zealand before coming to live in Perth, where he played for Claremont-Cottesloe with Graham McKenzie, Edwards, Laurie Mayne and myself. Oddly, Ross had begun his senior career as a wicketkeeper-batsman, but his 20 Tests, two centuries and an average of 40.38 proved that shedding the gloves had been a wise decision. Plus, he developed into a world-class cover fielder.

Bill and Ross only managed 10 and 11 runs respectively, but WA batted with more purpose in the second innings and, thanks to a 95 from Gordon Becker, 82 from Inverarity, and fine contributions from Murray Vernon and Jock Irvine, we set Victoria a target of 380.

When Victoria batted a second time, Tony Lock took five and we began what would turn out to be a successful campaign with outright victory – by 136 runs – over the reigning champions. As it turned out, the reverse clash, at the MCG late in the summer, was a virtual final. WA needed to win outright to snatch the crown … and we did just that! It was the state's first Shield win over a full schedule of games.

It was almost fitting that we would win the Shield with bookend outright wins over Victoria. There has been a rich history of West Australians sharing a feeling of disdain about Victorians. Historians suggest that this dates back to the Kalgoorlie gold rush, when hordes of Victorians came over to WA seeking their fortune – only to send their 'winnings' back home. This sense of dislike extended to the sports fields, and was reflected when Lock once put up a notice on the inside of our dressing-room door that read, 'AVAPs – All Vics Are Pricks'.

MATCH BETWEEN

WESTERN AUSTRALIA and VICTORIA

at W.A.C.A.

on 21-24 OCTOBER 1967.

1st. innings of VICTORIA

STUMPS 21/14/67 ~ 2/35 in. 59 ovs.

	Name	Runs as Scored	How Out	Bowler	Total
1	LAWRY. W.	111411>41113131217121112311√	c. BECKER	BRAYSHAW	47.
2	REDPATH. I.	1122430421√	Bowled	BRAYSHAW.	21
3	EASTWOOD. H.	1221√	c VERNON	BRAYSHAW	6
4	COWPER. R.	2111111√	Bowled	BRAYSHAW	7
5	POTTER. J.	√	BOWLED -	BRAYSHAW	0
6	STACKPOLE K	√	c IRVINE	BRAYSHAW	0
7	WATSON G.	24211111113114211√44√√	c INVERARITY.	BRAYSHAW	37
8	GRANT. F.	2442411111√	Bowled	BRAYSHAW	4
9	JORDAN R	113111√	c. BECKER	BRAYSHAW	9
10	BITMEAD. R.		NOT OUT		0
11	CONNOLLY. A.	√	c INVERARITY	BRAYSHAW w	0.
			Byes		
			Leg Byes 1		1
			Wides		
			No Balls		
				TOTAL	151

	1	2	3	4	5	6	7	8	9	10
Fall of Wickets	21-21	6-28	7-37	-0-37	-0-37	37-104	47-138	9-151	74-151	0-151
Batsman Out	REDPATH	EASTWOOD	COWPER	POTTER	STACKPOLE	WATSON	LAWRY.	JORDAN	GRANT	CONNOLLY
" Not Out	LAWRY. 1	LAWRY. 1	LAWRY.3	LAWRY. 3	LAWRY. 3	LAWRY. 32	GRANT. 20	BITMEAD 0	BITMEAD. 0	BITMEAD

50 Runs @ 11.55 ~ 84 min
100 " 1.17 " 161 "
150 " 2.53 " 207 "
151 " 3.17 " 221 "

ART PRINTING CO

This epithet stuck with that cohort of WA cricketers and manifested itself years later at a dinner party in Melbourne, when John Inverarity was sharing a table with Matthew Elliott, who had been a very good Victorian and Australian cricketer. Inverarity's son-in-law Scott chose a break in the conversation to raise the fact that one of his father-in-law's friends, Ian Brayshaw, had taken all ten in a first-class innings – which, he said, looking in John's direction, 'was a great effort'. To which John replied, 'Yes, but it was only against Victoria!'

TH AN AFTERNOON SEA BREEZE. MIN. 62DEG. MAX. 75DEG. (YESTERDAY, 57, 84.8)

West Australian

Telephone 21 0161; Phone-ads 21 0121.

PERTH, MONDAY, OCTOBER 23, 1967   44 PAGES 5c

Bowler's Day

ABOVE: West Australian fieldsman John Inverarity takes a diving catch to dismiss Victoria's last batsman in its first innings against W.A. at the W.A.C.A. Ground yesterday. The Victorian, Alan Connolly, was W.A. bowler Ian Brayshaw's tenth victim of the innings. Ross Edwards (W A) is

Brayshaw Ten For 44

By JACK LEE

Western Australia's Ian Brayshaw yesterday finished with ten Victorian wickets for 44 runs.

Brayshaw, a medium-pace right-hander, became the seventh Australian bowler to take ten wickets in an innings when Victoria was dismissed for 152 on a good wicket in the Sheffield Shield match at the

fieldsman John Inverarity and wicketkeeper Gordon Becker each took two spectacular catches sent down 17.6 overs, four of which were maidens.

He owed much of his success to the shrewd assessment by W.A. captain Tony Lock of the vagaries of a breeze that changed from easterly to south-westerly and to clever field-placings that restricted the bats-

1933. Wall sent down 12.4 overs, two of which were maidens and took his ten wickets at a cost of 36 runs. Queenslander Peter Allan equalled Wall's performance two years ago when he took ten wickets for 61 from 15.6 overs, three of which were maidens, against Victoria in Melbourne. Wall and Allan were on the losing side. Other Australians to perform the feat in first-class

CHAPTER 25

SPARE A THOUGHT

Before we go it seems only fair to remember, and commiserate with, the 'nearly' men and women, those who fell one wicket short of a ten-for. As you have read, there have been only 91 occasions when a ten-for was recorded in a first-class game. However, there have been many, many times when a bowler came up just one wicket short. In fact, at the time of writing, there had been 580 occasions where a nine-wicket haul had been posted.

Perhaps the most celebrated instance of nine-for was that recorded by England's Jim Laker in the first Australian innings of the fourth Test at Old Trafford in 1956. What makes it stand out was that Laker, of course, took all ten in the second innings. So coming up one short had been a very short-lived sense of disappointment for him. Spare a thought, though, for that long list of other trundlers who were very good, but not good (or lucky) enough, in a first-class match, to get that one additional wicket.

At the top of the 'almost-but-not-quite' ladder was Muttiah Muralitharan. Seventeen times a bowler has racked up a nine-for in Test cricket.[39] Two of these belong to Murali who retired from Test cricket in July 2010 having just become the first man to top 800 wickets at the supreme level. The jovial little wizard had done it all – well, apart from putting his name down on the ten-for list.

---

39 An eight-for, by contrast, is common. There have been 80 of them in Tests. Murali had three of those.

Murali is best described as a wrist-spinning off-spinner, whose unorthodox action was complemented by extraordinary sustained degrees of accuracy. I witnessed the man's stellar talents at first hand as coach when he came to play at Kent in 2003, during my time there. Testament to his control came the afternoon of his arrival in Canterbury. He went to the nets to roll his arm over and shake out the vestiges of his travel from Sri Lanka. After warming up, he placed a ball at his chosen line and length, bowled from his normal run-up ... and hit that ball three times in a row. He then left the nets feeling that, now, he had his range-finder fully fine-tuned.

There were many times during a sparkling six-week stay with the county when Murali completely bamboozled a class batsman. And that was before he had polished his new delivery – which he called the *doosra* – to the degree that he was ready to unveil it in competition. It was a batsman's nightmare: a biting leg-spinner, to a right-hand batsman, that looked for all the world like his standard off-spinner.

Let us now transport ourselves to Kandy in Sri Lanka on 4 January 2002. There's a Test match taking place, Sri Lanka versus Zimbabwe. The visitors have lost nine wickets, all of them taken by Murali. Now picture this situation, as described by Charlie Austin for ESPNcricinfo. 'Events on the field were dominated by Murali's failure to capture the last wicket in the morning,' Austin wrote. 'Hampered by torn ligaments in his ring finger, dislocated the night before, he would have surpassed fellow off-spinner Jim Laker's 10-53 against Australia in 1956 if Russel Arnold had not fumbled a simple bat-pad catch off the first ball of the day.

'Then, with the fifth ball, Murali spun an off-break sharply back into the pads of Travis Friend – only to see umpire [Srinivasaraghavan] Venkataraghavan rule in the batsman's favour. Next over Chaminda Vaas ran in and went through the motions, bowling gentle medium-pace at No. 11 Henry Olonga. But the dreadlocked tailender couldn't resist a swipe at the left-armer's last ball, and was caught behind by Kumar Sangakkara. There was a stifled appeal and a moment of silence – while the Sri Lankan players wondered whether they could just ignore the final wicket's fall – before umpire Asoka de Silva was forced to raise his finger.'

So, greatness was denied. And, as it turned out, not only once! The Sri Lankan genius had earlier been thwarted in a one-off Test against England at The Oval in August 1998. On that occasion he rolled out 54.2 overs for figures of 9-65 in England's second innings. This time, however, the *other* wicket was the fourth to fall, when Alec Stewart was run out. Murali had twice failed to enter a stratospheric galaxy.

Another who knocked on the same door was New Zealand pace bowler Richard Hadlee (now Sir Richard). The outstanding swing-and-seam merchant at one stage held the record for the most wickets in Tests, retiring at age 39 with 431 scalps at the miserly average of 22.29. For more than a decade he was the rock on which New Zealand's cricket fortunes were built.

Picture, then, his personal dilemma when, at the Brisbane Cricket Ground in 1985, a skied shot off the bat of Geoff Lawson came towards him at midwicket. Why was that play anything out of the ordinary? Well, it was to be the ninth Australian wicket to fall – and at that stage Hadlee had the first eight in his bag. Of course, Hadlee accepted the catch and the wicket went to off-spinner Vaughan Brown. This was the first of Brown's two Tests and his only wicket. Hadlee then knocked over Bob Holland for figures of 9-52. For Hadlee, the team always came first.

As impressive (and no doubt frustrating for the central protagonists) as those three nine-for examples are, the title of 'The Most Comprehensive Nine-for' in first-class cricket must surely go to a Victorian named Gideon Elliott, who peeled off 9-2 in a game for his state against Tasmania at Launceston back in February 1858. Elliott bowled 19 overs, including 17 maidens. But for Tom Wills – who clean bowled Tasmania's No. 3, Charles Evans – Elliott may well have found himself atop the ten-for list.

We acknowledged earlier the fact that among the 84 individuals who've taken first-class ten-fors, six members achieved the feat more than once – one of them, Tich Freeman, even managing a third instance. Now let us cast our eyes over the nine-for list, brushing it up against its ten-for counterpart. Each one of those six players features at least once in the nine-for bracket. In total there are 32 players from the ten-for list also on the nine-for list, some making a real meal of the achievement.

Three English bowlers each piled up an almost unbelievable roll of eight nine-for innings. For Tom Goddard and Charlie Parker this was on top of their all-ten innings. Not so for Jack Hearne, who produced his eight nine-fors without adding a single ten! Rated as a truly great bowler of his type, Hearne sent them down at medium-fast from a long run-up and a classic full-on action. He gained movement off even the most docile of wickets – plus swing if it was about. His high delivery release point also produced awkward bounce.

Hearne was a prodigious wicket-taker. In 1896, one noted as a consistently dry season that was generally unhelpful to bowlers, he produced his very best: a total of 257 wickets, including an amazing 56 at just over 13 apiece against the touring Australians. In five seasons he headed the first-class bowling averages and appeared in 12 Tests between 1892 and 1899, claiming 49 wickets at 22.08. In all first-class matches he had 3061 wickets at 17.75.

Other repeat offenders from the list were Frank Tarrant and Hedley Verity, each with seven nine-fors, and Kent's Tich Freeman and Colin Blythe with five. Also with five nine-fors to his name is, perhaps not surprisingly, William Lillywhite, the person who got our ten-for list off and running with his complete haul in 1837.

AFTERWORD

The scene was the WA dressing-room at the WACA Ground in January 1977. The end of day two against South Australia – and we had taken a firm grip on the game, having scored 340 and bowled our opponents out for 125. There were smiles all around the space, a warm, satisfied hush after two good days' work.

The sense of silent reverie came to an abrupt end. Rodney Marsh, our captain, with a wicked look on his face that we all knew so well, called the group to order. 'Don't know about you guys,' he said, 'but I'm seriously thinking about giving the game up … there's just not enough laughs!' No shortage of laughter followed hotly on the skipper's words.

Fact is, playing for WA in the Seventies *was* fun – and not just because we had so much success, winning five Sheffield Shield titles and four one-day competitions. We just loved the whole package of pulling on a black and gold cap and giving it our best shot, both individually and as a team.

Making everything easier during that marvellous decade was the presence of two men who stood tall for their nation, but willingly gave all for their state: Rod Marsh and Dennis Lillee. They were drivers of the team dynamic, adding significantly to what they brought to the table as players. They made the dressing-room hum – Rod with his wisecracks and Dennis with his practical jokes.

Of course, as players the rest of us were raised to another level whenever they were available to play, fitting in as many club games as their busy schedules would permit. I can well recall standing in the slips cordon at the Gabba on 31 October, 1969, when a young Dennis Lillee stormed in to fire down his first delivery for WA in a first-class game. If the batsman Sam Trimble's eyes were popping out, so were ours. The 20-year-old carried his follow-through down to within a couple of metres of the Queenslander and then offered up what was to become the trademark 'Lillee glare'.

Let me say, with those two around there was a guarantee of a lot of laughs, win, lose or draw. And we didn't lose too many!

By the time we had reached the mid-Seventies Rod and Dennis were very much part of the leadership team of which I was also a part. However, astride that vital cohort stood our captain, John Inverarity. With a firm yet pliant hand he guided and cajoled the group to be its best. He was a master tactician – with an amazing memory for the strengths and weaknesses of our opponents. We were always well prepared. No surprise John went on to the lofty position of chairman of national selectors and more's the pity he wasn't appointed Australian captain during the disruptive World Series Cricket years. His nurturing skills would have made him a natural for what was a difficult role.

I felt blessed to be a part of it: to be a senior player and occasional captain. To have the ear of two wonderful selectors in Allan Edwards and Laurie Sawle, who were on the constant lookout for opportunities to make a contribution to the team's performance. WA was the first state to appoint a '13th man' – Daryl Foster, who began as the squad coordinator and later became the coach. He saw to it that we were fit and ready for every game. Not to be overlooked, our wives and girlfriends played a huge part too. They not only got on well with each other, which helped when we were away on tour, but they also saw to it that there was a happy degree of socialising between us all.

All these puzzle pieces fitted into place created an environment in which team and individual success was fostered and nurtured. I loved every moment. So much so that when, in 1978, the time felt right to call it quits on my playing days, there wasn't a single regret.

Did I ever fret about not being given the Baggy Green cap? Not once. World Series Cricket floated onto the scene, but I wasn't their sort of player. Instead that arrival played into the hands of teammates Tony Mann, Wayne Clark and Craig Serjeant, who did wear the Australian colours, and I'm delighted they did.

It was a heady way to end my playing association with cricket at first-class level. I had just turned 36 and my team had just won both the Sheffield Shield and Gillette Cup competitions for the second year in a row. What, then, to do with my time in cricket from that moment on? I had no idea. Then came a fateful phone call from George Grljusich, head of the ABC's Perth sports department. Would I be interested in trying my hand as a radio broadcaster?

It would be a part-time engagement, still leaving me free to pursue my career as a print journalist. Sounded like a pretty good thing to me. A soft landing after all those years in harness. Almost too good to be true. 'I'd love to, George,' I replied. So began a decade of covering state and international cricket, which took me all around Australia again and again – and had me rubbing shoulders in the commentary box with the likes of Lindsay Hassett, Keith Miller (my childhood hero), Christopher Martin-Jenkins and Henry Blofeld.

Just as I had highlights on the pitch – one of which I've outlined in great detail in these pages, of course – so there were highlights from my days as a broadcaster and journalist. The latter, for instance, included filing daily reports for the *London Times* on a Pakistan tour to Australia. What an honour! The former saw me contribute to the coverage of the 1980 Centenary Test at Lord's – a Test in which my former WA teammate Kim Hughes adorned each of the five days with some of the most glorious strokeplay imaginable. Scores of 117 and 84 tell only part of the story. I picture him running down the wicket to Chris Old (no, not a spin bowler!), going down on one knee and flaying him to the cover-point boundary. He later put an Old delivery on to the roof of the Pavilion. I felt privileged to bear witness. Just as I was to see Lillee skittle the stumps of the great Viv Richards at the MCG in the dying moments of Boxing Day 1981.

Could it be called luck to have found myself sitting there in the ABC box at the MCG on 1 February 1981, for the third one-day international final between Australia and New Zealand? Going into the last over, to be bowled by Trevor Chappell, New Zealand needed 15 runs to win. By the time it got down to the final ball, the target was seven to win, six to tie – an unlikely, though not impossible, outcome. Brian McKechnie came out. I saw captain Greg Chappell approach his brother, who then approached the umpire … at which point I uttered these words: 'I think he's going to bowl under-arm!' Which he did. So, Australia won the game and the series, but it left a bitter taste in the mouth. To bowl under-arm was within the Laws – indeed it was once the only way to bowl, as explored earlier in this book – but in 1981 it was well outside the spirit of the game.

Since retiring from broadcasting and journalism, I've enjoyed living vicariously through the sporting endeavours of, first, two of my sons: Mark, who played AFL football for North Melbourne, and James, a very successful cricketer for WA and South Australia. I've then been able to appreciate the AFL careers of three grandsons, Angus, Hamish and Andrew, all sons of Mark and his wife, Debra.

With all this going on how often, you might wonder, does this 83-year-old turn his mind back to his playing days or, to be more specific, those incredible couple of days at the WACA back in October 1967? The answer is 'rarely'. We had a 'Seventies' reunion last year, when we did recall the thrill of winning the Sheffield Shield five times and the one-day competition three times. They were golden years for WA cricket, well worth remembering within the cohort.

At the time, of course, it was magic! We particularly remember the trip home from Melbourne after defeating Victoria to snatch the Shield from their grasp. I don't know why, but our flight had a one-hour break in Adelaide – when Eileen Hardy, a close friend of Tony Mann's father, legendary wine man Jack, had hastily set up a room at the airport and made some of her best vintages available. And some 5000 people were at Perth airport for our arrival, which was played live on local television. That *was* heady stuff.

Now, though, it takes a lot to get me dusting off the memories. With mates our age, conversation is more likely to be about our grandchildren, and our aching bones. I am sure we would all say how, privately, we remain very proud of the part we played in taking WA cricket from the 'easy beats' to a force to be reckoned with.

Ian Brayshaw's 1967 trophy

TEN WICKETS IN AN INNINGS
IN FIRST-CLASS CRICKET

Compiled by Steven Lynch

William Lillywhite: 10-?*^, Players v Gentlemen, Lord's, 1837
An early adopter of round-arm bowling and a fixture in the MCC team. Took 1576 wickets in first-class games at 1.54 apiece.

Edmund Hinkly: 10-?*, Kent v England, Lord's, 1848
A left-handed round-arm bowler with 189 first-class wickets at 7.13 apiece.

John Wisden: 10-?*, North v South, Lord's, 1850
All ten victims were bowled, which remains unique in first-class cricket. Later founded the famous *Wisden Cricketers' Almanack*. Took 1109 first-class wickets at 10.32 each.

John Wisden: 10-58^, All England Eleven v Yorkshire, Sheffield, 1851
A second ten-for, this one for the professional touring side 'All England'. Yorkshire had 14 players.

Vyell 'Edward' Walker: 10-74, England v Surrey, The Oval, 1859
Also scored 108 in the second innings. Made 3384 runs at 17.26 and took 334 wickets at 14.45 apiece.

EM Grace: 10-69^, Gentlemen of MCC v Gentlemen of Kent, Canterbury, 1862
Brother of the legendary WG Grace; also carried his bat for 192. Although the opposition had 12 players, only 11 batted in the second innings, so took all ten wickets to fall. Played one Test match. In all first-class games scored 10,025 runs at 18.66 and took 305 wickets at 20.37 each.

George Tarrant: 10-40^, England v Kent, Lord's, 1863
A round-arm bowler from Cambridge. Achieved the feat against a 13-man team. Took 421 wickets at 11.60 in first-class games.

George Wootton: 10-54, All England Eleven v Yorkshire, Sheffield, 1865
A round-arm pace bowler – and a butcher – from Nottinghamshire. Took just one wicket in the first innings, and 983 wickets at 13.00 in first-class cricket.

Vyell 'Edward' Walker: 10-104, Middlesex v Lancashire, Manchester, 1865
Second ten-for – not including another taken in a non first-class match for the Gentlemen of Middlesex in 1864.

William Hickton: 10-46, Lancashire v Hampshire, Manchester, 1870
Another round-arm pace bowler. Like George Wootton, became a butcher. Took 284 wickets at 14.15 in first-class games.

Samuel Butler: 10-38, Oxford University v Cambridge University, Lord's, 1871
The only instance in the long-running varsity match. A round-arm seamer; never played county cricket. Took 116 wickets at 12.33 in first-class games.

James Lillywhite: 10-129, South v North, Canterbury, 1872

Sent down 60.2 four-ball overs, but the North still won by an innings. In 1877, captained England in the first-ever Test match. Took eight wickets at 15.75; in all first-class games captured 1210 at 15.23.

WG Grace: 10-92^, Gentlemen of MCC v Kent, Canterbury, 1873

Both teams had 12 players. Better known as the father of modern batting. Also a considerable bowler.

Alfred Shaw: 10-73, MCC v North, Lord's, 1874

Three years after this ten-for, the Nottinghamshire medium-pacer took the first wicket in the first-ever Test match. Claimed 12 wickets at 23.75. In all first-class matches had 2027 at 12.12.

Edward Barratt: 10-43, Players v Australians, The Oval, 1878

A left-arm spinner for Surrey. In all first-class matches Barratt took 790 wickets at 17.54 apiece.

George Giffen: 10-66, Australian XI v Combined XI, Sydney, 1884

The first instance outside England. Seven victims would play Tests for Australia. Played 31 Tests and made 1238 runs at 23.35 and took 103 wickets at 27.09. In all first-class games scored 11,517 runs at 29.61 and took 1022 wickets at 21.31 each.

WG Grace: 10-49, MCC v Oxford University, Oxford, 1886

Earlier made 104, then bowled the students out for 90 to seal an innings win. Played 22 Tests and scored 1098 runs at 32.29, also taking nine wickets. In all first-class games scored 54,211 runs at 39.45 and claimed 2809 wickets at 18.14.

George Burton: 10-59, Middlesex v Surrey, The Oval, 1888

A bearded slow bowler who did not play a first-class match until 30 (in 1881). Took 608 wickets at 17.18 apiece in first-class games.

Albert Moss: 10-28, Canterbury v Wellington, Christchurch, 1889

Taken on his first-class debut, still the only instance in New Zealand. Played four first-class games, taking 26 wickets at 10.96 each.

Sammy Woods: 10-69, Cambridge University v CI Thornton's XI, Cambridge, 1890

Played Test cricket for both England and his native Australia – and rugby for England. Played six Tests for ten wickets at 25. In all first-class games scored 15,499 runs and had 1040 wickets at 20.81.

Tom Richardson: 10-45, Surrey v Essex, The Oval, 1894

A lion-hearted fast bowler. Took 1944 wickets in England in the 11 seasons from 1893 to 1903. Played 14 Tests and claimed 88 wickets at 25.22. In all first-class games took 2104 at 18.43 apiece.

Harry Pickett: 10-32, Essex v Leicestershire, Leyton, 1895

A stocky medium-pacer. Took the first ten-for in the English County Championship, which began officially in 1890. Claimed 134 wickets at 24.39 in first-class cricket.

Ted Tyler: 10-49, Somerset v Surrey, Taunton, 1895

A tall, flighty slow left-armer with a peculiar action. Played lone Test in South Africa the following winter. In all first-class games took 895 wickets at 22.09 apiece.

Bill Howell: 10-28, Australians v Surrey, The Oval, 1899
Sydney medium-pacer. Started maiden first-class match in England by demolishing Surrey for 77. Played 18 Tests and claimed 49 wickets at 28.71. In all first-class games took 519 wickets at 21.49.

Cyril Bland: 10-48, Sussex v Kent, Tonbridge, 1899
A quick bowler from Lincolnshire. Took 553 wickets in eight seasons for Sussex. Claimed 557 wickets at 24.28 in first-class games.

Johnny Briggs: 10-55, Lancashire v Worcestershire, Manchester, 1900
Slow left-armer and the first to take 100 Test wickets. In final season when taking ten-for. Played 33 Tests and took 118 wickets at 17.75. In all first-class games had 2221 wickets at 15.95.

Albert Trott: 10-42, Middlesex v Somerset, Taunton, 1900
Played Tests for England and Australia, and remains the only man to hit a ball over the pavilion at Lord's. Played five Tests for 26 wickets at 15. In all first-class matches returned 1674 wickets at 21.09.

Fitz Hinds: 10-36^, A. B. St Hill's XI v Trinidad, Port-of-Spain, 1901
Both sides had 12 players. Opened the bowling, hailed from Barbados. Played 12 first-class games, taking 29 wickets at 15.

Arthur Fielder: 10-90, Players v Gentlemen, Lord's, 1906
The Gentlemen (amateurs) v Players (professionals) match was a highlight of the English summer. Played six Tests for 26 wickets at 27.34. In all first-class games captured 1277 wickets at 21.02.

George Dennett: 10-40, Gloucestershire v Essex, Bristol, 1906
Slow left-armer. Finished with more than 2000 wickets and took ten in a match 57 times. Took 2151 wickets at 19.82 each.

Ernie Vogler: 10-26, Eastern Province v Griqualand West, Johannesburg, 1906

The first instance in South Africa. A leg-spinner, took 6-12 in the first innings and also scored 79. Played 15 Tests and claimed 64 wickets at 22.73. In all first-class games took 393 wickets at 18.27.

Colin Blythe: 10-30, Kent v Northamptonshire, Northampton, 1907

Slow left-armer. Took 7-18 in the second innings, the same day. Played 19 Tests for 100 wickets at 18.6. In all first-class games took 2503 wickets at 16.8 apiece.

Bart King: 10-53, Gentlemen of Philadelphia v Gentlemen of Ireland, Haverford, 1909

A brisk swing bowler from Pennsylvania. Rated among the best in the world around this time. Took 415 first-class wickets at 15.66 each.

Alonzo Drake: 10-35, Yorkshire v Somerset, Weston-super-Mare, 1914

Left-armer; played only one more first-class match. Died of ill-health in 1919, aged 34. Took 480 wickets at 18.03 in first-class games.

Frank Tarrant: 10-90, Maharaja of Cooch-Behar's XI v Lord Willingdon's XI, Poona, 1918–19

Followed up with a 182 not out. A superb all-rounder from Melbourne. Missed out on Test cricket plying trade in England and India. In first-class games scored 17,952 runs at 36.41 and took 1512 wickets at 17.49.

Billy Bestwick: 10-40, Derbyshire v Glamorgan, Cardiff, 1921

At 46 years 116 days, remains the oldest man to take ten-for in a first-class innings. Took 1457 wickets at 21.28 apiece.

Jack White: 10-76, Somerset v Worcestershire, Worcester, 1921

Slow left-armer. Completed the feat on the same day as Billy Bestwick (20 June). Played 15 Tests and took 49 wickets at 32.3. In all first-class games claimed 2355 wickets at 18.6.

Tom Rushby: 10-43, Surrey v Somerset, Taunton, 1921

A 40-year-old seamer playing last season and the 222nd of 229 first-class matches. Took 954 first-class wickets at the average of 20.58.

Charlie Parker: 10-79, Gloucestershire v Somerset, Bristol, 1921

Left-arm spinner. Piled up more than 3000 wickets – but played only Test a week before this feat. Took 3278 first-class wickets at 19.46, just two of them in Tests.

Arthur Mailey: 10-66, Australians v Gloucestershire, Cheltenham, 1921

Whimsical leg-spinner from Sydney. Called 1958 autobiography *10 for 66 and All That*. Played 21 Tests and took 99 wickets at 33.91. In all first-class games had 779 dismissals at 24.09.

George Collins: 10-65, Kent v Nottinghamshire, Dover, 1922

A Gravesend-born seamer. Took 6-18 in the first innings, then ten-for in the follow-on. Claimed 379 wickets at 23.91 in first-class games.

Harry Howell: 10-51, Warwickshire v Yorkshire, Birmingham, 1923

A local paceman. Bowled out that season's eventual county champions for 113. Took seven wickets in Tests, and a total of 975 at 21.23 in all first-class games.

Alex Kennedy: 10-37, Players v Gentlemen, The Oval, 1927

Scotsman who won five England caps. Took over 2500 wickets for Hampshire. Played five Tests taking 31 wickets at 28.74. In all first-class games scored 16,586 runs at 18.53 and took 2874 wickets at 21.23.

Gubby Allen: 10-40, Middlesex v Lancashire, Lord's, 1929

Fast bowler with a famously smooth action. Bowled eight of his victims, and later captained England. Played 25 Tests for 750 runs at 24.19 and 81 wickets at 29.37. In all first-class games scored 9233 runs at 28.67 and claimed 788 wickets at 22.23.

Tich Freeman: 10-131, Kent v Lancashire, Maidstone, 1929

A leg-spinner who finished with 3776 wickets – a season-record 304 of them in 1928. Was 41 years old here when taking the first of three ten-fors.

George Geary: 10-18, Leicestershire v Glamorgan, Pontypridd, 1929

Glamorgan needed only 84 to win – but skittled for 68. Took 46 wickets at 29.41 in Tests. In all first-class games captured 2063 wickets at 20.03.

Clarrie Grimmett: 10-37, Australians v Yorkshire, Sheffield, 1930

Canny leg-spinner. Ten-for haul included six Test players (another, Wilfred Rhodes, remained not out). Played 37 Tests and took 216 wickets at 24.21. In all first-class games claimed 1424 wickets at 22.28.

Tich Freeman: 10-53, Kent v Essex, Southend-on-Sea, 1930

Second ten-for. Added 6-41 in the second innings setting up a thumping 277-run win.

Hedley Verity: 10-36, Yorkshire v Warwickshire, Leeds, 1931

In his second season after succeeding the legendary Wilfred Rhodes as Yorkshire's slow left-armer. Played 40 Tests, scoring 669 runs at 20.90 and taking 144 wickets at 24.37. In all first-class games scored 5603 runs at 16.07 and captured 1956 wickets at 14.90.

Tich Freeman: 10-79, Kent v Lancashire, Manchester, 1931

By now 43, became the first – and still only – bowler to take all ten three times in first-class matches.

Vallance Jupp: 10-127, Northamptonshire v Kent, Tunbridge Wells, 1932

Was 41 at the time, and well on the way to completing the 1000-run/100-wicket seasonal double for the ninth time. Played eight Tests, taking 28 wickets at 22.00. In all first-class matches had 703 wickets at 24.73.

Hedley Verity: 10-10, Yorkshire v Nottinghamshire, Leeds, 1932

The best figures in all first-class cricket. A whole book was devoted to this feat in 2014.

Tim Wall: 10-36, South Australia v New South Wales, Sydney, 1933

NSW's 113 included 56 from Don Bradman and 43 from Jack Fingleton; the others made seven runs between them. Played 18 Tests and took 56 wickets at 35.89. In all first-class games claimed 330 wickets at 29.93.

Tommy Mitchell: 10-64, Derbyshire v Leicestershire, Leicester, 1935

A bespectacled leg-spinner, and something of a spare part on the 1932–33 Bodyline tour. Played five Tests and took eight wickets. In all first-class games claimed 1483 wickets at 20.59.

Jack Mercer: 10-51, Glamorgan v Worcestershire, Worcester, 1936

A seamer and a member of the magicians' Magic Circle. Tricks were too much on this day. Took 1591 wickets at 23.40 in first-class games.

Tom Goddard: 10-113, Gloucestershire v Worcestershire, Cheltenham, 1937
An off-spinner with huge hands. Played on past the age of 50 and
took almost 3000 wickets. Claimed 22 wickets at 26.72 in Tests.
Overall first-class tally was 2979 at 19.84.

Frank Smailes: 10-47, Yorkshire v Derbyshire, Sheffield, 1939
Mixing seamers with off-breaks, skittled Derby for 97 – an
improvement on their first innings of 20. Played one Test. In all
first-class games scored 5892 runs at 19.25 with three centuries,
while also taking 822 wickets at 20.81.

Eddie Watts: 10-67, Surrey v Warwickshire, Birmingham, 1939
A sturdy seamer. Often opened Surrey's bowling with brother-in-
law Alf Gover, later a famous coach. Scored 6158 runs at 21.38, with
two centuries, and took 729 wickets at 26.06 apiece.

Eric Hollies: 10-49, Warwickshire v Nottinghamshire, Birmingham, 1946
Leg-spinner. Did not require any assistance: seven victims bowled
and three lbw. Played 13 Tests and took 44 wickets at 30.27. In all
first-class games had 2323 dismissals at 20.94.

Jim Sims: 10-90, East v West, Kingston-upon-Thames, 1948
Took all ten at a September festival to round off a season dominated
by Don Bradman's 'Invincibles'. Leg-spinner. Played four Test
matches; in all first-class games took 1581 wickets at 24.92.

Ken Graveney: 10-66, Gloucestershire v Derbyshire, Chesterfield, 1949
A modest seamer and older brother of Tom Graveney, who would
play 79 Tests for England. Took 173 wickets at 27.85 in first-class
games.

Trevor Bailey: 10-90, Essex v Lancashire at Clacton-on-Sea, 1949

Despite the efforts of 'Barnacle' Bailey, an England regular throughout the 1950s, Lancashire still made 331. Played 61 Tests and scored 2290 runs at 29.74, also taking 132 wickets at 29.21. In all first-class games scored 28,641 runs at 33.42 and took 2082 wickets at 23.13.

Bob Berry: 10-102, Lancashire v Worcestershire, Blackpool, 1953

A slow left-armer; the first to be capped by three different English counties. Played two Tests and in all first-class games took 703 wickets at 24.73.

Subhash Gupte: 10-78, Bombay v Pakistan, Combined Services & Bahawalpur XI, Bombay, 1954

Rated the best leg-spinner of all by many: 'Better than Shane Warne,' thought Garry Sobers. Played 36 Tests and took 149 wickets at 29.55, taking in all first-class games 530 wickets at 23.71.

Jim Laker: 10-88, Surrey v Australia, The Oval, 1956

Off-spinner. Warmed up for Ashes heroics by demolishing the Aussies early on their 1956 tour. Played 46 Tests and took 193 wickets at 21.24 each. In all first-class games captured 1944 wickets at 18.41.

Ken Smales: 10-66, Nottinghamshire v Gloucestershire, Stroud, 1956

Yorkshire-born off-spinner, later became secretary of Nottingham Forest Football Club. Played 161 first-class games for a total of 389 wickets at 30.70.

Tony Lock: 10-54, Surrey v Kent, Blackheath, 1956

Fiery slow left-armer. Became the second Surrey bowler of the season to take all ten. Played 49 Tests and took 174 wickets at 25.58. In all first-class games captured 2844 wickets at 19.23. For WA, took 316 wickets at a cost of 22.51 runs apiece.

Jim Laker: 10-53, England v Australia, Manchester, 1956

Second first-class ten-for and the first all-ten in a Test – contributing to the best first-class match figures, having taken 9-37 in the first innings.

Premangsu Chatterjee: 10-20, Bengal v Assam, Jorhat, 1957

First instance in India's Ranji Trophy. Left-arm seamer, took 134 wickets at 17.75 in first-class games.

Jack Bannister: 10-41, Warwickshire v Combined Services, Birmingham, 1959

Later became a TV commentator. Services team included several players with first-class experience. In first-class games took 1198 wickets at 21.91.

Tony Pearson: 10-78, Cambridge University v Leicestershire, Loughborough, 1961

Student who also played for Somerset. Backed up by three catches from the young Mike Brearley. Took 139 wickets at 28.18 in first-class games.

Ian Thomson: 10-49, Sussex v Warwickshire, Worthing, 1964

This feat on his home club ground helped win selection for England's tour of South Africa, aged 35. Played five Tests. In all first-class games claimed 1597 wickets at 20.58.

Peter Allan: 10-61, Queensland v Victoria, Melbourne, 1966

Feat came after being dropped from Australia's Test side for the home series against England. Played one Test. In all first-class games took 206 wickets at 26.10.

Ian Brayshaw: 10-44, Western Australia v Victoria, Perth, 1967

Right-arm medium-pacer. Relied on movement both ways through the air. In first-class cricket, took 178 wickets at 25.08.

Shahid Mahmood: 10-58, Karachi Whites v Khairpur, Karachi, 1969
Left-arm seamer. Played one Test in England in 1962. Took 89 first-class wickets at 21.64.

Eddie Hemmings: 10-175, International XI v West Indies XI, Kingston, 1982
The most expensive of all the first-class ten-fors. In Tests, took 43 wickets at 42.44; in first-class matches 1515 wickets came at 29.30.

Pradeep Sunderam: 10-78, Rajasthan v Vidarbha, Jodhpur, 1985
Seamer from the 'Pink City' of Jaipur. Added 6-76 in the second innings. Took 145 wickets at 28.78 in first-class games.

Steve Jefferies: 10-59, Western Province v Orange Free State, Cape Town, 1987
A left-arm opening bowler from Cape Town. Had spells with three English County sides. Took 478 wickets at 27.62 in first-class games.

Imran Adil: 10-92, Bahawalpur v Faisalabad, Faisalabad, 1989
The first instance in Pakistan's Patron's Trophy. At 18 years 344 days, the youngest to achieve the feat. Played 79 first-class matches for 186 wickets at 27.52.

Pramodya Wickramasinghe: 10-41, Sinhalese Sports Club v Kalutara, Colombo, 1991
A long-serving seamer. Was in the Sri Lankan team that won the 1996 World Cup final. Took 186 wickets at 27.52 in first-class games.

Richard Johnson: 10-45, Middlesex v Derbyshire, Derby, 1994
A swarthy seamer. Played three Tests, taking two Zimbabwean wickets in first Test over. In all first-class games took 528 wickets at 28.58.

Naeem Akhtar: 10-28, Rawalpindi B v Peshawar, Peshawar, 1995

A seamer who never won a Test cap. Produced the best figures in Pakistan's Quaid-e-Azam Trophy. Took 322 wickets at 21.46 in first-class games.

Anil Kumble: 10-74, India v Pakistan, Delhi, 1999

Bowled brisk leg-breaks. The second instance in Tests – and a big win for India over their neighbours. Played 132 Tests and took 619 wickets at 29.65 each. In all first-class games claimed 1136 wickets at 25.38; in ODIs had 337 at 30.89; in List A games returned 514 at 27.58; and in T20 games 57 at 24.36.

Debasis Mohanty: 10-46, East Zone v South Zone, Agartala, 2001

Haul included seven Test players. A seamer, played two Tests plus 45 one-day internationals. In first-class games took a total of 417 wickets at 21.05 each.

Ottis Gibson: 10-47, Durham v Hampshire, Chester-le-Street, 2007

A popular Barbadian. Won only two Test caps but later coached West Indies and South Africa. Played two Tests and in all first-class cricket took 659 wickets at 27.79 apiece.

Mario Olivier: 10-65, Warriors v Eagles, Bloemfontein, 2007

Four Test bowlers in the Warriors' attack but the much-travelled seamer took all the wickets. Played first-class cricket from 2005 to 2012, taking 168 wickets at 32.87 each.

Zulfiqar Babar: 10-143, Multan v Islamabad, Multan, 2009

The slow left-armer made his Test debut when almost 35. Played 15 Tests and took 54 wickets at 39.42. In first-class games captured 509 wickets at 23.38.

Malinda Pushpakumara: 10-37, Colombo Cricket Club v Saracens, Moratuwa, 2019

Slow left-armer. Followed 6-73 first innings with all ten, bowling unchanged as Saracens slumped to defeat. Played four Tests and in all first-class games took 863 wickets at 20.09 each.

Sean Whitehead: 10-36, South Western Districts v Easterns, Oudtshoorn, 2021

Another left-arm spinner. Achieved the feat in South Africa's second-tier competition. In first-class matches has taken 74 wickets at 23.32 apiece.

Ajaz Patel: 10-119, New Zealand v India, Mumbai, 2021

Slow left-armer. Wheeled down 47.5 overs to take all ten in his city of birth – but *against* India. Has played 21 Tests and taken 85 wickets at 29.75. In all first-class games has 393 wickets at 33.06.

Anshul Kamboj: 10-49, Haryana v Kerala, Lahli, 2024

Lively fast-medium right-armer. The third to take all ten in the Ranji Trophy competition. By the end of 2024 had taken 57 wickets at 24.47 in first-class games.

* Runs conceded and overs bowled were not routinely recorded at the time
^ Was achieved against teams containing more than 11 players (which was allowed in some early first-class matches)

ACKNOWLEDGEMENTS

First and foremost, I wish to acknowledge and thank Steven Lynch for his significant contribution to this work. His vast experience as a historian, archivist and statistician, much of it under the umbrella of *Wisden*, was of great value to me in chasing down matters, some of them from many years ago. I thank him sincerely for his sage counsel. Therefore I must also thank Scyld Berry, English cricket writer, former editor of *Wisden* and plain good bloke, for it was he who introduced me to Steven from the outset. My sincere gratitude – even admiration – goes to editor Paul Connolly, who painstakingly took a mountain of information and turned it into a much more readable manuscript. Thanks, too, to Kent County Cricket Club's heritage officer Ian Phipps and heritage trust chair Jo Rice for opening doors in county cricket. On the 'home front' I am also indebted to Stephen Hall, museum coordinator at the WA Cricket Association, and to Joanne Winter, digital presentation coordinator at the Melbourne Cricket Club. Finally, to my mate and former teammate, Dennis Lillee, for his contribution to the front cover design.

REFERENCES

Richard Cashman (Ed.), *Oxford Companion to Australian Cricket,*
Oxford University Press, 1996

Jack Fingleton, *Brightly Fades the Don,* Pavilion, 1985

Bill Frindall (Ed.), *The Wisden Book of Test Cricket 1876–77 to
1977–78,* MacDonald and Jane's, London, 1978

WG Grace, *Cricket,* JW Arrowsmith, 1891

Alan Hill, *Hedley Verity,* Mainstream Publishing, 2000

Garrie Hutchinson and John Ross (Eds.), *The 200 Seasons of
Australian Cricket,* Macmillan, 1997

David Lemmon, *Tich Freeman and the Decline of the Leg-break
Bowler,* Allen & Unwin, 1982

Arthur Mailey, *10 For 66 And All That,* The Sportsman's Book
Club, 1959

Jack Pollard, *Australian Cricket: The Game and the Players,* Angus
& Robertson, 1989

EW Swanton (Ed.), *Barclays World of Cricket,* Harper Collins,
1980

PICTURE CREDITS

Page 6 Ian Brayshaw with his 1967 trophy *Photograph taken by Liam Brick*
Page 16 William Lillywhite
Page 21 John Wisden
Page 26 V. E. Walker
Page 28 Henry 'Harry' Pickett *Supplied courtesy of Essex County Cricket Club*
Page 29 Cyril Bland *Supplied courtesy of Sussex Cricket Museum*
Page 33 Edwin James 'Ted' Tyler
Page 38 William Gilbert 'WG' Grace *Supplied courtesy of Roger Gibbons and Gloucestershire County Cricket Club*
Page 40 William Gilbert 'WG' Grace
Page 41 William Gilbert 'WG' Grace *Supplied courtesy of Roger Gibbons and Gloucestershire County Cricket Club*
Page 45 Edward Mills 'EM' Grace *Supplied courtesy of Roger Gibbons and Gloucestershire County Cricket Club*
Page 51, 56 Alfred Percy 'Tich' Freeman
Page 63, 68, 71 Hedly Verity
Pages 76, 79 James Charles 'Jim' Laker
Pages 84, 85, 86 Colin 'Charles' Blythe *Supplied courtesy of Kent County Cricket Club*
Page 87 George Geary
Page 90 James Morton 'Jim' Sims *Supplied courtesy of Middlesex County Cricket Club*
Page 92 George Christopher Collins
Page 93 Anthony John Grayhurst 'Tony' Pearson *Supplied courtesy of the Downside School, UK*
Page 95 Norman Ian Thomson *Supplied courtesy of Sussex Cricket Museum*
Page 101 Alfred Arthur Mailey
Page 103 Alfred Arthur Mailey *Supplied courtesy of Melbourne Cricket Club Museum*
Page 104 George Giffen *Supplied courtesy of the South Australian Cricket Association*
Page 105 George Giffen *Supplied courtesy of Melbourne Cricket Club Museum*
Page 107 Kenneth 'Ken' Smales *Supplied courtesy of Nottinghamshire County Cricket Club*
Page 109 John Kenneth Richard 'Ken' Graveney *Courtesy New York Public Library*
Page 110 Match record when Ken Graveney bowled all 10 out in 1949. *Supplied courtesy of Gloucestershire County Cricket Club*
Page 114 William 'Eric' Hollies

Page 123 William Peter 'Bill' Howell
Page 124 Bill Howell's ball *Supplied courtesy of Melbourne Cricket Club Museum*
Page 126 Clarence Victor 'Clarrie' Grimmett *Supplied courtesy of Melbourne Cricket Club Museum*
Page 128 Clarence Victor 'Clarrie' Grimmett
Page 130 Thomas Welbourn 'Tim' Wall *Supplied courtesy of Melbourne Cricket Club Museum*
Page 133 Peter John Allan *Supplied courtesy of Queensland Cricket Association*
Page 140, 141 Johnny Briggs *Supplied courtesy of Lancashire County Cricket Club*
Page 143 John 'Jack' Mercer *Supplied courtesy of Glamorgan Cricket Archives The Museum of Welsh Cricket*
Page 144 Arthur Fielder
Page 147 Thomas Bignall 'Tommy' Mitchell *Supplied courtesy of the Derbyshire County Cricket Club Archive*
Page 149 Thomas Francis 'Frank' Smailes
Page 151 Edward Alfred 'Eddie' Watts *Supplied courtesy of Surrey County Cricket Club*
Page 152, 153 Edward George Dennett *Supplied courtesy of Gloucestershire County Cricket Club*
Page 154 Vallance William Crisp Jupp
Pages 188, 159 Anil Kumble
Page 161 Ajaz Yunus Patel
Pages 166, 167 John Barton 'Bart' King
Page 172 William 'Billy' Bestwick *Supplied courtesy of the Derbyshire County Cricket Club Archive*
Page 174 John Cornish 'Jack' White *Supplied courtesy of Somerset County Cricket Club Museum*
Page 175 Thomas 'Tom' Rushby *Supplied courtesy of Surrey County Cricket Club*
Page 177 Charles Warrington Leonard 'Charlie' Parker *Supplied courtesy of Gloucestershire County Cricket Club*
Page 180 Subhash Pandharinath 'Fergie' Gupte
Page 182 Albert Edward Ernest Vogler
Page 184 Delmont Cameron St Clair 'Fitz' Hinds
Page 187 Albert Edward Moss
Page 191 James Lillywhite *Wikipedia*
Page 195 Albert Edwin Trott *Supplied courtesy of Middlesex County Cricket Club*
Page 196 Samuel Moses James 'Sammy' Woods *Supplied courtesy of Somerset County Cricket Club*
Page 198 Francis Alfred 'Frank' Tarrant
Page 199 Alonzo Robson Drake *Wikipedia*
Page 201 Thomas 'Tom' Richardson
Page 203 Thomas William John 'Tom' Goddard *Supplied courtesy of Gloucestershire County Cricket Club*
Page 214 Robert 'Bob' Berry *Supplied courtesy of Lancashire County Cricket Club*
Page 217 Richard Leonard Johnson
Page 219 Trevor Edward Bailey *Supplied courtesy of Essex County Cricket Club*
Page 223 Edward Ernest 'Eddie' Hemmings
Page 226 Graham Anthony Richard 'Tony' Lock

TEN OUT!

Pages 228, 231 Graham Anthony Richard 'Tony' Lock *Supplied courtesy of Surrey County Cricket Club*
Page 238 Mario Wickus Olivier *Copyright Chevrolet Warriors*
Page 239 Sulfiqar Babar
Page 241 Pawuluge Malinda Pushpakumara
Page 249 Score sheet for Western Australia v Victoria 1967 when Ian Brayshaw bowled all 10 out *Supplied courtesy of the Western Australia Cricket Association Archives*
Page 250 *The West Australian*, Monday, October 23, 1967
Page 259 Ian Brayshaw's trophy from 1967 *Photograph taken by Liam Brick*